A *Primer on*
DECISION MAKING

How Decisions Happen

James G. March

with the assistance of Chip Heath

The Free Press
New York London Toronto Sydney

THE FREE PRESS
A Division of Simon & Schuster Inc.
1230 Avenue of the Americas
New York, NY 10020

THE FREE PRESS and colophon are trademarks
of Simon & Schuster Inc.

Manufactured in the United States of America

10

Library of Congress Cataloging-in-Publication Data

March, James G.
    A primer on decision making: how decisions happen / James G.
March; with the assistance of Chip Heath.
        p.   cm
    Includes bibliographical references and index.

    1. Decision-making.   I. Heath, Chip.   II. Title.
    HD30.23.M368   1994
    658.4'03—dc20   95—4414
    ISBN-10: 1-4391-5733-2   CIP
    ISBN-13: 978-1-4391-5733-6

Contents

Acknowledgments

This book is based on lecture notes from a course I have given at Stanford University for several years. The lectures have profited from a steady flow of intelligent and enjoyable students in the Stanford course. If there are ideas worth crediting here, they deserve much of the credit. The book has been written with the assistance of Chip Heath. He made a rough preliminary draft from my lecture notes and persuaded me to undertake the writing. He has also provided comments on the chapters as they emerged. He should not have to take any responsibility for any of it, but I am grateful for his help.

The essays in the book, like the lectures on which they are based, are best seen as a secretary's report to a collection of extraordinarily able friends and collaborators with whom I have worked on problems of decision making. Among the many, in addition to Chip Heath, I should like to cite particularly Ingmar Björkman, Nils Brunsson, Glenn Carroll, Søren Christensen, Michael D. Cohen, Richard M. Cyert, Omar El Sawy, Julie Elworth, Lars Engwall, Martha S. Feldman, Henrich Greve, J. Richard Harrison, Kaj Hedvall, Scott R. Herriott, Kristian Kreiner, Theresa Lant, Charles A. Lave, Daniel A. Levinthal,

Barbara Levitt, David Matheson, John W. Meyer, Stephen Mezias, Anne Miner, Johan P. Olsen, Jeffrey Pfeffer, Martin Schulz, W. Richard Scott, Guje Sevón, Zur Shapira, Herbert A. Simon, Jitendra Singh, Lee S. Sproull, Arthur L. Stinchcombe, Suzanne Stout, Michal Tamuz, Risto Tainio, and Xueguang Zhou.

Despite this dependence on the work of others, the book is footnoted only sparsely. While that may be taken as a manifestation of laziness, it is also an effort to make the essays more a form of personal conversation than a scholarly treatise. Anyone who knows the research literature will recognize the influence of innumerable colleagues in the assertions and speculations I make, but if asked for a reference for any specific one, I fear I will claim only that I believe it. I have included a brief list of additional readings at the end of the book.

The ability to do this kind of thing is a luxury bestowed by support from the Spencer Foundation, the Stanford Graduate School of Business, and the Scandinavian Consortium for Organizational Research. And by a wife, who certainly could have thought of better things for me to do but often refrained from saying so.

Preface

This book is a primer, a little compendium of ideas for thinking about how decisions happen. The ideas are not novel. They are familiar to students of decision making and are elaborated at length in the research literature. They are presented here in their starkest, least elaborate form, a first introduction to decisions.

The essays in the book are concerned primarily with how decisions actually happen rather than how they ought to happen. They sometimes draw on theories that purport to say how decisions ought to be made, and the last chapter provides a few observations on how intelligence is (or is not) achieved through decision making. For the most part, however, the book sticks to a simple collection of ideas that might be useful in understanding decision making as we observe it and participate in it.

Understanding any specific decision in a specific situation requires a great deal of concrete contextual knowledge—details about the historical, social, political, and economic worlds surrounding the decision and about the individuals, organizations, and institutions involved. Such details are not presented in this book. There are no stories of the rich drama of decision, no elaborations of history. The text tries to be faithful to what is known about decision making as it actually takes place, but the focus is on ideas that can be used to understand decisions generally, not on the particular details of any particular decision.

Chapter 1 examines ideas of rational choice, particularly limited rationality. Chapter 2 considers ideas of identity, appropriateness, and history-dependent rules. Chapters 3 and 4 look at multiple-person decision making, decisions made in the face of inconsistency in preferences or identities. Chapter 5 treats the consequences for decision making of ambiguity in preferences, identities, and experience. Finally, Chapter 6 considers the prospects for decision engineering.

Underlying these clusters of ideas are several different perspectives on decision making, with numerous variations. Students of decision making draw from all the disciplines of social science—anthropology, cognitive and decision science, economics, organization studies, political science, psychology, and sociology. As ideas from those disciplines are woven into the story of decision making, new forms of old issues are encountered: issues of reason and ignorance, of intentionality and fate, of coherence and conflict, of institutions, identities, and rules, of learning and selection, of meaning and interpretation, of preferences and obligations.

Those topics will arise naturally in their places, and their details will not be anticipated here. It may, however, be useful to note four relatively deep (and not entirely independent) issues that persistently divide students of decision making:

> The first issue is whether decisions are to be viewed as choice-based or rule-based. Do decision makers pursue a logic of consequence, making choices among alternatives by evaluating their consequences in terms of prior preferences? Or do they pursue a logic of appropriateness, fulfilling identities or roles by recognizing situations and following rules that match appropriate behavior to the situations they encounter?
>
> The second issue is whether decision making is typified more by clarity and consistency or by ambiguity and inconsis-

tency. Are decisions occasions in which individuals and institutions achieve coherence and reduce equivocality? Or are they occasions in which inconsistency and ambiguity are exhibited, exploited, and expanded?

The third issue is whether decision making is an instrumental activity or an interpretive activity. Are decisions to be understood primarily in terms of the way they fit into a problem solving, adaptive calculus? Or are they to be understood primarily in terms of the way they fit into efforts to establish individual and social meaning?

The fourth issue is whether outcomes of decision processes are seen as primarily attributable to the actions of autonomous actors or to the systemic properties of an interacting ecology. Is it possible to describe decisions as resulting from the intentions, identities, and interests of independent actors? Or is it necessary to emphasize the ways in which individual actors, organizations, and societies fit together?

These issues are not resolved here, but they are exercised a bit.

CHAPTER ONE

Limited Rationality

B y far the most common portrayal of decision making is one that interprets action as rational choice. The idea is as old as thought about human behavior, and its durability attests not only to its usefulness but also to its consistency with human aspirations. Theories of rational choice, although often elaborated in formal and mathematical ways, draw on everyday language used in understanding and communicating about choices. In fact, the embedding of formal theories of rationality in ordinary language is one of their distinctive features. Among other things, it makes them deceptively comprehensible and self-evident. This chapter examines the idea of rational choice and some ways in which theories of limited rationality have made that idea more consistent with observations of how decisions actually happen.

1.1 The Idea of Rational Choice

Like many other commonly used words, "rationality" has come to mean many things. In many of its uses, "rational" is approximately equivalent to "intelligent" or "successful." It is used to describe actions that have desirable outcomes. In other uses, "rational" means "coldly materialistic," referring to the spirit or values in terms of which an action is taken. In still other uses, "rational" means "sane," reflecting a judgment about the mental health displayed by an action or a procedure for taking action. Heterogeneous meanings of rationality are also characteristic of the literature on decision making. The term is used rather loosely or inconsistently.

In this book, "rationality" has a narrow and fairly precise meaning linked to processes of choice. Rationality is defined as a particular and very familiar class of procedures for making choices. In this procedural meaning of "rational," a rational procedure may or may not lead to good outcomes. The possibility of a link between the rationality of a process (sometimes called "procedural rationality") and the intelligence of its outcomes (sometimes called "substantive rationality") is treated as a result to be demonstrated rather than an axiom.

1.1.1 The Logic of Consequence

Rational theories of choice assume decision processes that are consequential and preference-based. They are *consequential* in the sense that action depends on anticipations of the future effects of current actions. Alternatives are interpreted in terms of their expected consequences. They are *preference-based* in the sense that consequences are evaluated in terms of personal preferences. Alternatives are compared in terms of the extent to which their expected consequences are thought to serve the preferences of the decision maker.

A rational procedure is one that pursues a logic of consequence. It makes a choice conditional on the answers to four basic questions:

1. The question of *alternatives:* What actions are possible?
2. The question of *expectations:* What future consequences might follow from each alternative? How likely is each possible consequence, assuming that alternative is chosen?
3. The question of *preferences:* How valuable (to the decision

maker) are the consequences associated with each of the alternatives?

4. The question of the *decision rule:* How is a choice to be made among the alternatives in terms of the values of their consequences?

When decision making is studied within this framework, each of these questions is explored: What determines which alternatives are considered? What determines the expectations about consequences? How are decision maker preferences created and evoked? What is the decision rule that is used?

This general framework is the basis for standard explanations of behavior. When asked to explain behavior, most people "rationalize" it. That is, they explain their own actions in terms of their alternatives and the consequences of those alternatives for their preferences. Similarly, they explain the actions of others by imagining a set of expectations and preferences that would make the action rational.

A rational framework is also endemic to theories of human behavior. It is used to understand the actions of firms, marriage partners, and criminals. It underlies many theories of bargaining, exchange, and voting, as well as theories of language and social structure. Rational choice processes are the fundamentals of microeconomic models of resource allocation, political theories of coalition formation, statistical decision theories, and many other theories and models throughout the social sciences.

1.1.2 Rational Theories of Choice

Within rational processes, choice depends on what alternatives are considered and on two guesses about the future: The first guess is a guess about future states of the world, conditional on the choice. The second guess is a guess about how the decision maker will feel about that future world when it is experienced.

PURE THEORIES OF RATIONAL CHOICE

Some versions of rational choice theory assume that all decision makers share a common set of (basic) preferences, that alternatives and their consequences are defined by the environment, and that decision makers have perfect knowledge of those alternatives and their consequences. Other versions recognize greater inter-actor subjectivity but nevertheless assume perfect knowledge for any particular decision—that all alternatives are known, that all consequences of all alternatives are known with certainty, and that all preferences relevant to the choice are known, precise, consistent, and stable.

These pure versions of rational choice have well-established positions in the prediction of aggregate behavior, where they are sometimes able to capture a rational "signal" within the subjective "noise" of individual choice. They are sources of predictions of considerable generality, for example the prediction that an increase in price will lead (usually) to an aggregate decrease in demand (although some individuals may be willing to buy more at a higher price than at a lower one).

In spite of their utility for these qualitative aggregate predictions, pure versions of rational choice are hard to accept as credible portraits of actual individual or organizational actors. Consider the problem of assigning people to jobs in an organization. If it were to satisfy the expectations of pure rationality, this decision would start by specifying an array of tasks to be performed and characterizing each by the skills and knowledge required to perform them, taking into account the effects of their interrelationships. The decision maker would consider all possible individuals, characterized by relevant attributes (their skills, attitudes, and price). Finally the decision maker would consider each possible assignment of individuals to tasks, evaluating each possible array of assignments with respect to the preferences of the organization.

Preferences would be defined to include such things as (1) profits, sales, and stock value (tomorrow, next year, and ten years from now); (2) contributions to social policy goals (e.g. affirmative action, quality of life goals, and the impact of the assignment on the family); and (3) contributions to the reputation of the organization among all possible stakeholders—shareholders, potential shareholders, the employees themselves, customers, and citizens in the community. The tradeoffs among these various objectives would have to be known and specified in advance, and all possible task definitions, all possible sets of employees, and all possible assignments of people to jobs would have to be considered. In the end, the decision maker would be expected to choose the one combination that maximizes expected return.

A considerably less glorious version of rationality—but still heroic—would assume that a structure of tasks and a wage structure are given, and that the decision maker assigns persons to jobs in a way that maximizes the return to the organization. Another version would assume that a decision maker calculates the benefits to be obtained by gathering any of these kinds of data, and their costs.

Virtually no one believes that anything approximating such a procedure is observed in any individual or organization, either for the job assignment task or for any number of other decision tasks that confront them. Although some people have speculated that competition forces the outcomes of actual decision processes to converge to the outcomes predicted from a purely rational process, even that speculation has been found to be severely restricted in its applicability. Pure rationality strains credulity as a description of how decisions actually happen. As a result, there have been numerous efforts to modify theories of rational choice, keeping the basic structure but revising the key assumptions to reflect observed behavior more adequately.

RATIONAL DECISION MAKING AND
UNCERTAINTY ABOUT CONSEQUENCES

The most common and best-established elaboration of pure theories of rational choice is one that recognizes the uncertainty surrounding future consequences of present action. Decision makers are assumed to choose among alternatives on the basis of their expected consequences, but those consequences are not known with certainty. Rather, decision makers know the likelihoods of various possible outcomes, conditional on the actions taken.

Uncertainty may be imagined to exist either because some processes are uncertain at their most fundamental levels or because decision makers' ignorance about the mechanisms driving the process make outcomes look uncertain to them. The food vendor at a football game, for example, knows that the return from various alternative food-stocking strategies depends on the weather, something that cannot be predicted with certainty at the time a decision must be made.

Since a decision maker does not know with certainty what will happen if a particular action is chosen, it is unlikely that the results of an action will confirm expectations about it. Postdecision surprise, sometimes pleasant sometimes unpleasant, is characteristic of decision making. So also is postdecision regret. It is almost certain that after the consequences are known (no matter how favorable they are) a decision maker will suffer regret—awareness that a better choice could have been made if the outcomes could have been predicted precisely in advance. In such a spirit, investors occasionally rue the gains they could have realized in the stock market with perfect foresight of the market.

The most commonly considered situations involving uncertainty are those of decision making under "risk," where the precise consequences are uncertain but their probabilities are known. In such situations, the most conventional approach to predicting decision making is to assume a decision maker will choose the alternative that maximizes expected value, that is, the alternative that would, on average, produce the best outcome if this particular choice were to be made many times. The analog is gambling and the choice of the best gamble. An expected-value analysis of choice involves imagining a decision tree in which each branch represents either a choice to be made or an "act of nature" that cannot be predicted with certainty. Procedures for constructing and analyzing such trees constitute a large fraction of modern decision science.

In more elaborate rational theories of choice in the face of risk, an alternative is assessed not only by its expected value but also by its uncertainty. The value attached to a potential alternative depends not only on the average expected return but also on the degree of uncertainty, or risk, involved. For risk-averse decision makers, riskiness decreases the value of a particular alternative. For risk-seeking decision makers, riskiness increases the value.

The riskiness of an alternative is defined in different ways in different theories, but most definitions are intended to reflect a measure of the variation in potential outcomes. This variation has a natural intuitive measure in the variance of the probability distribution over outcome values. For various technical reasons, such a measure is not always used in studies of choice, but for our purposes it will suffice. When risk is taken into account, a decision is seen as a joint function of the expected value (or mean) and the riskiness (or variance) of the probability distribution over outcomes conditional on choice of a particular alternative.

MODIFYING THE ASSUMPTIONS

The introduction of risk and the development of ways to deal with it were major contributions to understanding and improving decision making within a rational framework. Such developments were, however, just the first step in modifying the knowledge assumptions of rational choice. Most modern theories of rational choice involve additional modifications of the pure theory. They can be distinguished by their assumptions with respect to four dimensions:

1. *Knowledge:* What is assumed about the information decision makers have about the state of the world and about other actors?
2. *Actors:* What is assumed about the number of decision makers?
3. *Preferences:* What is assumed about the preferences by which consequences (and therefore alternatives) are evaluated?
4. *Decision rule:* What is assumed to be the decision rule by which decision makers choose an alternative?

Although most theories "relax" the assumptions of the pure theory on at least one of these dimensions, they tend to be conservative in their deviations from the assumptions underlying a pure conception of rationality. For example, most theories of limited knowledge are not simultaneously theories of multiple actors; most theories of multiple actors (for example, microeconomic versions of game theory) are not simultaneously theories of limited knowledge; and virtually none of the limited knowledge or multiple-actor theories introduce conceptions of ambiguous or unstable preferences. In that sense at least, the pure model still permeates the field—by providing an overall structure and significant (though different) parts for various different theories.

1.1.3 Enthusiasts and Skeptics

Enthusiasts for rational models of decision making notice the widespread use of assumptions of rationality and the successes of such models in predictions of aggregates of human actors. They easily see these symptoms of acceptance and usefulness as impressive support for the models. Skeptics, on the other hand, are less inclined to give credence to models based on their popularity, noting the historical fact that many currently rejected theories have enjoyed long periods of popularity. They are also less inclined to find the models particularly powerful, often emphasizing their less than perfect success in predicting individual behavior. They easily see these symptoms of conventionality and imperfection as making the models unattractive.

Both enthusiasts and skeptics endorse limited rationality, the former seeing limited rationality as a modest, natural extension of theories of pure rationality, and the latter seeing limited rationality as a fundamental challenge to pure rationality and a harbinger of much more behaviorally based conceptions of decision making.

1.2 Limited (or Bounded) Rationality

Studies of decision making in the real world suggest that not all alternatives are known, that not all consequences are considered, and that not all preferences are evoked at the same time. Instead of considering all alternatives, decision makers typically appear to consider only a few and to look at them sequentially rather than simultaneously. Decision makers do not consider all consequences of their alternatives. They focus on some and ignore others. Relevant information about consequences is not sought, and available information is often not used. Instead of having a complete, consistent set of preferences, decision makers seem to have incomplete and inconsistent goals, not all of which are considered at the same time. The decision rules used by real decision makers seem to differ from the ones imagined by decision theory. Instead of considering "expected values" or "risk" as those terms are used in decision theory, they invent other criteria. Instead of calculating the "best possible" action, they search for an action that is "good enough."

As a result of such observations, doubts about the empirical validity and usefulness of the pure theory of rational choice have been characteristic of students of actual decision processes for many years. Rational choice theories have adapted to such observations gradually by introducing the idea that rationality is limited. The core notion of limited rationality is that individuals are intendedly rational. Although decision makers try to be rational, they are constrained by limited cognitive capabilities and incomplete information, and thus their actions may be less than completely rational in spite of their best intentions and efforts.

In recent years, ideas of limited (or bounded) rationality have become sufficiently integrated into conventional theories of rational choice to make limited rationality viewpoints generally accepted. They have come to dominate most theories of individual decision making. They have been used to develop behavioral and evolutionary theories of the firm. They have been used as part of the basis for theories of transaction cost economics and game theoretic, information, and organizational economics. They have been applied to decision making in political, educational, and military contexts.

1.2.1 Information Constraints

Decision makers face serious limitations in attention, memory, comprehension, and communication. Most students of individual decision making seem to allude to some more or less obvious biological constraints on human information processing, although the limits are rarely argued from a strict biological basis. In a similar way, students of organizational decision making assume some more or less obvious information constraints imposed by methods of organizing diverse individuals:

1. *Problems of attention.* Time and capabilities for attention are limited. Not everything can be attended to at once. Too many signals are received. Too many things are relevant to a decision. Because of those limitations, theories of decision making are often better described as theories of attention or search than as theories of choice. They are concerned with the way in which scarce attention is allocated.

2. *Problems of memory.* The capabilities of individuals and organizations to store information is limited. Memories are faulty. Records are not kept. Histories are not recorded. Even more limited are individual and organizational abilities to retrieve information that has been stored. Previously learned lessons are not reliably retrieved at appropriate times. Knowledge stored in one part of an organization cannot be used easily by another part.

3. *Problems of comprehension.* Decision makers have limited capacities for comprehension. They have difficulty organizing, summarizing, and using information to form inferences about the causal connections of events and about relevant features of the world. They often have relevant information but fail to see its relevance. They make unwarranted inferences from information, or fail to connect different parts of the information available to them to form a coherent interpretation.

4. *Problems of communication.* There are limited capacities for communicating information, for sharing complex and specialized information. Division of labor facilitates mobilization and utilization of specialized talents, but it also encourages differentiation of knowledge, competence, and language. It is difficult to communicate across cultures, across generations, or across professional specialties. Different groups of people use different frameworks for simplifying the world.

As decision makers struggle with these limitations, they develop procedures that maintain the basic framework of rational choice but modify it to accommodate the difficulties. Those procedures form the core of theories of limited rationality.

1.2.2 Coping with Information Constraints.

Decision makers use various information and decision strategies to cope with limitations in information and information-handling capabilities. Much of contemporary research on choice by individuals and organizations focuses on those coping strategies, the ways choices are made on the basis of expectations about the future but without the kind of complete information that is presumed in classical theories of rational choice.

THE PSYCHOLOGY OF LIMITED RATIONALITY

Psychological studies of individual decision making have identified numerous ways in which decision makers react to cognitive constraints. They use stereotypes in order to infer unobservables from observables. They form typologies of attitudes (liberal, conservative) and traits (dependent, extroverted, friendly) and categorize people in terms of the typologies. They attribute intent from observing behavior or the consequences of behavior. They abstract "central" parts of a problem and ignore other parts. They adopt understandings of the world in the form of socially developed theories, scripts, and schemas that fill in missing information and suppress discrepancies in their understandings.

The understandings adopted tend to stabilize interpretations of the world. For the most part, the world is interpreted and understood today in the way it was interpreted and understood yesterday. Decision makers look for information, but they see what they expect to see and overlook unexpected things. Their memories are less recollections of history than constructions based on what they thought might happen and reconstructions based on what they now think must have happened, given their present beliefs.

A comprehensive review of psychological studies of individual information processing and problem solving would require more space and more talent than are available here. The present intention is only to characterize briefly a few of the principal speculations developed as a result of thatresearch, in particular speculations about four fundamental simplification processes: editing, decomposition, heuristics, and framing.

Editing. Decision makers tend to edit and simplify problems before entering into a choice process, using a relatively small number of cues and combining them in a simple manner. Complex problems or situations are simplified. Search may be simplified by discarding some available information or by reducing the amount of processing done on the information. For example, decision makers may attend to choice dimensions sequentially, eliminating all alternatives that are not up to standards on the first dimension before considering information from other dimensions. In other situations, they may consider all information for all alternatives, but weight the dimensions equally rather than weight them according to their importance.

Decomposition. Decision makers attempt to decompose problems, to reduce large problems into their component parts. The presumption is that problem elements can be defined in such a way that solving the various components of a problem individually will result in an acceptable solution to the global problem. For example, a decision maker might approach the problem of allocating resources to advertising projects by first decomposing the global advertising problem of a firm into subproblems associated with each of the products, then decomposing the product subproblems into problems associated with particular geographic regions.

One form of decomposition is working backward. Some problems are easier to solve backward than forward because, like mazes, they have only a few last steps but many first steps. Working backward is particularly attractive to decision makers who accept a "can do" decision making ideology, because it matches an activist role. Working backward encourages a perspective in which decision makers decide what they want to have happen and try to make it happen.

Decomposition is closely connected to such key components of organizing as division of labor, specialization, decentralization, and hierarchy. An important reason for the effectiveness of modern organization is the possibility of decomposing large complex tasks into small independently manageable ones. In order for decomposition to work as a problem solving strategy, the problem world must not be tightly interconnected. For example, if actions taken on one advertising project heavily affect the results of action on others, deciding on the projects independently will produce complications. The generality of decomposition strategies suggests that the world is, in fact, often only loosely interconnected, so subproblems can be solved independently. But that very generality makes it likely that decomposition will also be attempted in situations in which it does not work.

Heuristics. Decision makers recognize patterns in the situations *they face and apply rules of appropriate behavior to those situations.* Studies of expertise, for example, generally reveal that experts substitute recognition of familiar situations and rule following for calculation. Good chess players generally do more subtle calculations than novices, but their great advantage lies less in the depth of their analysis than in their ability to recognize a variety of situations and in their store of appropriate rules associated with situations. Although the problem solving of expert salespersons has been subjected to less research, it appears to be similar.

As another example, people seem not to be proficient at calculating the probability of future events by listing an elaborate decision tree of possible outcomes. However, they are reasonably good at using the output of memory to tell them how frequently similar events have occurred in the past. They use the results of memory as a proxy for the projection of future probability.

Such procedures are known to the literature of problem solving and decision making as "heuristics." Heuristics are rules-ofthumb for calculating certain kinds of numbers or solving certain kinds of problems. Although psychological heuristics for problem solving are normally folded into a discussion of limited rationality because they can be interpreted as responses to cognitive limitations, they might as easily be interpreted as versions of rule-following behavior that follows a logic quite different from a logic of consequence (see Chapter 2).

Framing. Decisions are framed by beliefs that define the problem to be addressed, the information that must be collected, and the dimensions that must be evaluated. Decision makers adopt paradigms to tell themselves what perspective to take on a problem, what questions should be asked, and what technologies should be used to ask the questions. Such frames focus attention and simplify analysis. They direct attention to different options and different preferences. A decision will be made in one way if it is framed as a problem of maintaining profits and in a different way if it is framed as a problem of maintaining market share. A situation will lead to different decisions if it is seen as being about "the value of innovation" rather than "the importance of not losing face."

Decision makers typically frame problems narrowly rather than broadly. They decide about local options and local preferences, without considering all tradeoffs or all alternatives. They are normally content to find a set of sufficient conditions for solving a problem, not the most efficient set of conditions. Assigning proper weights to things in the spatial, temporal, and causal neighborhood of current activity as opposed to things that are more distant spatially, temporally, or causally is a major problem in assuring decision intelligence (see Chapter 6). It is reflected in the tension between the frames of decision makers, who often seem to have relatively short horizons, and the frames of historians, who (at least retrospectively) often have somewhat longer horizons.

The frames used by decision makers are part of their conscious and unconscious repertoires. In part they are encased in early individual experiences that shape individual approaches to problems. In part they are responsive to the particular se-quences of decision situations that arise. There is a tendency for frames to persist over a sequence of situations. Recently used frames hold a privileged position, in part because they are more or less automatically evoked in a subsequent situation. In addition, past attention strengthens both a decision maker's skills in using a frame and the ease of justifying action to others within the frame.

These internal processes of developing frames and using them is supplemented by an active market in frames. Decision makers adopt frames that are proposed by consultants, writers, or friends. They copy frames used by others, particularly others in the same profession, association, or organization. Consequential decision making itself is, of course, one such frame. Prescriptive theories of decision making seek to legitimize a consequential frame for considering decisions, one that asks what the alternatives are, what their expected consequences are, and what the decision maker's preferences are.

THE STATISTICS OF LIMITED RATIONALITY

Faced with a world more complicated than they can hope to understand, decision makers develop ways of monitoring and comprehending that complexity. One standard approach is to deal with summary numerical representations of reality, for example income statements and cost-of-living indexes. The numbers are intended to represent phenomena in an organization or its environment: accounting profits, aptitude scores, occupancy rates, costs of production. The phenomena themselves are elusive—real but difficult to characterize and measure. For example, income statements confront a number of uncertainties. How quickly do resources lose their value (depreciate or spoil)? How should joint costs be allocated to various users? How should inventory be counted and valued? How can the quality of debts be assessed? What is the value of a contract? Of a good name? There is ambiguity about the facts and much potential for conflict over them. As a result, the numbers are easily described as inventions, subject to both debate and ridicule. They have elements of magic about them, pulled mysteriously from a statistician's or a manager's hat. For example, estimates of U.S. government subsidies to nuclear power went from $40 billion under one administration to $12.8 billion under another with no change in actual programs.

The numbers are magical, but they also become quite real. Numbers such as those involved in a cost-of-living index or an income (profit and loss) statement come to be treated as though they were the things they represent. If the cost-of-living index goes down, decision makers act as though the cost of living has gone down—even though they are well aware of the many ways in which, for many people, the cost of living may actually have gone up. Indeed, the whole concept of "cost of living" moves from being an abstract hypothetical figure to being a tangible reality.

Three main types of such numbers can be distinguished:

1. Representations of *external reality* are numbers purporting to describe the environment in which decision makers exist. Measures of external reality include such numbers as the balance of payments with another country, the number of five-year olds in a school district, the number of poor in a country, the cost of living, the unemployment rate, and the number of people watching a particular television program on a given night.

2. Representations of *processes* are numbers purporting to measure "work" performed. They include the fraction of the time of a machinist or lawyer that is allocated to a particular product or client, the total number of hours worked, and the length of time taken to produce a product. They also include records of how resources were allocated—for example, how much was spent on administration, on pure versus applied research, and on graduate versus undergraduate education.

3. Representations of *outcomes* are numbers purporting to report the outcomes of decisions or activities. In a business firm, this includes outcomes such as sales or profits. In a school, student achievement is represented by a number. Numbers are also constructed to measure such outcomes as number of enemy killed, changes in crime rates, and budget deficits.

The construction of these magic numbers is partly problem solving. Decision makers and professionals try to find the right answer, often in the face of substantial conceptual and technical difficulties. Numbers presuppose a concept of what should be measured and a way of translating that concept into things that can be measured. Unemployment numbers require a specification of when a person is "seeking employment" and "not employed". The concepts and their measurement are sufficiently ambiguous to make the creation of unemployment statistics a difficult technical exercise. Similarly, the definition and measurement of corporate profits, gross national product (GNP), or individual intelligence are by no means simple matters. They involve professional skills of a high order.

The construction of magic numbers is also partly political. Decision makers and others try to find an answer that serves their own interests. Unemployment levels, profits, GNP, individual intelligence, and other numbers are negotiated among contending interests. If the cost-of-living index affects prices or wages, affected groups are likely to organize to seek a favorable number. If managers are evaluated in terms of their profits, they will seek to influence transfer prices, depreciation rates, and the application of accounting rules and conventions that affect the "bottom line." If political leaders care about GNP, they will involve themselves in the negotiation of those numbers. Management involves account and number management as much as it involves management of the things that the numbers represent.

These simultaneous searches for truth and personal advantage often confound both participants and observers. Realist cynics portray the pursuit of truth as a sham, noticing the·many ways in which individuals, experts, and decision makers find it possible to "discover" a truth that happens to be consistent with their own interests. Idealist professionals portray the pursuit of personal advantage as a perversion, noticing the many ways in which serious statisticians struggle to improve the technical quality of the numbers without regard for policy consequences. Both groups have difficulty recognizing the ways in which the process subtly interweaves truth seeking and advantage seeking, leaving each somewhat compromised by the other, even as each somewhat serves the other.

The tenuousness and political basis of many key numbers is

well-known to decision makers. They regularly seek to improve and influence the numbers. At the same time, however, decision makers and others have an interest in stabilizing the numbers, securing agreement about them, and developing shared confidence in them as a basis for joint decision making and communication. The validity of a number may be less important than its acceptance, and decision makers may be willing to forgo insisting on either technical correctness or immediate political advantage in order to sustain social agreement.

1.2.3 Satisficing and Maximizing

Most standard treatments of rational decision making assume that decision makers choose among alternatives by considering their consequences and selecting the alternative with the largest expected return. Behavioral students of decision rules, on the other hand, have observed that decision makers often seem to *satisfice* rather than *maximize*. Maximizing involves choosing the best alternative. Satisficing involves choosing an alternative that exceeds some criterion or target.

The shopkeeper in a small retail store could determine price by assessing information about the complete demand of the relevant population at a set of various prices and selecting the price that best serves her or his preferences. Alternatively he or she could use a simple mark-up over cost in order to ensure an acceptable profit margin on each item. A maximizing procedure for choosing equipment at a new manufacturing facility would involve finding the best combination of prices and features available. A satisficing strategy would find equipment that fits specifications and falls within budget. A marketing manager could seek to find the best possible combination of products, pricing, advertising expenses, and distribution channels; or he or she could create a portfolio of products that meets some sales, market share, or profit target.

DO DECISION MAKERS SATISFICE OR MAXIMIZE?

Neither satisficing nor maximizing is likely to be observed in pure form. Maximizing requires that all possible alternatives be compared and the best one chosen. Satisficing requires only a comparison of alternatives with a target until one that is good enough is found. Maximizing requires that preferences among alternatives meet strong consistency requirements, essentially requiring that all dimensions of preferences be reducible to a single scale—although that scale need not exist in conscious form. Satisficing specifies a target for each dimension and treats the targets as independent constraints. Under satisficing, a bundle that is better on each criterion will not be chosen over another bundle that is good enough on each criterion if the latter bundle is considered first. Satisficing also makes it possible that no bundle will satisfy all criteria, in which case a decision will not be made.

In personnel decisions, a maximizing procedure would involve finding the best possible combination of persons and tasks. A satisficing procedure, on the other hand, would involve finding a person good enough to do the job. A decision maker would define a set of tasks adequate to accomplish the job, and would set targets (performance standards, job requirements) for performance on the job. A decision maker would consider candidates sequentially, perhaps by looking at the current job holder or an immediate subordinate, and would ask whether that person is good enough. When universities consider granting tenure to professors, or when individuals consider mates, for example, they can choose among a host of decision rules varying from relatively pure satisficing rules ("Does this person meet the standards set for satisfactory performance as a tenured professor or spouse?") to relatively pure maximizing rules ("Is this person the best possible person likely to be found—and available—for tenure or marriage in the indefinite future?").

There are problems with using empirical data to tell whether (or when) decision makers maximize or satisfice. The usual difficulties of linking empirical observations to theoretical statements are compounded by the ease with which either vision can be made tautologically "true." True believers in maximization can easily use circular definitions of preferences to account for many apparent deviations from maximizing. True believers in satisficing can easily use circular definitions of targets to account for many apparent deviations from satisficing.

Assessing whether organizations satisfice or maximize involves inferring decision rules from one or more of three kinds of data: (1) data drawn from listening to participants as they talk about the process, (2) data drawn from observing decision processes, and (3) data drawn from observing decision outcomes. The different kinds of data lead to different impressions.

When participants talk about the process, they seem generally to accept the ideology of maximization, but their descriptions sound a lot like satisficing. There is a strong tendency for participants to talk about targets as critical to the process of decision. Although there are frequent efforts to reduce a few separate goals to a common measure (e.g. profit), separate targets are treated as substantially independent constraints unless a solution satisfying them all cannot be found. In addition, alternatives are considered semisequentially. It may not be true that only one alternative is considered at a time (as in the pure form of satisficing), but only a few seem to be considered at a time.

In observations of the process of decision making, targets frequently appear as components of both official and unofficial practices. It is common to specify goals as constraints, at least at first. There is a tendency for only a few alternatives to be considered at a time, but consideration often continues for some more or less predetermined time, rather than strictly until the first satisfactory alternative is found. Decision makers sometimes seem to maximize on some dimensions of the problem and satisfice on others. Sometimes they seem to try to maximize the chance of achieving a target. Targets seem to be especially important when they are defined in terms of surviving until the next period, meeting a deadline, or fulfilling a contract. The pure maximization model seems not to fit the data, although in some situations people might be described as maximizing within a much-edited choice set.

When decision outcomes are observed, it is difficult to differentiate maximizing from satisficing. Most decisions are interpretable in either way, so it is necessary to find situations in which the two yield distinctively different outcomes. Maximization emphasizes the relative position of alternatives. A maximizing procedure is sensitive to nonhomogeneous shifts in alternatives, when one alternative improves relative to another. A maximizing search is sensitive to changes in expected return and costs. Satisficing, on the other hand, emphasizes the position of alternatives relative to a target. A satisficing procedure is sensitive to a change in the absolute value of the current choice, and thus to homogeneous downward shifts in alternatives if they include the chosen one. A satisficing search is sensitive to current position relative to the target.

It is necessary to find situations in which the position of the chosen alternative is changing relative to either other alternatives or the target, but not both. As an example, take the willingness of people to pursue energy conservation. Maximizers will be sensitive to shifts in relative prices but not to whether they reach a target or not (except secondarily). Satisficers will be sensitive to whether they are reaching a target but not to shifts in relative prices (except secondarily). Observations of actual decision making in such domains as new investments, energy conservation, and curricular decisions indicate that satisficing is an aspect of most decision making but that it is rarely found in pure form.

Beyond the evidence that such a portrayal seems to match many observations of decision making behavior, there are two broader theoretical reasons—one cognitive and one motivational—why behavioral students of decision making find satisficing a compelling notion. From a cognitive perspective, targets simplify a complex world. Instead of having to worry about an infinite number of gradations in the environment, individuals simplify the world into two parts—good enough and not good enough. From a motivational perspective, it appears to be true that the world of psychological sensation gives a privileged position to deviations from some status quo.

SATISFICING, ADAPTIVE ASPIRATIONS, AND THE STATUS QUO

In classical theories of rational choice, the importance of a potential consequence does not depend on whether it is portrayed as a "loss" or as a forgone "gain." The implicit aspiration level represented by the status quo is irrelevant. This posture of the theory has long been resisted by students, and generations of economists have struggled to persuade students (and managers) to treat cash outlays and forgone gains as equivalent. The resistance of students has a natural satisficing explanation. Satisficing assumes that people are more concerned with success or failure relative to a target than they are with gradations of either success or failure. If out-of-pocket expenditures are treated as decrements from a current aspiration level (and thus as unacceptable) and forgone gains are not, the former are more likely to be avoided than the latter. A satisficing decision maker is likely to make a distinction between risking the "loss" of something that is not yet "possessed" and risking the loss of something that is already considered a possession.

The tendency to code alternatives as above or below an aspiration level or a status quo has important implications for decision making. Whether a glass is seen as half-empty or half-full depends on how the result is framed by aspiration levels and a decision maker's history. The history is important because aspiration levels—the dividing line between good enough and not good enough—are not stable. In particular, individuals adapt their aspirations (targets) to reflect their experience. Studies of aspiration level adjustment in situations in which information on the performance of others is lacking indicate that decision makers revise aspirations in the direction of past performance but retain a bit more optimism than is justified by that experience. Thus, current aspirations can be approximated by a positive constant plus an exponentially weighted moving average of past experience.

If aspirations adapt to experience, then success contains the seeds of failure, and failure contains the seeds of success. In a very general way, empirical data seem to support such a conception. Although there are some signs that chronically impoverished individuals are less happy than chronically rich individuals, studies of lottery winners reveal that they are no more happy than other people, and studies of paraplegics reveal that they are no less happy than others. This pattern of results has led some people to describe life as a "hedonic treadmill." As individuals adapt their aspirations to their experience, both their satisfactions and their dissatisfactions are short-lived.

The world is more complicated than such a simple model would suggest, of course. Aspirations adapt not only to one's own experience but also to the experience of others. They can become attached not just to the level of reward but to the rate of change of reward. They do not adapt instantaneously, and they appear to adapt upward more rapidly than downward. As a result, deviations in a negative direction seem to be more persistently noticed than positive deviations. This "predisposition to dissatisfaction" is, of course, a strong stimulus for search and change in situations where it exists.

1.3 Theories of Attention and Search

In theories of limited rationality, attention is a scarce resource. The evoked set, of alternatives, consequences, and preferences, and the process that produces the evoked set, take on an importance not found in models of infinitely rational decision makers. Not all alternatives are known, they must be sought; not all consequences are known, they must be investigated; not all preferences are known, they must be explored and evoked. The allocation of attention affects the information available and thus the decision.

Ideas that emphasize the importance of attention are found throughout the social and behavioral sciences. In psychology, the rationing of attention is central to notions of editing, framing, and problem solving "set"; in political science, it is central to the notion of agendas; in sociology, it is central to the notion that many things in life are "taken as given" and serve as constraints rather than as decision alternatives. In economics, theories of search are a central concern of the study of decisions. The study of decision making is, in many ways, the study of search and attention.

1.3.1 The Rationing of Attention

In contrast to traditional societies, which are ordinarily described as short of physical and human resources rather than short of time, the modern world is usually described as stimulus-rich and opportunity-filled. There are more things to do than there is time to do them, more claims on attention than can be met. The importance of scheduling and time, and concerns about "information overload," are distinctive complaints. Industries have arisen to compete for the attention of individuals, as well as to advise people on proper time management. The problems are conspicuously not ameliorated by information technology. Time pressures are further dramatized and probably accentuated by telefaxes, car phones, and systems of electronic mail. Computers seem to have done more to increase information load than to reduce it.

The problems of time, attention, and information management are critical to research on decision making. Limitations on attention and information raise dilemmas for actors in the system and cause difficulties for those who would try to understand decisions. If attention is rationed, decisions can no longer be predicted simply by knowing the features of alternative and desires. Decisions will be affected by the way decision makers attend (or fail to attend) to particular preferences, alternatives, and consequences. They will depend on the ecology of attention: who attends to what, and when. Interested participants may not be present at a given decision because they are somewhere else. Something may be overlooked because something else is being attended to. Decisions happen the way they do, in large part, because of the way attention is allocated, and "timing" and "mobilization" are important issues.

Decision makers appear to simplify the attention problem considerably. For example, they respond to deadlines and the initiatives of others. They organize their attention around well-defined options. Insofar as decisions about investments in attention are made consciously, they are delayed as long as possible. The simplifications do not always seem appropriate to students of decision making. Decision makers are often criticized for poor attention management. They are criticized for dealing with the "wrong" things, or for dealing with the right things at the "wrong" time. Short-run problems often seem to be favored over long-run. Crises seem to preempt planning.

1.3.2 Rational Theories of Information and Attention

Investments in information and attention can be examined using the same rational calculations used to make other investments. No rational decision maker will obtain all possible information (unless it has some direct consumption value—as in the case of rabid sports fans). Rational decision makers can be expected to invest in information up to the point at which the marginal expected cost equals the marginal expected return. The cost of information is the expected return that could be realized by investing elsewhere the resources expended to find and comprehend the current information. There are times when information has no decision value. In particular, from the point of view of decision making, if a piece of information will not affect choice, then it is not worth acquiring or attending to.

Since information is costly, rational decision makers can be expected to look for ways to reduce the average costs of attention, computation, calculation, and search. By assuming that actual decision makers and organizations do in fact make such efforts and are effective in optimizing with respect to information costs, information and transaction cost economists generate a series of predictions about the organization of communication, incentives, contracts, and authority. For example, they consider the possibilities for using other resources to "buy" time. Owners hire managers to act in their interests. Managers delegate responsibility to employees. Since agents may not know the interests of those who delegate to them or may not take those interests fully to heart, the use of agents incurs costs of delegation that are experienced in terms of time as well as money.

As a classic example of rationalizing information and its use, consider the design of optimal information codes. A rational code would be designed to minimize the expected cost of sending messages. People typically tell others to "yell if you're in trouble" rather than to "yell as long as you're okay." Yelling takes energy and so should be conserved. Since "being in trouble" is a less likely state than "being okay," energy expenditure is minimized by associating it with the former state rather than the latter. Similarly, if we assume the early American patriot

Paul Revere was an optimal code designer, then we know that he must have calculated the expected cost of alternative codes in signaling an attack by the British as they moved out of Boston. Under such assumptions, his code of "one if by land, two if by sea" tells us that he thought an attack by land was more likely than an attack by sea (assuming, of course, that he assumed the British would not know about his code).

Organizations use many specially designed codes for recording, retrieving, and communicating information. Accounting systems, human resource management systems, and inventory systems are examples. But the most familiar form of information code is a natural language. Languages and other codes partition continuous worlds into discrete states. Language divides all possible gradations of hues into a relatively small number of colors. Language recognizes a small set of kin relationships (a different set in different cultures) among the many relations that could be labeled. Insofar as a natural language can be imagined to have developed in response to considerations of the costs and benefits of alternative codes, it should make decision relevant distinctions easier to communicate than distinctions that are not relevant to decisions. Where fine gradations in colors are important for decisions, the language will be elaborated to reflect fine gradations. Where color distinctions are unimportant for decisions, they will tend to disappear.

It is not trivial to imagine a process of code development that will optimize a code or language, and it would not be overly surprising to observe suboptimal codes. Decision alternatives are often ambiguous, overlapping, and changing, as are costs and benefits. Decisions require tradeoffs across time and space that are not easy to make. And languages are likely to endure for some time after decision options have changed. Moreover, there are strategic issues involved. If codes distinguish possible actions efficiently from the point of view of a decision maker, they simultaneously provide a guide for the strategic manipulation of that decision maker's choices. Since natural languages have evolved in the face of these complications, one speculation is that some puzzling elements of languages—particular their ambiguities, inconsistencies, and redundancies—are actually efficient solutions to the many ways in which the world does not match the simplifications of rational models of information.

Rational theories of attention, information, and information structures have become some of the more interesting and important domains of modern economics and decision theory. They have been used to fashion substantial contributions to the practices of accounting, communication, and information management. They have also been used to predict important features of organizational forms and practices. However, there is a kind of peculiarity to all such theories. Determining the optimal information strategy, code, investment, or structure requires complete information about information options, quality, processing, and comprehension requirements. It requires a precise specification of preferences that resolve complicated tradeoffs over time and space. In effect, the problem of limits is "solved" by a solution that presumes the absence of limits. Behavioral students of attention, search, and information have generally pursued a different set of ideas.

1.3.3 Satisficing as a Theory of Attention and Search

Rather than focus on rationalizing attention and information decisions, behavioral students of attention are more likely to build on ideas of satisficing. In its early formulations, satisficing was commonly presented as an alternative decision rule to maximizing. Emphasis was placed on the step function characteristics of the satisficing utility function. Actually, satisficing is less a decision rule than a search rule. It specifies the conditions under which search is triggered or stopped, and it directs search to areas of failure. Search is controlled by a comparison between performance and targets. If performance falls below target, search is increased. If performance achieves its target, search is decreased. As performance rises and falls, search falls and rises, with a resulting feedback to performance.

Thus, satisficing has close relatives in the psychology of decision making. The idea that decision makers focus on targets to organize their search and decision activities is standard. The "elimination by aspects" model of choice assumes that decision makers do not engage in tradeoffs, they simply consider each criterion sequentially—usually in order of importance—and eliminate alternatives that do not exceed a threshold. The "prospect theory" of choice assumes that decision makers are more risk-averse when returns are expected to be above a target than when they are expected to be below a target.

FAILURE-INDUCED SEARCH

The most important step in a satisficing model of search is the comparison of achievements to targets. Decision makers set aspiration levels for important dimensions—firms for sales and profits, museums for contributions and attendance, colleges for enrollments and placements. Achievements are evaluated with respect to those aspirations. Failure increases search, and success decreases search. In a pure satisficing model, search continues as long as achievement is below the target and ends when the target is exceeded. A natural modification of the pure model would allow search to vary with the discrepancy between achievement and the target, with a decreasing effect as the discrepancy increases.

There are three principal features of satisficing as a theory of search:

1. Search is *thermostatic.* Targets (or goals) are essentially search branch points rather than ways of choosing among alternatives directly. They are equivalent to discrimination nets or thermostats; they begin and end search behavior. As a result, researchers frequently learn more about the real operational goals of decision makers by asking for their search triggers than by asking about their "goals."

2. Targets are considered *sequentially.* A satisficing search process is serial rather than parallel; things are considered one at a time—one target, one alternative, one problem. Since decision makers generally act as though they assume a solution will be found in the neighborhood of a symptom of a problem, the first alternatives they consider tend to be local. If sales fall in Texas, then they look for the problem and the solution in Texas. In this way, order effects become important, and better alterna-

tives are likely to be overlooked if inferior, but acceptable, alternatives are evoked earlier.

3. Search is *active in the face of adversity.* In many ways, standard decision theory is a passive theory. It emphasizes making the best of a world as it exists. Decision theory instructs decision makers to calculate the odds, lay the best bet they can, and await the outcome. Satisficing stimulates a more active effort to change adverse worlds. A satisficing decision maker faced with a host of poor alternatives is likely to try to find better ones by changing problem constraints. A maximizing decision maker is more likely to select the best of the poor lot.

SLACK

Satisficing theories of limited rationality assume two adaptive processes that bring aspirations and performance close to each other. First, aspirations adapt to performance. That is, decision makers learn what they should expect. Second, performance adapts to aspirations by increasing search and decreasing slack in the face of failure, decreasing search and increasing slack when faced with success.

Such theories predict that as long as performance exceeds aspirations, search for new alternatives is modest, slack accumulates, and aspirations increase. When performance falls below aspirations, search is stimulated, slack decreases, and aspirations decrease. Search stops when targets are achieved, and if targets are low enough, not all resources will be effectively used. The resulting cushion of unexploited opportunities and undiscovered economies—the difference between a decision maker's realized achievement and potential achievement—is slack.

Slack includes undiscovered and unexploited technological, marketing, and cost reduction opportunities. It includes undiscovered and unexploited strategies. Variations in search intensity or efficiency result in variations in slack. Since knowledge about opportunities may not be shared generally within an organization, organizational slack resources may be preemptively expropriated by subunits. Some units may not work as hard as others. Some managers may fly first class or may have more elegant offices and more support staff. Professionals may become "more professional"; engineers may satisfy their love of a beautiful design rather than build the most efficient machine.

Slack has the effect of smoothing performance relative to potential performance. Slack stored in good times becomes a buffer against bad times—a reservoir of potential performance. Thus, variations in realized performance will be smaller than variations in environmental munificence. Because performance is managed in this way, slack conceals capabilities. The level of slack is difficult to determine, and it is hard to estimate what level of performance can be achieved if necessary. Individuals and organizations that appear to be operating close to their capacities frequently are able to make substantial improvements in the face of adversity. The lack of clarity about the level of slack, however, makes slack reduction a highly strategic activity in which each part of an organization (and each individual decision maker) seeks to have the other parts give up their slack first.

Thus, slack is managed. A decision maker may choose to have slack as a hedge against adversity, to smooth fluctuations in profits or resources, or as a buffer against the costs of coordination. Slack may be used to inhibit the upward adjustment of aspirations. Decision makers deliberately reduce performance in order to manage their own expectations about the future. Even more, they do so in order to manage the expectations of others. They restrict their performance in order to avoid overachieving a target and causing the target to rise.

ELABORATING THE SEARCH MODEL

Not all search by decision makers is due to failure. Social systems and organizations may take a deliberate anticipatory approach to search. They may create "search departments" both to solve problems (strategy, planning, research and development) and to find them (quality control, customer complaints). This search tends to be orderly, standardized, and somewhat independent of success or failure.

However, the simple thermostat model of satisficing search captures some important truths. Failure-induced search, the basic idea of the model, is clearly a general phenomenon. Necessity is often the mother of invention, and decision makers threatened with failure often discover ways to cut costs, produce better products, and market them more effectively. Slack serves as a buffer, accumulating in good times and decreasing in bad times. The simple model of search, which involves comparing changing performance with a fixed aspiration, does not capture all that is known about satisficing search, however.

First, *aspirations change* over time, and they change endogenously. They are affected by the past performances of the particular individual or organization and by the past performances of those individuals and organizations perceived as comparable. In general, as performances improve, so do aspirations; as performances decline, so do aspirations.

Adaptive aspirations and have very general effects on organizations. The way they, along with failure-induced search, tend to bring performance and aspirations together has already been noted. When performance exceeds the target, search is reduced, slack is increased, and the target is raised. On average, this tends to reduce performance. When performance is below the target, search is increased, slack is decreased, and the target is lowered. On average, this tends to increase performance.

Thus the process of target adjustment can be seen as a substitute for slack adjustment. If targets adapt rapidly, then slack and search will not adapt rapidly, and vice versa. By virtue of the adaptation of aspirations, subjective definitions of success and failure (which control search behavior and—as will be developed later—both risk taking and learning from experience) depend not only on current performance but also on current aspirations for performance (and thus on a performance history).

Second, search is *success-induced* as well as failure-induced. When the presence of slack relaxes coordination and control pressures, decision makers are free to pursue idiosyncratic, local preferences. They may act opportunistically or imperialistically. If they are members of an organization, they may assert independence from the organization or may pursue linkages with outside constituents (professional organizations or community interests). These activities are forms of slack search, stimulated by success rather than failure.

Slack search differs in character, as well as timing, from search under adversity. It is less tightly tied to key objectives and less likely to be careful. It involves experiments that are, on average, probably inefficient, particularly in the short run, relative to the primary goals of a decision maker or organization. Most such experiments are probably disadvantageous, but they allow for serendipity, foolishness, and variation. The outcomes of slack search are likely to have a lower mean and higher variance than the outcomes of failure-induced search or institutionalized search. The possibility that such activities find a protective cover in the "waste" of slack plays an important role in an expanded theory of long-run adaptation.

Third, search is *supply-driven* as well as demand-driven. Search is a possible way of describing information acquisition in decision making, but the metaphor has its limits if search is seen as prospecting, seeking alternatives and information that lie passively in the environment. A significant feature of contemporary life is that information is not passive. In some circumstances, a better analogy for information acquisition might be to mating, where information is seeking users even as users are seeking information (for example, in the purchase of equipment). Or the proper analogy might be to hunting, where information is actively eluding information seekers (for example, military secrets) or where information "seekers" are actively eluding information sources (for example, investors and stock salespeople). In general, the market in information is a joint consequence of behavior by the recipient and behavior by the transmitter of the information. It cannot be understood without considering both sides of the transaction.

The general structure of an expanded model of satisficing search is sketched in Figure 1. It displays the close relations among changes in aspirations, changes in slack, and changes in search, the direct and indirect effects of slack on performance, and the exogenous effects of institutionalized search, supply-

Figure 1
Expanded Model of Satisficing Search

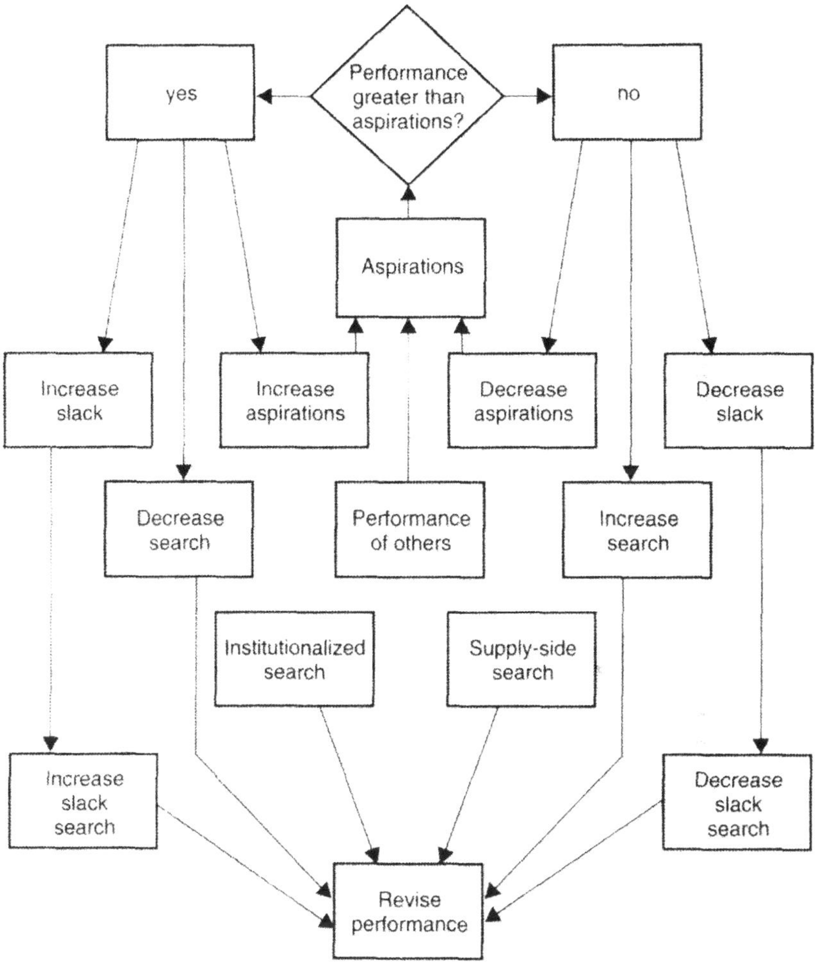

side search, and the performance of others on the dynamics of the system.

UNDERSTANDING INNOVATION

It is possible to use the general ideas of satisficing search to speculate about the long-run dynamics of individual and institutional change: Do those who have been successful in the past continue to be successful, or does success sow the seeds of failure? Do the rich get richer or poorer?

There are no simple answers to such questions. Both success and failure stimulate mechanisms that encourage subsequent success, and both success and failure stimulate other mechanisms that encourage subsequent failure. However, an important part of the answer to the stability of success depends on the richness of the search environment. Failure-induced search increases efficiency and reduces foolishness. Success-induced search introduces more risky alternatives. It tends to produce more distant search and introduces bigger changes with lower odds of success. The rich get richer if success-induced search (slack search) gives better returns than failure-induced search or if prior success was produced by either institutionalized search or supply-side search that continues.

In technologically mature worlds, success will tend to breed failure. Slack will produce inefficiencies and unproductive success-induced search. In technologically young worlds, on the other hand, success will tend to breed success. The specific innovation that will provide a breakthrough is hard to identify in advance, so there is a good deal of chance in the outcome from any particular innovation. But slack search provides the resources for relatively frequent experiments, thus increases the chance of an important discovery.

Will there then be persistent innovators? Assuming that all actors are competent, within the satisficing search theory major successful innovations are produced by foolishness, which in turn is produced by a combination of slack (thus success) and luck. Individuals or organizations must be foolish enough to look and lucky enough to find something. A few innovative ideas will be successful, thus marking the individuals and organizations involved as "innovative." Success will lead to slack and thus to more foolish innovative ideas.

As a result, persistently successful organizations will tend to be more innovative than others. However, since most innovative ideas will not be successful, most innovators will not repeat their successes, and their resources will fall, leading them to produce fewer and fewer potentially innovative ideas. Thus, success in innovation increases the amount of innovative activity. By increasing the amount of innovative activity, it increases the likelihood of new success. But unless the pool of opportunities is rich, it may not increase the likelihood enough to pay the increased costs incurred by the search. Under those circumstances, it leads to long-term decline.

1.4 Risk and Risk Taking

As has been suggested above, understanding risk and risk taking is a serious concern of rational theories of choice. In fact, "risk" is sometimes used as a label for the residual variance in a theory of rational choice. The strategy is to assume that risk preference accounts for any deviation in observed behavior from the behavior that would be observed if decision makers had utilities for money that were linear with money and made decisions by maximizing expected monetary value. This strategy has some appeal for many formal theorists of choice and for many students of aggregate decision behavior.

Behavioral students of decision making are inclined to take a different route. They try to understand the behavioral processes that lead to taking risks. The emphasis is on understanding individual and organizational risk taking rather than fitting the concept into aggregate predictions. As a result, behavioral students of risk are more interested in characterizing the way variability in possible outcomes affects a choice.*

The factors that affect risk taking in individuals and organizations can conveniently be divided into three sets:

1. *Risk estimation.* Decision makers form estimates of the risk involved in a decision. Those estimates affect the risk actually taken. If the risk is underestimated, decisions will reflect greater risk taking than is intended. If the risk is overestimated, decisions will reflect less risk taking than is intended.

2. *Risk-taking propensity.* Different decision makers seem to

---

*This section draws from work done jointly with Zur Shapira.

have different propensities to take risk. In some choice theories, decision makers are described as having "preferences" for risk. Observations of risk taking suggest that the term "preferences" may incorrectly imply that individual risk propensities are primarily conscious preferences, whereas they appear to arise only partly through conscious choice.

3. *Structural factors* within which risk taking occurs. Both risk estimation and risk-taking propensity are affected by the context in which they occur. Features of organizing for decisions introduce systematic effects into risk taking.

1.4.1 Estimating Risk

Decision makers seek to form estimates of risk that are both technically and socially valid. Technically valid estimates are those that reflect the true situation faced by the decision maker. Socially valid estimates are those that are shared by others, are stable, and are believed with confidence. Neither technical nor social validity can be assured, nor can either be described as distinct.

IMPROVING TECHNICAL VALIDITY

Decision makers typically attribute uncertainty about outcomes to one or more of three different sources: an inherently unpredictable world, incomplete knowledge about the world, and incomplete complete contracting with strategic actors. Each produces efforts to reduce uncertainty.

Inherently Unpredictable Worlds. Some uncertainties are seen as irreducible, inherent in the mechanisms of the universe. For uncertainties that are thought to arise from inherently uncertain environmental processes, decision makers try to judge the likelihood of events. There are numerous studies of individual estimates of the likelihood of uncertain future events. In general, the studies indicate that experienced decision makers are by no means helpless when it comes to estimating future probabilities. They do rather well in situations in which they have experience.

On the other hand, the mental machinery they use to anticipate the future contains some flaws. For example, future events are rated as more likely to the extent that similar events can be remembered in the decision maker's own past. This is one of the reasons why experienced decision makers do reasonably well in the domain of their experience. The sample from which they draw is related to the universe about which they make predictions. Biases are produced by differences between the universe of relevant events and the sample stored in memory.

Decision makers also assess the likelihood of an event by considering how closely it conforms to a prototypical image of what such an event would look like. Events are judged to be more likely to the extent they are "representative." The most prototypical events are, however, not always the most frequent. In particular, decision makers tend to overlook important information about the base rates of events. Even though the greatest hitters in history were successful only about 40 percent of the time in their best seasons, there is a tendency to expect great baseball hitters to hit whenever they bat, because hitting is what is prototypical of great hitters. Similarly, although great designers produce exceptional designs only a few times in a lifetime, every failure of a great designer to produce a great design is experienced as a surprise.

There are indications that decision makers, in effect, seek to deny uncertainty by focusing on events that are certain to occur or certain not to occur and by ignoring those that are highly uncertain. This is accentuated by the tendency to round extreme probabilities either to certainty or to impossibility. Very few decision makers have the experience necessary to distinguish an event with a probability of 0.001 from one with a probability of 0.00001, although the difference is extremely large and, in some cases, critical.

Incomplete Knowledge. Decision makers tend to exaggerate their control over their environment, overweighting the impacts of their actions and underweighting the impact of other factors, including chance. They believe things happen because of their intentions and their skills (or lack of them) more than because of contributions from the environment. This tendency is accentuated by success. As a result, although decision makers certainly recognize that some uncertainties are unresolvable, there is a strong tendency to treat uncertainty as something to be removed rather than estimated.

Some of these "avoidable" uncertainties are seen as a result of ignorance or lack of information, incomplete knowledge of the world. For uncertainties that arise from gaps or ambiguities in their knowledge of the environment, decision makers assume that uncertainty can be removed by diligence and imagination. They try to judge and, if possible, improve the quality of information. They have a strong tendency to want their knowledge about what will happen to be couched in terms that deny doubt. They are more likely to seek to confirm their existing information than to acquire or notice disconfirming information. For example, purchasing agents spend a few minutes forming an impression of a potential product, then devote the rest of their time to seeking information consistent with their initial hypothesis.

Since their strategies for understanding uncertain worlds involve forming firm estimates, decision makers appear to prefer stories to more academic information. They prefer information about specific cases to information about general trends. They prefer vivid information to pallid information. They prefer concrete information to abstract statistics. When confronted with inconsistent information, they tend to rely on one cue and exclude others from consideration.

Incomplete Contracting. Some uncertainties are seen as a result of incomplete contracting, the failure to establish understandings with critical people in the environment. Many of the other actors in the environment have interests at variance with those of any particular decision maker. Each decision maker acts on the basis of the probable actions of the others, knowing that they are doing the same. The resulting indeterminacy leads to intelligence systems designed to spy on the intentions of others. It leads to the pursuit of resources to remove dependence on them. And it leads to negotiations to bind others to desired future actions, rather than to efforts to predict them probabilistically.

The tendency to negotiate and control the environment rather than predict it is consistent with what has already been observed. Uncertainty is treated the same way any other problem is treated—as something to be removed. Decision makers seek control over the uncontrolled part of their environments. Deadlines and guarantees are more common than time-dependent or performance-dependent variable prices, and the latter are more common than time and performance gambles.

IMPROVING SOCIAL VALIDITY

Individuals, social systems, and systems of knowledge all require reasonable stability and agreement in understandings of the world. Without such social validity, decision makers may have difficulty acting, and social systems may have difficulty enduring. The social robustness of beliefs is threatened by the ambiguities of experience and meaning and by the numerous alternative interpretations of reality that can be sustained. Processes toward differentiation persistently break down tendencies toward agreement. Successes lead to decentralization and experimentation in beliefs; failures lead to rejection of beliefs and disagreement.

Countering these pressures toward heterogeneity and instability are an assortment of mechanisms fostering shared and stable estimates of risk. Experience is edited to remove contradictions. Individuals recall prior beliefs as more consistent with present ones than they are. Incongruous data or predictions are likely to be forgotten. Information is gathered to sustain decisions rather than change them. Beliefs are adjusted to be consistent with actions. They are shaped by the beliefs of others.

Preferences for vivid and detailed information and for redundant, overly idiosyncratic information fit this picture of augmenting robustness and building confidence. Detailed stories tend to be filled with redundant and arguably irrelevant information, thus probably inefficient and misleading from the standpoint of making more valid estimates of risk. Nevertheless, decision makers show a preference for detailed stories. Insofar as the goal of the decision process is to see the world with confidence rather than accuracy, the double counting of evidence becomes an asset rather than a liability. In social contexts, this justification could possibly be explained as the confounding of social influence with personal preference, but the same kind of effect seems to occur even within individuals who are merely trying to justify their choices to themselves. Confidence increases with the amount of information processed, even though accuracy typically does not.

The view of decision makers as seekers of stable, shared estimates in which they can have confidence is consistent with research on reactions to alternative gambles. At one point, it was speculated that decision makers might be averse not just to uncertainty about outcomes but also to uncertainty about the probabilities of those outcomes. In fact, people seem to seek not certainty of knowledge but social validity. They actually reject clear bets in favor of those with ill-defined probabilities in domains where they feel their estimates and actions are based on valid beliefs. They avoid bets with ill-defined probabilities in domains where they lack such a sense of socially valid knowledge or competence.

1.4.2 Risk-Taking Propensity

The level of risk taking observed in organizations is affected not only by the estimation of the risk but also by the propensity of a risk taker to seek or avoid a particular level of expected risk. Consider four different understandings of risk-taking propensity: (1) risk-taking propensity as a personality trait, (2) risk-taking propensity as a reaction to targets, (3) risk-taking propensity as a reasoned choice, and (4) risk-taking propensity as an artifact of reliability.

RISK-TAKING PROPENSITY AS TRAIT

In one interpretation of risk-taking propensity, propensities for risk are described as individual traits. For example, in many theories of rational choice, particularly those in which risk is measured by nonlinearities in the utility for money, individuals are assumed to be risk-averse. They are assumed to prefer an alternative that will yield a given return with certainty to any alternative having the same expected value but some chance of higher and lower returns. The assumption of risk aversion is sometimes taken as an unexplained attribute of human beings, sometimes linked to an assumption of decreasing marginal utility of money, sometimes given a somewhat casual competitive advantage survival interpretation.

If people are risk-averse, it is argued, risk taking must be rewarded. Thus, it is expected that risky gambles will be accepted only if they have higher expected returns than those without risk or, more generally, there should be a positive relation between the amount of risk in an investment and the return provided. The argument is impeccable if one accepts the risk-aversion trait assumption and an assumption that markets in risk are efficient. Such assumptions are not universally accepted, and direct observation often produces a negative correlation between risk and return. The assumptions seem to have somewhat greater merit in narrow finance markets than elsewhere— or at least somewhat greater acceptance.

Skepticism about a generic trait of risk aversion, however, does not preclude the possibility that any one individual has a risk-taking propensity that is stable over time but that propensities vary among individuals. In this interpretation, different individuals have different characteristic tastes for risk, some being inherently more risk-averse and some more risk-seeking. Those tastes for risk are seen as established relatively early in life and to be maintained as stable personality traits in adulthood.

The distribution of risk takers in a population (e.g. in a given organization), therefore, is assumed to be affected primarily by selection. Risk-averse people are assumed to select (and to be selected by) different professions and different organizations from those chosen by people more comfortable with risk. The people who become underwater welders or racing drivers will be different kinds of people from those who become postal workers or professors. Thus the solution to creating an organization with a certain "risk propensity" is to attract the right kind of people.

The evidence for variation among decision makers in individually stable risk-taking propensities is mixed, but it seems plausible to suspect that some such variations exist, that there may be consistent differences among people, even consistent differences among cultures or subcultures. However, the evidence also seems to indicate that, at least within a given culture, the risk-taking effects attributable to trait differences in risk propensity are relatively small when compared with other effects.

RISK-TAKING PROPENSITY AS TARGET-ORIENTED

In most behavioral studies of risk taking, individual risk-taking propensity is not seen as a stable trait of an individual but as varying with the situation. Probably the best established situational effect stems from the way decision makers distinguish between situations of success (or expected success) and situations of failure (or expected failure). Risk-taking propensity varies with the relationship between an individual's position and a target or aspiration level, and thus between contexts of success and failure.

When they are in the neighborhood of a target and confront a choice between two items of equal expected value, decision makers tend to choose the less risky alternative if outcomes involve gains, and the more risky alternative if outcomes involve losses. This is a relatively robust empirical result, true for college students, business executives, racetrack bettors, and small granivorous birds.

When individuals find themselves well above the target, they tend to take greater risks—partly because, presumably, in that position they have little chance of failing, and partly because they may be inattentive to their actions as a result of the large cushion. The risk-taking propensities of decision makers who are well below a target are more complicated, especially when their position puts them in danger of not surviving. On the one hand, as they fall farther and farther below their targets, they tend to take bigger and bigger risks, presumably to increase the chance of achieving their targets. On the other hand, as they come closer and closer to extinction, they tend to become rigid and immobile, repeating previous actions and avoiding risk.

Since falling farther from a target and falling closer to extinction are normally correlated, the effect of failure on risk taking appears to depend on whether decision makers focus attention on their hopes (organized around their aspiration level target) or their fears (organized around their extinction level).

These links between success (outcomes minus aspirations) and risk taking are complicated by two important feedbacks:

First, outcomes are affected by risk taking. At the least, decision makers who take greater risks realize a higher variance in their returns than those who take lower risks. In situations where risk and return are positively correlated, risk takers will, on average, do better than risk avoiders. In situations where risk and return are negatively correlated, risk avoiders will, on average, do better.

Second, aspiration levels (targets) adapt to outcomes. Success leads to higher aspirations; failure leads to lower aspirations. In general, adaptive aspirations tend to moderate the effects of success and failure by making very successful people less risk taking, and by making unsuccessful people less risk taking. Thus adaptive aspirations smooth system performance and risk taking. Explorations of the dynamic properties and long-run competitive consequences of this system suggest that there are some survival advantages in variable risk preferences when combined with adaptive aspiration levels.

RISK-TAKING PROPENSITY AS CHOICE

In a third view of risk-taking propensity, risky behavior is treated not as a function of personality or of aspirations, but as a reasoned choice. In the spirit of the present chapter, individuals can be imagined as rationally calculating what level of risk they think would serve them best. Consider, for example, risk-taking strategy in a competitive situation where relative position makes a difference. Suppose that someone wishes to finish first, and anything else is irrelevant. Such an individual might want to choose a level of risk that maximizes the chance of finishing first. In general, strategies for maximizing the chance of finishing first are quite different from strategies for maximizing expected value.

For example, suppose one were challenged to a tennis match and given the option of specifying the number of points in the match. Given a choice, how long a game would a rational tennis player choose to play, assuming that the length of the game itself had no intrinsic value? The key to answering this question lies in recognizing how the probability of outscoring an opponent depends both on the probability of winning any particular point and on the length of the game. As the length of the game increases, the better player is more and more likely to win, because the variability in outcomes declines with "sample" size (relatively rapidly, in fact). The game's outcome becomes more and more certain, less and less risky.

Any disadvantaged player (i.e., any player who on average loses, for example, a weaker tennis player or a customer at a casino) increases the chance of reaching a positive outcome by decreasing the number of trials (that is, by increasing the sampling error or risk). That is one reason why better students might prefer majors, courses, and examinations with relatively little random error in their evaluations, and poorer students might prefer majors, courses, and examinations with relatively large random error.

Anticipating somewhat the spirit of Chapter 2, it is also possible to observe that individuals might make a reasoned choice of risk that depends not on calculations of expected consequences but on fulfilling the demands of an identity. A culture might define appropriate risk behavior for different roles. For example, it is sometimes reported that teachers seem to expect (and observe) greater playground risk taking by boys than by girls. Rites of passage into different groups require different risk preferences. Similarly, managerial ideology contains a large number of recommendations about the appropriate levels of risk that should be assumed. Management is often defined in terms of taking risks, acting boldly, making tough choices, and making a difference.

RISK-TAKING PROPENSITY AS AN ARTIFACT OF RELIABILITY

Risks may also be taken without consciousness, as a consequences of unreliability—breakdowns in competence, communication, coordination, trust, responsibility, or structure. Cases of risk taking through lack of reliability are easy to overlook, because they have none of the intentional, willful character of strategic, deliberate, or situational risk-taking. Nevertheless, they can be important parts of the risk-taking story.

For example, risk-taking behavior is influenced by changes in the knowledge of a decision maker. Those effects stem from the relation between knowledge and reliability. Ignorance is a prime source of variability in the distribution of possible outcomes from an action. The greater the ignorance of decision makers or of those implementing the decisions, the greater the variability of the outcome distribution conditional on the choice. That is, the greater the risk. Thus, increases in knowledge have two principal effects on a performance distribution: On the one hand, an increase in knowledge increases the mean performance that can be expected in a decision situation. At the same time, knowledge also increases the reliability of the outcome (that is, decreases the risk in the situation). Thus, as decision makers become more knowledgeable, they improve their average performance and reduce their risk taking.

Similarly, social controls tend to increase reliability, thus decrease risk taking. The mechanisms by which controls grow looser and tighter, or become more or less effective, are only marginally connected to conscious risk taking. In general, reliability increases with education and experience, decreases with organizational size. Organizational slack tends to increase in good times and to reduce reliability; it tends to decrease in poor times and to increase reliability. Diversity in organizational tasks or organizational composition tends to reduce reliability. All of these changes affect the actual level of risk exhibited by decision makers.

1.4.3 Organizational Effects on Risk Taking

Organizations often form the context in which riskiness is estimated and risk-taking propensities are enacted into the taking of risks. That context makes a difference. The forms and practices of organizing shape the determinants of risk and thereby the levels of risk taking observed.

BIASES IN ESTIMATION OF RISK

The estimation of risk by decision makers is systematically biased by the experiences they have in organizations. Decision maker experience is not random but is strongly biased in at least two ways: Decision makers are characteristically successful in their past performance in the organization, and they rarely experience rare events. These two mundane facts produce systematic effects in the estimation of risk.

Success-induced Bias. Organizations provide a context of success and failure, both for individuals and for the organizations as a whole. Success and failure, in turn, affect the estimation of risk. Suppose that all outcomes are a mix of ability and luck (risk). Then biases in the perception of the relative contributions of ability and luck to outcomes will translate into biases in the estimation of risk. Any inclination to overattribute outcomes to luck will be associated with overestimating risk, thus with decreasing risk taking. Similarly, any inclination to overattribute outcomes to ability will be associated with underestimating risk, thus with increasing risk taking.

Research on individual attributions of causality to events indicates that success and failure produce systematic biases in attribution. Individuals are more likely to attribute their successes to ability and their failures to luck than they are to attribute their successes to luck and their failures to ability. They are likely to experience lucky successes as deserved and to experience unlucky failures as manifestations of risk. Persistent failure leads to a tendency to overestimate the amount of risk involved in a situation because of oversampling cases in which luck was bad. Persistent success leads to a tendency to underestimate the amount of risk involved because of oversampling cases in which luck was good.

Since organizations promote successful people to positions of power and authority, rather than unsuccessful ones, it is the biases of success that are particularly relevant to decision making. Success makes executives confident in their ability to handle future events; it leads them to believe strongly in their wisdom and insight. They have difficulty recognizing the role of luck in their achievements. They have confidence in their ability to beat the apparent odds. The same conceits may be found in organizational cultures. Successful organizations build a "can do" attitude that leads people in them to underestimate risk. This "can do" attitude is likely to be especially prevalent in young, successful high-growth organizations where the environment conspires to induce decision makers to believe they know the secrets of success. As a result, successful managers (and others who record their stories) tend to underestimate the risk they have experienced and the risk they currently face, and decision makers who are by intention risk-averse may actually be risk-seeking in behavior.

This organizational inducement of risk underestimation may, of course, be useful for the organization. On the one hand, it is a way of compensating for the negative effects of success and upward aspiration adjustments on risk taking. On the other hand, it is a way of inducing the individually self-sacrificing risk taking that serves the organization and the larger society. In situations where risks must be taken in order to be successful, most of those overconfident decision makers will undoubtedly fall prey to the risks they unwittingly face. But only the overconfident will be heroes. Actors in high-performance, quick-decision, high-risk professions (neurosurgery, air force pilots, investment bankers) all share a professional stereotype of being unusually confident. Overconfidence is still overconfidence and often leads to disaster, but in some situations organizations profit from the individual foolishness that unwarranted self-confidence provides.

Biases in Estimating Extreme Probabilities. As has already been observed, there appears to be a tendency for human subjects to assume that extremely unlikely events will never occur and that extremely likely events will occur. This tendency is accentuated by ordinary experiential learning in an organizational setting. Consider an event of great importance to an organization and very low probability. Individuals in the organization can be expected to estimate the probability of the event and to update their estimates on the basis of their experience.

Suppose, for example, that an event of great importance is so unlikely that it is expected to occur only once every hundred years. Examples might be a disaster in a nuclear power facility, an unprecedented flood, or a dramatic scientific discovery. The rare individual or organization that actually experiences a rare event will come to overestimate the likelihood of the event as a result of that experience. However, most individuals in most organizations will never experience such an unlikely event. As a result, experience will lead most individuals in most organizations to underestimate the likelihood of a very unlikely event.

The effects of this underestimation are twofold. First, in cases where the event being estimated is outside the control of the organization (e.g. natural disasters, revolutions), the underestimation leads to a perversity in planning. The tendency is for plans to ignore extremely unlikely events, to treat them as having no chance of occurring. When planning scenarios exclude extremely unlikely events, they tend to overlook (1) that many of these very unlikely events would have very substantial consequences if they were to occur, and (2) that although each one of these events is extremely unlikely to occur, the chance of *none* of them occurring is effectively zero. Predicting precisely which extremely unlikely event with important consequences will occur is impossible, but some such event will almost certainly occur. Yet plans tend to ignore *all* such events. As a result, plans are developed for a future that is known (with near certainty) to be inaccurate.

Second, in cases where the event being estimated is within the control of an organization, underestimating the likelihood of an extremely unlikely event may have perverse motivational and control consequences. Consider the case of "high-reliability" organizations (e.g. nuclear power plants, air traffic control systems, the space program), where organizations go to great lengths to avoid accidents—to manage the system so that an accident becomes an extremely rare event. In such high-reliability systems, most individual decision makers never experience a failure. They come to think the system is more reliable than it is. This exaggerated confidence in the reliability of the system is likely to lead to relaxation of attention to reliability and to a degradation of reliability over time.

Consider, similarly, research and development organizations looking for a rare discovery. Innovative breakthrough discoveries are extremely unlikely events. Most individuals in research never experience them. They come to think breakthroughs are actually rarer than they are. This reduces the motivation to seek such breakthroughs, and thus further reduces the probability.

Most individuals in these two situations learn over time to modify their estimates of risk in directions that are organizationally perverse. Individuals in high-reliability situations underestimate the danger of breakdown and, as a result, increase the danger. Individuals in breakthrough creativity situations underestimate the possibility of discovery and, as a result, reduce the likelihood. The two situations are not entirely parallel, however. The perversities involved in high-reliability are—at some substantial cost—self-correcting. Degradation of reliability leads to increasing the likelihood that individuals will experience a breakdown and recognize that they have underestimated the danger. On the other hand, the perversities in research are not self-correcting in the same way. Reduced motivation to seek discoveries leads to reduced likelihood of such discoveries, thus confirming the earlier underestimate.

SELECTION ON INDIVIDUAL TRAITS

Insofar as risk-taking propensity is an individual trait, the main way in which organizational risk taking can be affected is by affecting the entrance, exit, and promotion of individuals with particular risk-taking propensities.

Who Enters? Who Leaves? Entry into and exit from an organization are commonly seen as voluntary matchmaking and matchbreaking, acts of deliberate consequential choice. In such a vision, a match is established or continued if (and only if) it is acceptable to both the individual and the organization. Thus, in effect, the match between an individual and an organization continues as long as neither has a better alternative. This hypersimple rational model of entries and exits is, of course, subject to a variety of qualifications of the sort considered in this book. But as long as it is taken as a very loose frame, it may serve to highlight a few features of the process by which individuals and organizations select each other.

In particular, it is possible to ask whether entry or exit processes are likely to be affected by risk-taking propensity. One possibility is that an organization systematically monitors risk-taking propensity and explicitly includes that consideration in its decisions to hire or retain an individual. If risk-taking propensity is observable, the only question is whether one would expect an organization to prefer risk seekers or risk avoiders. The most common speculation is that organizations, particularly those using formal hiring and firing procedures, tend to prefer risk avoiders to risk seekers. The argument is straightforward: Since big employment mistakes are more visible, more attributable, and more connected to the reward system than big employment triumphs, rational employment agents prefer reliable employees to high-risk ones. The argument is plausible, but very little evidence exists for gauging the extent to which it is true.

A second possibility is that organizations do not (or cannot) monitor risk-taking propensity but monitor other things that are, perhaps unknowingly, correlated with risk-taking propensity. For example, suppose employers seek competence. As they assess competence and secure it, they favor individuals who are able to gain and exhibit competence. Since an important element of competence is reliability—being able to accomplish something within relatively small tolerances for error—competence itself selects individuals by traits of risk-avoidance. Thus, unwittingly, an organization in pursuit of ordinary competence disproportionately selects risk avoiders.

Who Moves Up? If risk taking is considered to be a trait that varies from individual to individual, we need to ask not only which individuals enter or exit an organization but also which individuals move toward the top in a hierarchy. As before, it can be imagined that an organization has some preference for risk-seeking or risk-avoiding managers, monitors the behavior of candidates for promotion, and favors those who have the right traits. Also as before, the most common prediction is that (for reasons similar to those given above) an organization will tend to favor risk-avoiding managers for promotion. As a result, it is predicted that the average risk-taking propensity of higher-level managers will be less than that of lower-level managers.

Surprisingly enough, the small amount of information available to test the prediction indicates that the prediction is wrong. The average risk-taking propensity of higher-level managers appears to be somewhat higher than that of lower-level managers. One possibility is, of course, that organizations monitor risk-taking propensity and differentially promote managers who are prone to take risks. Alternatively, however, it is possible that risk-prone managers are promoted not because the organization consciously seeks risk-seeking executives but because it promotes those who do particularly well.

To explore how this might come to pass, consider the following simple model: Assume that there is a hierarchy within the organization, that there is competition for promotion, and that promotion is based on comparative reputation. Reputation is accumulated over a series of performances on the job. Each single performance on a job is a draw from a distribution having a mean equal to the individual's ability level and a variance equal to the individual's risk-taking propensity. Individuals accumulate reputations over a series of performances. Their reputations are averages of their realized performances. Whenever a vacancy occurs in the organization, the person with the highest reputation on the next lower level is promoted.

Let us assume that individual risk-taking propensity is a trait (individuals do not consciously choose to take risks, they are simply either risky people or cautious people), and that abilities and risk-taking propensities are independent. Then, as the size of the performance samples becomes very large, the reputations of individuals approach their true abilities. The assignment of individuals to levels is determined entirely by the relative abilities of employees. Average ability increases as you move up the hierarchy, and average risk preference is approximately equal at every level in the organization.

However, in real organizations performance samples are typically rather small. For very small performance samples (with moderate variability in both ability and risk-taking propensity), reputation no longer depends exclusively on ability but is a joint consequence of ability and risk-taking propensity. If the hierarchy is steep (that is, only a few people are promoted from one level to another), the assignment of individuals to levels is heavily dependent on risk preference. Average ability increases very little as you move up the hierarchy, while average risk preference increases substantially. Thus, a procedure that appears to promote people on the basis of their abilities actually moves them ahead on the basis of the amount of risk they take.

EXPERIENCE, LEARNING, AND RELIABILITY

If experience on a job leads to an accumulation of skills and knowledge, then this cumulative knowledge should both increase average performance and increase reliability, decreasing the variance in the performance. As long as competition, promotion, and order effects are relatively small, people with experience will be more likely to stay in a job and in an organization because of their higher average performance, and the increased reliability associated with longer tenure in a job should be manifested in less risk taking.

Moreover, organizations are adept at cumulating experience across individuals to increase both average performance and reliability. They use rules, procedures, and standard practices to ensure that the experiences of earlier individuals are transferred to newer members of the organization. This process of routinization is a powerful factor in converting collective experience into improved average performance. It is also a powerful influence on reliability and should tend to make the average level of risk taken by individuals within an organization decline as the organization ages.

RISK STRATEGIES

In a competitive world, of course, the positive effects of increases in the mean performance must be weighed against the (potentially negative) performance effects of increased reliability. Increasing both competence and reliability is a good strategy for getting ahead on average. But finishing first in a large field requires not just doing things others do well but doing something different and being lucky enough to have your particular deviation pay off.

In particular, experience gains that increase reliability substantially and mean performance only a little (e.g. standardization, simplification) are not good for competitive advantage when the number of competitors is large. It may be no accident that while experience (as reflected in years of prior work) and knowledge of standard beliefs (as reflected by success in school) are fair predictors of individual success in organizations on average, very conspicuous success in highly competitive situations is not closely related to either experience or knowledge as conventionally defined.

The competitive situation inside and outside an organization affects optimal risk-taking strategies. Suppose that risk can be chosen deliberately and strategically by individual decision makers competing for hierarchical promotion (as above). Any particular individual's reputation will depend on a sample of performances, and the sample mean will depend on two things: ability (which is fixed) and risk taken (which can be chosen). If a hierarchy is relatively steep and reputations are based on relatively small samples of performances, a low-ability person can win only by taking high risks. But if low-ability persons take high risks, the only way a higher-ability person can win in a highly competitive situation is also by taking substantial risks. If the level of risk can be taken arbitrarily to any level, anyone who wants to get ahead will choose to take maximum risks. In this situation there is no screening on ability at all. The "noise" of risk makes it impossible to detect the "signal" of ability. The average ability level will be approximately the same at all levels in the organization, and the average risk preference at all levels will be identical and high.

It should be observed that fluctuations in the importance of risk taking for hierarchical promotion also have implications for the selection of organizations by individuals. If individuals who are ambitious for promotion can choose organizations based on organizational characteristics, then high-ability individuals will prefer situations where their ability is correctly identified. They will choose situations where reputation is established through large performance samples, where absolute performance is more important than relative performance, and where strategic risk taking is constrained as much as possible. Thus large, steep hierarchies that use small performance samples to establish reputations will be differentially attractive to low-ability people who are ambitious for promotion.

1.4.4 "Risk Taking" and "Risk Preference"

The concept of "risk-preference," like other concepts of preferences in theories of rational choice, divides students of decision making into two groups. The first group, comprising many formal theorists of choice, treats risk preference as revealed by choices and associates it with deviations from linearity in a revealed utility for money. For this group, "risk" has no necessary connection to any observable behavioral rules followed by decision makers. It is simply a feature of a revealed preference function. The second group, consisting of many behavioral students of choice, emphasize the behavioral processes by which risky choices are made or avoided. This group finds many of the factors in risk taking to be rather remote from any observable "preference" for taking or avoiding risk.

To be sure, decision makers often attend to the relationship between opportunities and dangers, and they are often concerned about the latter; but they seem to be relatively insensitive to probability estimates when thinking about taking risks. Although theories of choice tend to treat gambling as a prototypic situation of decision making under risk, decision makers distinguish between "risk taking" and gambling, saying that while they should take risks, they should never gamble. They react to variability more by trying actively to avoid it or to control it than by treating it as a tradeoff with expected value in making a choice.

Sometimes decision makers take greater risks than they do at other times, but ideas of risk, risk taking, and risk preference are all, to some extent, inventions of students of decision making. Often the taking of risk is inadvertant, as is the avoiding of risk. Decision makers take larger or smaller risks because they make errors in estimating the risks they face, because they feel successful or not, because they are knowledgeable or ignorant, because they find themselves in a particular kind of competition.

CHAPTER TWO

Rule Following

Chapter 1 portrayed decision making as resulting from intendedly rational calculation. Pure rationality and limited rationality share a common perspective, seeing decisions as based on an evaluation of alternatives in terms of their consequences for preferences. This logic of consequences can be contrasted with a logic of appropriateness by which actions are matched to situations by means of rules organized into identities. This chapter considers a perspective in which decision making is seen as resulting from rule following and the fulfillment of an identity.

2.1 Decision Making as Rule Following

When individuals and organizations fulfill identities, they follow rules or procedures that they see as appropriate to the situation in which they find themselves. Neither preferences as they are normally conceived nor expectations of future consequences enter directly into the calculus.

2.1.1 The Logic of Appropriateness

Rule following is grounded in a logic of appropriateness. Decision makers are imagined to ask (explicitly or implicitly) three questions:

1. The question of *recognition*: What kind of situation is this?
2. The question of *identity*: What kind of person am I? Or what kind of organization is this?
3. The question of *rules*: What does a person such as I, or an organization such as this, do in a situation such as this?

The process is not random, arbitrary, or trivial. It is systematic, reasoning, and often quite complicated. In those respects, the logic of appropriateness is quite comparable to the logic of consequences. But rule-based decision making proceeds in a way different from rational decision making. The reasoning process is one of establishing identities and matching rules to recognized situations.

2.1.2 The Familiarity and Centrality of Identities and Rules

Rule- and identity-based decision making is familiar to modern experience. Social systems socialize and educate individuals into rules associated with age, gender, and social position identities. Decisions are shaped by the roles played by decision makers—family roles, school roles, organizational roles. Individuals learn what it means to be a mother, a manager, a college student, or a man. Universities teach appropriate rules for members of professions. Individuals learn how a doctor or an engineer acts.

Rule following as a way of decision making is also familiar to theories of behavior. Economists and political scientists talk about the importance of institutions, anthropologists about culture and norms, sociologists about roles, and psychologists about identities, production systems, and schema. Each discipline, in its own way, sees decision making as organized by a logic of appropriateness.

Rules and identities are so obvious that they are more likely to be regarded as a context for behavior than as an interesting phenomenon in their own right. Not only do decision makers take them for granted, so also do observers. Within an ideology of choice, any detectable willfulness is exalted, no matter how circumscribed by rules. The stories told in history and journalism tend to glorify strategies of rational maneuver within the rules. They tend to ignore the rich processes by which identities and rules are created, maintained, interpreted, changed, and ignored. In that spirit, some rational theorists of choice treat rules as the outcome of a higher-order rational process. They endogenize rules by rationalizing them.

Students of rule following, on the other hand, tend to regard the rational model of choice described in Chapter 1 as simply one version of rule following associated with the identity of the decision maker. Rationality is a rule that requires decisions to be made consequentially. It is a common rule, so actions following its structure are also common, as are procedures that reassure actors and observers that rationality is being practiced. Within such conceptions, it is rule following that is fundamental. Rationality is derivative.

2.2 Rules, Identities, and Action

Rules and identities provide a basis for decision making in every aspect of life: in families, informal groups, markets, political campaigns, and revolutions. Individuals and social systems depend on rules and on the standardization, routinization, and organization of actions that they provide. From this perspective, any decision in any context can be seen as being shaped by identities and a logic of appropriateness.

Studying decision making within a rule-following frame involves a set of questions different from those that guide research on the logic of consequence: How are situations interpreted and recognized? How are organizational identities defined? How are those definitions and identities created and changed? How are they preserved and transmitted? How is the match between situations and identities made? Why are the rules what they are?

2.2.1 Rules and Identities in Organizations

The ubiquity of rules and identities can be illustrated by considering their role in formal organizations. Most people in an organization execute their tasks most of the time by following a set of well-specified rules that they accept as a part of their identity. This is true of doctors in hospitals, workers on assembly lines, sales representatives in the field, teachers in a classroom, and police officers on a beat. It is also true for those people in organizations whose tasks primarily involve making decisions. Organizational rules define what it means to be an appropriate decision maker.

There are rules about what factors are to be considered in decisions (e.g. return on investment); who has access to a decision process; and how decisions should be timed, reported, and justified. Examples include hiring the applicant with the highest test scores or setting price by totaling costs and adding 40 percent. There are rules controlling information flows and use, specifying how it should be gathered and who should gather it, how it should be summarized and filtered, how it should be communicated and to whom, and how it is to be stored and for how long. Examples are admonitions to go "through channels" with a particular request, or rules about the appropriate forums for announcing meetings or job positions. There are rules specifying the criteria to be used to assess and monitor performance. Examples are performance standards such as production plans and personnel performance contracts.

Organizations select individuals with preexisting identities and rules. When an engineer, machinist, clerk, or truck driver is hired, the organization hires those identities, mixed as they are with an assortment of other identities that any one individual accepts—parent, friend, member of an ethnic or religious group. Organizations also define identities specific to themselves, train individuals in them, and socialize individuals to adopt the identities as their own. Formal and informal organizational rules are woven into, utilize, and help define organizational identities and roles. Tasks are organized around sets of skills, responsibilities, and rules that define a role. Roles and their associated rules coordinate and control organizational activities.

Organizations also have identities. For an organization to be a proper business firm, or a proper military unit, it must organize and act in a particular way. Organizations are described in terms of their legal structures, their national or regional characters, their technological configurations, and sets of individual identities. As organizations seek to confirm such descriptions, they frame organizational forms and procedures in ways consistent with them. They achieve standing as legitimately representing what they are.

To say that individuals and organizations follow rules and identities, however, is not to say that their behavior is always easily predicted. Rule-based behavior is freighted with uncertainty. Situations, identities, and rules can all be ambiguous. Decision makers use processes of recognition to classify situations; they use processes of self-awareness to clarify identities; they use processes of search and recall to match appropriate rules to situations and identities. The processes are easily recognized as standard instruments of intelligent human behavior. They require thought, judgment, imagination, and care. They are processes of reasoned action, but they are quite different from the processes of rational analysis.

2.2.2 *The Concept of Identity and Individual Action*

The logic of appropriateness is tied to the concept of identity. An identity is a conception of self organized into rules for matching action to situations. When Don Quixote says "I know who I am," [1] he claims a self organized around the identity of "knight-errant." When an executive is enjoined to "act like a decision maker," he or she is encouraged to apply a logic of appropriateness to a conception of an identity.

Individuals describe themselves in terms of their occupational, group, familial, ethnic, national, and religious identities.

Identities are both constructed by individuals and imposed upon them. Creating or accepting an identity is a motivational and cognitive process by which order is brought to the concept of self and to individual behavior. It involves learning to act in a particular way. Identity development is a part of individual development, closely linked to the development of language and to an understanding of the physical and social environment.

INDIVIDUALIZATION AND SOCIALIZATION

Conceptions of identity are embedded in a broader cultural context. In many of the cultures found in the United States, for example, defining an identity is pictured as ultimately a task of *individualization.* Individuals are assumed to be independent and unique, defined by the complex assortment of behaviors and roles that they endorse. Identity is seen as a matter of "self," and the metaphors of self are metaphors of discovery and creation. Such expressions as "finding oneself" or "being in touch with oneself" are common. In this process of creation, individuals are encouraged to take an active role in deriving their identities from observations of their own behavior or their internal thoughts, emotions, or motivations. They are seen as struggling to differentiate their identities from others (particularly parents and other figures of authority and convention) by exhibiting distinctive dress, behavior, and thoughts.

Alternatively, identities can be seen as arising from a process of socialization into socially defined relationships and roles. Individuals are taught how to behave as proper accountants or proper soldiers. They learn the rules of accountancy or warfare. They are taught appropriate codings of situations and appropriate responses to them. Educational systems, religions, and legal systems spend a great deal of time educating people on the meaning of identities and on applications of principles of proper behavior to specific life situations.

In a socialization perspective, identity is adopted or imposed rather than discovered or created. The imagery of self is less inclined to emphasize being true to idiosyncratic individual goals and desires, and more inclined to emphasize being true to important relationships and cultural expectations. Individuals see identities as establishing and celebrating their ties with others and their place in a social order of relationships that they honor. Attention is directed outward toward real or imagined groups rather than inward toward individual opinions, abilities, and judgments. Identities shift from situation to situation as each situation highlights a different set of relationships.

The differences between the metaphorical images conjured by these two visions of identity formation are important. In the image of individualization, actions are imagined to arise from self-imposed standards or self-selected roles and rules. In the image of socialization, actions are imagined to arise from learned obligations, responsibilities, or commitments to others. Thus the first perspective, even though it emphasizes the ways identities constrain behavior, portrays identities as in some sense chosen voluntarily. The second perspective sees identities as followed, but not chosen.

The differences are important, but they are as much statements of alternative ideologies as they are alternative descriptions of the world. Most studies of identity formation report an *interaction* between processes of *individualization* and *processes* of belonging. Particular cultures may glorify one or the other side of this interaction, both in their behavior and in their theories of that behavior. But more "individualistic" cultures exhibit strong effects of socialization, and more "social" cultures exhibit strong elements of individual deviance. Moreover, the two are intertwined. As many parents and children in many cultures can testify, the process of adolescent identity formation and revolt is a complicated mixture of individualistic differentiation and socialization into group conformity.

THE SOCIAL BASIS OF IDENTITY

Someone who says, "I am a good accountant. I do what good accountants do," is making a statement that is both a confirmation of an individual identity and a recognition of the social basis of individual action. Individuals adopt rules of behavior from families, schools, religious groups, age cohorts, and companies. They build their own understandings of themselves using socially based distinctions. As collections of individuals define and solve problems posed by their environments, they develop shared rules for behavior and shared attitudes toward experience. Those rules and attitudes are organized in terms of social roles or identities from which individual identities are formed. Being a "good accountant" means knowing, accepting, and following a variety of socially constructed and maintained rules that control individual behavior in considerable detail. The individual self is drawn using social templates.

Socially defined identities are templates for individual identities in three senses. First, they define the *essential nature* of being an accountant, or manager, or plumber, permitting individuals to deal with identities as meaningful things. In this sense, identities are like other labels through which cognition is organized. Individuals in a society distinguish a police officer from a postal carrier in much the same way they distinguish a dog from a cat—by looking for properties and actions that are associated with the label. Recognizing a dentist involves knowing how dentists behave and associating observed behavior with that role. Being a dentist involves knowing how dentists behave and acting appropriately.

The second sense in which social identities are templates is that they are prepackaged *contracts.* Individuals accept them in return for receiving things they value. Groups facilitate the construction of an identity by rewarding behavior consistent with the definition of the identity and penalizing inconsistent behavior. The social specification of what it means to act as an accountant details the terms of the contract by which an individual agrees to assume the accountant role. An individual agrees to behave in a way consistent with the socially defined identity in order to gain certain compensation. The "compensation" will often be monetary in an organizational setting, but it need not be. Individuals also accept identities as long as they receive group approval or love in return. In particular, social acceptance of an individual as a legitimate accountant (father, teacher, etc.) may be precious not only to individual self-esteem but also to the ability to function effectively. Decision makers who fail in their contractual obligations are likely to lose legitimacy and authority.

In principle, contractual identities could be idiosyncratic—everybody's job could be unique. More commonly, however, identities are, at least to some extent, standardized. The social standardization of identities makes them well-defined clusters of reliable rules, building blocks of a social system. Standardized identities simplify thinking about the structure of an organized system, and they simplify implementing it. They simplify labor markets and management. They simplify education and training. Consider, for example, the dependence of a traffic system on the socially standardized identity of a "proper driver."

The third sense in which social identities are templates for individual action is that they frequently come to be *assertions of morality*, accepted by individuals and society as what is good, moral, and true. An individual "internalizes" an identity, accepting and pursuing it even without the presence of external incentives or sanctions. The identity is protected by a conscience and by such emotions as pride, shame, and embarrassment. Social reactions to inappropriate behavior include accusations of immorality and lack of propriety. Shame and guilt are important components of social control based on a logic of appropriateness. Decision makers can violate a logic of consequence and be considered stupid or naïve, but if they violate the moral obligations of identity, they will be condemned as lacking in elementary virtue. Among other things, the fact that logics of appropriateness are imbued with such moral content increases the emotionality of decision making.

INCENTIVES AND THE INTERNALIZATION OF IDENTITIES

There is a complicated relationship between the provision of incentives for following rules associated with identities and their internalization. On the one hand, there is a strong tendency for individuals (and organizations) to accept identities that are easy or rewarding to perform—that confirm their competences. As learning and experience increase competence at an identity, they simultaneously increase the likelihood of internalization of the identity. People are likely to internalize roles and rules that they fulfill effectively more than those that they do not. Professionals who feel competent in their profession are more likely to internalize the norms of the profession. Individuals are likely to regard those identities in which they or their friends excel as more important than others.

In hierarchical organizations, for example, top-level executives have experienced their own competence in decision making and tend to internalize the role of decision maker. They are likely to think of themselves as decision makers. They act appropriately as decision makers because they have come to believe that the proper way is not only a way to gain social approval but also a way to conform to their own standards. On the other hand, individuals who have experienced failures in decision making, or who lack experience at it, are less likely to have internalized the role. As a result, experienced, successful decision makers become socially more reliable in their decision making, and inexperienced, unsuccessful decision makers become less reliable.

Since competence leads to internalization of an identity and its rules, one might be tempted to speculate that any rewarded identity will tend to be internalized, that contractual identities inexorably become internalized identities. Such a speculation is not, in general, true. If anything, the data seem to support a "conservation of motivation" hypothesis: The extent to which an identity is internalized (at least in the short run) is inversely related to the strengths of external incentives provided for adopting it. As individuals observe and interpret their own behaviors, they construct internal motives (internalized identities) where coercive external motives (contractual identities) are inadequate to account for their behavior. Strong external threats or dramatic rewards can be used to explain behavior without the need of internal commitment, so fail to stimulate internalization. Internalized identities are likely to be imagined (and thus formed) where external incentives are weak.

Studies of commitment seem to show that internalization of identities is associated with the development of internal interpretations of one's own behavior rather than directly with incentives. One standard strategy for increasing the internalization of an identity is to highlight the identity implications of a certain (typically small) behavior. People are asked, for example, to sign a petition to show they are ecology- or community-minded. The act is minor, but the interpretation of being a certain kind of citizen is made explicit by outsiders. This is, of course, usually in the context of being rewarded for being that kind of citizen, but the key strategy is not rewarding behavior but rewarding an interpretation of identity. Later, a much larger favor requiring a larger sacrifice is solicited. People are willing to engage in a much more onerous task in order to avoid violating their new identity.

Such strategies are often effective. Children are more likely to clean up their classrooms after having been induced to think of themselves as the kind of people who maintain clean places than after being threatened for being unclean. This is a kind of character change by grace: bestowing on an individual an identity that he or she values but has not earned, in hopes that external confimration of an identity will lead to its acceptance and fulfillment. Treat the statue of a young woman as the woman herself and it will come to life.* There are limits to Pygmalionic magic, of course. Like most strategies, strategies of interpretation are well known and often detected as manipulative. Even when an interpretation is accepted, its ultimate stability depends on experiential confirmation, so interpretations that are totally unrealistic will be eroded by subsequent disconfirmation. Since experiential disconfirmation itself is subject to interpretation, Pygmalionic identities can be protected by defining them ambiguously (at the cost of making their mandates less precise also).

For now, however, the strategic elements of identity formation are less important than an awareness of the interplay of social processes that shape individual and collective identities. Identities are created by external incentives and sanctions, by senses of competence or autonomy, and by learning the accepted meanings of roles. Identities are socially constructed con-

---

*With a little help from Aphrodite, of course.

tracts, motives, and cognitions that connect to organizational rule structures. And this fine tapestry of obligations controls much of what is called decision making.

2.2.3 Which Identity? Which Situation? Which Rule?

To make decisions within a logic of appropriateness, decision makers need to be able to determine what their identities are, what the situation is, and what action is appropriate for persons such as they in the situation in which they find themselves. Most decisions could call up a number of relevant identities and rules, and attention is as important in rule following as it is in consequential action. When reminded of the role of citizen, a decision maker may well act in a way that is different from the way that results from being reminded of the role of family member. Motivational, cognitive, and organizational factors all play a role in evoking one identity or rule rather than another. Likewise, since identities and rules rarely specify everything unambiguously, motivational, cognitive, and organizational factors play a role in determining behavior within the identities and rules evoked.

MULTIPLE IDENTITIES, MULTIPLE RULES

The singularity of the term "identity," along with various popular enthusiasms for personal integration and consistency, leads to a tendency to imagine an internally coherent self—"a well-rounded and integrated personality" in which actions reflect stable and consistent qualities of the actor's identity. In fact, of course, any particular actor has multiple identities, not just one. The self is a collection of incompletely integrated identities.

The problem of multiple identities is well known to the literature on human behavior. A decision maker is a parent as well as a police officer, a friend as well as a physician, a lover as well as a woman. The apparent inconsistency between the variety of roles accepted by any one individual and the concept of a coherent self is mitigated by having the multiple identities of any one individual fit together in a mutually supportive way. Such integration is accomplished partly by clustering consistent identities and partly by interpreting any one identity with a consciousness of the others. Openness in the meaning of being a "decision maker" allows that identity to be made consistent with different other roles at different times.

Although the collection of images that constitute a personal identity achieves a limited amount of structure, the self is not a seamless whole. An individual is likely to have sets of diverse self-images, which shift and alter as the context shifts. More peripheral aspects of the self are less elaborated, less frequently evoked, and less burdened with requirements of consistency than are more central aspects. They may be developing and tentative rather than fully accepted. The pursuit of appropriateness involves experimentation with new identities, inconsistency, and "self-discovery."

In a similar fashion, the rules of an identity are rarely unique or precise. The same identity may evoke inconsistent rules. A parent is expected to be firm and loving. A decision maker is expected to be thoughtful and decisive. The same set of standard operating procedures may mandate and forbid the same behavior. Good practice may be vague, particularly in new domains.

EVOKING IDENTITIES AND RULES

Not all parts of an individual's identity are available at the same time. Different behavior, different attitudes about the self and others, and different motivations may be invoked in different environments or different relationships. Accountants do not act like accountants in all situations, nor do men see "manliness" as equally relevant to all situations. Seemingly subtle environmental changes have a strong impact on behavior. Seemingly clear constraints on behavior can be overcome. For example, in experimental settings, ordinary people have proved themselves willing to deliver electric shocks to other people when instructed in such a way as to evoke a role consistent with such an action.

In the same way, not all potentially relevant rules are evoked. Some rules are overlooked. Noticing the relevance of identities or rules in a situation comes from an interaction among at least four common psychological mechanisms. The first mechanism is *experiential learning*. Individuals learn to evoke (or not to evoke) an identity in a situation by experiencing the rewards and punishments of having done so in the past. Identities with which they have had extensive positive experience are more likely to be evoked than will those with less extended or less positive experience.

The second mechanism involved in evoking identities and rules is *categorization*. Responses to situations tend to be organized around a few central conceptions of identity. Central aspects of the self are likely to be evoked more frequently and maintained more consistently than others. Thus, people who always see the world in terms of competition are likely to see the central categorizing feature of a situation to be its competitive character, while others may focus on other categorizing features. Individuals judge others on identities that are central to their concept of themselves. They process information about central identities more quickly and in larger chunks. In dealing with a central aspect of their conception of self, they are likely to elaborate more information and to draw more extreme conclusions about their behavior and the behavior of others. Individuals with single-category taxonomies for classifying the world exhibit behavior that is less dependent on the process of evoking (and presumably less carefully calibrated to the world) than do people with richer taxonomies.

The third mechanism is *recency*. Identities and rules that have recently been evoked are likely to be evoked again. This leads to intertemporal and intersituational stability, which may create problems. An individual who has been working in the role of executive all day carries that identity over into the role of spouse when she comes home. An individual who has been negotiating a tough contract as an antagonistic lawyer carries that identity over to the role of diner in a restaurant or driver on a highway.

The fourth mechanism is the social *context of others*. The real or imagined presence of others highlights social definitions of identities and situations rather than personal ones and leads to closer conformity to social expectations. For example, evoking an identity that emphasizes the presence of others leads people to use a norm of equality in distributing rewards, while a focus on self leads them toward norms of "equity" or "fairness." Distinctiveness is a social setting also evokes identities. A single redhead in a crowd of others is likely to focus on hair color as a salient characteristic. One or two younger people are likely to notice their youth in a group of older people. The first-order effect is for distinctive people to become more aware of their own identities. The second-order effect is for this identity confirmation and differentiation among the small group to evoke the dimension of difference in the predominant group.

ORGANIZATIONAL FACTORS IN THE USE OF IDENTITIES AND RULES

Social institutions, such as formal organizations, play important parts in organizing the application of identities and rules to situations. Organizations shape individual action both by providing the content of identities and rules and by providing appropriate cues for invoking them. They not only define appropriate behavioral rules to attach to appropriate identities (teaching recruits how a proper manager or a proper professor behaves in a wide variety of contexts) but also structure the occasions for evoking one identity or rule or another. The boundaries between organizations and the outside world and among subunits in an organization regulate the awareness of inconsistencies in individual identities and rules.

The organized structure of identities and rules is not static but changes in response to external and internal pressures. For example, in recent years many organizations in the Western world have struggled with the complexity of moving from a segregation of work, gender, and familial identities to various forms of greater integration. In the process, familial, gender, and organizational identities have been reconstructed, the procedures for evoking them have been changed, and ideologies about proper solutions to problems of multiple simultaneous identities have been redefined.

Providing Models. Much of the formal and informal training that occurs in an organization is training in defining identities, categorizing situations, and applying appropriate rules. This training involves providing models, exemplars of proper behavior. New workers and managers model themselves after more experienced ones. They imitate. They emulate. They learn. Every organization, as every society, provides leaders, teachers, and priests who serve in positions that are socially highlighted to model prototypical behavior and to save others the trouble of deriving it. The modern term is "mentoring," a concept that combines the cognitive and motivational aspects of modeling identities.

As individuals seek models for their own identities and behavior, they draw from the organization's repertoire of examples. They also rely on organizational interpretation of the models. Rules of appropriate behavior are supplied with concrete meaning in concrete situations through elaboration and clarification within an organization. Decision makers coach decision makers and seek coaching. Social workers seek to understand the implications of their identities by talking with their clients and with other social workers.

Providing Cues. Organizations can be pictured not as writers of contracts and providers of incentives, but as writers of scripts and providers of cues and prompts. Organizations are stage managers. They provide prompts that evoke particular identities in particular situations, and they organize the temporal and spatial cues to minimize identity inconsistencies. They manage conflict not by arranging negotiation and bargaining but by managing attention. They reduce the chance that conflicting identities will be evoked at the same time and place by highlighting shared identities at appropriate times.

Organizations highlight identities through language, providing appropriate labels for people ("Mr. President," "Doctor," "Boss") and situations ("This is an engineering . . . finance . . . human resources . . . managerial problem"). Group members use acronyms and jargon to define their community, and formal and informal language to define situations (e.g. using different terminology in a meeting as opposed to a chat at the lunch table). They also use dress to invoke appropriate roles for both organizational participants and outsiders who interact with organizational members. Common uniforms signal a common fate and may smooth even unpredictable and unscriptable encounters. A doctor's uniform is a marker and a reminder of one's identity as a physician. It also reminds patients of their roles as patients. The act of putting on or taking off "work clothes" thus brings different identities to the surface.

Organizations remind people of their situation by landscaping: Formal locations (e.g. boardrooms) are constructed as a reminder of the appropriateness of formal behavior. Changes in geography invoke different rules. The behavior of a laboratory scientist changes as the scientist moves from the workbench to corporate headquarters. Features of location and physical space are used to segregate personal lives and their associated identities from organizational lives and identities.

Providing Experience. An organization is an arena in which identities and rules are exercised. Identities are evoked, rules are followed, results are monitored. Experience with pursuing an identity produces learning, by which the rules of identity are changed. The experiences are managed to stabilize a consistent set of identities within any given organization. The management is, however, never complete. Experience also develops norms, rules, and identities that thwart managerial control, sharpening their effectiveness through trial and error and differential survival. The experiential elements of rule development are elaborated briefly later in subsections 2.3.3 and 2.3.4.

2.2.4 Violations of Rules

Most of the time behavior follows the rules. At the same time, it is hard to imagine a social system without violations of rules. Rules are overlooked or ignored. Decision makers do things they are not supposed to do, and they fail to do things that they are supposed to do. Sometimes violations of rules involve large numbers of individuals. Sometimes they involve single, isolated cases.

IGNORANCE, INCONSISTENCY, AND INCOMPATABILITY

Many deviations from rules are unintentional. Decision makers may lack the ability to follow the rules because of lack of resources or competence. An action may be mandated without the resources required to make it possible, particularly when an action is mandated by one set of authorities and resources are provided by another. Decision makers may be unaware of rules, particularly where the number and complexity of rules is great. The rules may be ambiguous, particularly when they are new or are the result of political compromises.

Many deviations from rules are necessitated by inconsistencies among them. If every situation evoked one and only one identity and every identity evoked one and only one rule, rule-based decision making would be more routine than it is. Situations often evoke several identities or several rules. Sometimes there is clear conflict between the demands of alternative identities. When national interests conflict with class interests, a worker may have a problem. When the demands of work roles conflict with the demands of family roles, a family member may have a problem.

Rules may be imposed by legitimate but independent authorities, as in the conflict between institutional rules and professional standards or the conflict between auditing rules and performance rules. Decision makers may be faced with deadlines that are inconsistent with required procedures. They may be required both to engage in widespread consultation and to maintain secrecy. Violations of rules due to inconsistent demands will increase as rules multiply and become more complex, where devices for coordination are weak, and where independent authorities have the right to impose rules (e.g. company rules versus professional rules in the accounting industry).

Not all deviations from rules are unintentional or the result of inconsistency in rules, however. Many are deliberate, conscious violations of known rules. Rule making and rule enforcing sometimes involve different coalitions. They address different interests and require different mobilization patterns. The forces that have adopted a rule may be different from the forces that are asked to implement it. Political winners characteristically have a greater stake in the observance of rules that result from a political process than do political losers. The losers are likely to believe that the rules are inappropriate. They may want to continue the political debate through the implementation process. They may be upset by their defeat and want to create trouble.

The conflict of interest of politics is not, of course, the only conflict of interest involving rules. One of the most common reasons for rules is the expectation that individuals might not act "correctly" because it is not in their personal self-interest to do so. In the modern literature, this problem is often labeled "incentive incompatibility" between principals (in this case the ownership, management, or governing body of the organization) and agents (in this case the individual members or workers). Incompatible rules produce similar conflicts. Agents pursuing their own identities and rules may act in ways that are inconsistent with their principals' identities and rules. For example, professional ethics may conflict with organizational profits.

TOLERANCE, COLLUSION, AND CORRUPTION

Sometimes rule violations are justified or sanctioned (even demanded) by an organization or the larger society. Sometimes tolerance for deviation stems from a belief that flexibility is advantageous. Rules cannot fit every situation, and there is need to "fine-tune" them to meet the demands of a variable environment. Knowing when to bend the rules is one of the hallmarks of an experienced decision maker. Tolerance for rule violation is a form of delegation to individuals who have a more refined capability for accomplishing the intent of the rule in a special case. Organizations also allow variation in interpreting rules in order to experiment with what they might come to mean.

Violations in the name of effectiveness are more likely when the rules are relatively rigid than when they are easily changed. They are more likely when it is possible to point to performance measures that demonstrate the good sense of ignoring rules than where accepted performance measures are lacking. Thus, the bending of rules should be more prevalent in young organizations than in older ones, more prevalent in business organizations than in public organizations.

Social systems also may ignore cheating because rules are less designed to control behavior than to proclaim virtue. "Winking" at violations of virtuous but bothersome rules serves the social function of maintaining the shared values of the system while avoiding the costs of living up to them. In such cases, a social system is likely to be particularly tolerant of cheating if the violations are private. In many such cases implicit, informal agreements are made to accept rule breaking. Participants, in effect, agree that even though not everything is what it appears to be, and even though the parties know it, no party wishes to acknowledge the discrepancy. This kind of hypocrisy preserves the rules, sustains the sense of community within the social system, and allows accommodation to pressures for rule flexibility.

Sometimes this tolerance of variability is less benign. It reflects a way of placing individual actors "at risk." When individuals must violate one rule to serve another, or are allowed to violate rules in order to accomplish personal or group objectives, they are made vulnerable to a subsequent accusation of rule violation. Disparities between the rules that are espoused and the rules that are observed make any significant decision maker liable to exposure and disgrace. In this way, organizations gain a modicum of control over members who are constantly vulnerable by virtue of being in violation of some rule. The possibility of delicate (and often not so delicate) blackmail of this sort is a common feature of modern life.

2.3 Rule Development and Change

Much of the research on rule-based decision making treats rules, forms, procedures, and practices as given. The research identifies decision heuristics, standard organizational practice, or institutionalized norms and explores the implications of those rules for decision behavior. It elaborates how behavior is molded by rules, how decision makers operate within rules, and how they deal with uncertainties about rules. That strategy was reflected in section 2.2.

Examining how rules are evoked, interpreted, and used is , however, only part of the story. The logic of appropriateness is a logic attached to an evolving conception of propriety. Decision makers follow rules, but the rules change. Identities endure, with individuals learning and pursuing the rules of behavior consistent with the roles, but the rules themselves change through a mixture of analysis, negotiation, learning, selection, and diffusion. As the rules change, decision making behavior changes. As a result, the study of rule-based decision making is not only a study of how identities and situations are defined and rules applied but also a study of rule development. Since identities and rules are social constructions, developed within a context of other decision makers and historical experience, understanding the actions of any particular decision maker involves understanding how those social and historical contexts have molded them and how the continued unfolding of history will mold them in the future.

How is the process by which rules come to exist to be understood? How are rules modified as a result of experience; as a consequence of observing the rules used by others; as a result of deliberate strategic action; as a result of political conflict? How are rules maintained in memory and transmitted to new cohorts of decision makers? How does the distribution of rules change over time as a result of differential survival and growth of institutions? In short, how do the rules come to be the way they are?

2.3.1 *Alternative Visions of How Rules Change*

Identities and rules change as part of the process by which institutions adapt to their environments. The idea that individuals, institutions, and their environments adapt to each other is central to many modern theories of behavior. Such theories presume that individuals and institutions survive and prosper as their standard practices come to match environmental requirements. In the case of an institution, those requirements include both the demands of an institution's internal structures and coalitions and the demands and opportunities of the external world.

Rules and their environments adapt to each other by means of several intertwined processes:

1. *Analysis*, through the anticipation and evaluation of future consequences by intentional decision makers
2. *Bargaining*, through negotiation, conflict, and compromise among decision makers with inconsistent preferences and identities
3. *Imitation*, through the copying of rules, practices, and forms used by others
4. *Selection*, through differential birth and survival rates of unchanging rules and the decision making units that use them
5. *Learning*, through experience-based changes of routines and of the ways routines are used

Those are the processes by which identities and rules come to anticipate the future or reflect the past. Analysis is forward looking. Theories based on analysis as the primary mechanism of adaptation presume that rules reflect expectations of the future. Selection and learning are backward looking. Theories based on selection or learning presume that rules reflect history. Bargaining is either forward looking or backward looking (or both), depending on the bases of the behavior of the bargainers. Imitation is either forward looking or backward looking (or both), depending on the bases of the behavior of those who are imitated.

2.3.2 Capturing the Future: Plans and Contracts

Much modern thinking about decision making presumes that the expectations and willful actions of human beings enact the future in the present. The presumption is reflected in theories of rational action and power, including theories of strategic action. Rational actor models explain adaptation in organizational rules and form as a result of the preferences of actors and their calculations of future consequences. In this view, actors compete for resources and adjust rationally to each other's strategies over time. Identities, rules, and forms change as a result of a consequential action in the context of competition. From this perspective, individuals and groups create rules consciously as instruments of control. They construct identities and conceptions of proper behavior in order to control the actions of others as well as their own. They accept their own obligations as part of the process of creating a coherent system of social relationships that can enact an attractive future.

In these perspectives, change stems from imagining the future and imposing it on the present. Visions of the future, or destinies, are confirmed by following courses of action necessary for their fulfillment. The visions may be seen as extrahuman, in which case the theory links adaptation to destiny within some ultimate purpose or design. Alternatively, the visions are sometimes portrayed as inventions of human decision makers, in which case the theory is one of anticipatory individual or institutional choice. Adaptation is seen as reflecting wills and desires and the conscious intention to achieve them.

In traditions of studies of organized action, the future is captured particularly in plans and contracts. Contracts are made in order to avoid the uncertainty implicit in the future. Plans are developed on the basis of expectations of the future, then are implemented in such a way as to enact the future they anticipate. Budgets are a conspicuous example. Budgets are based on forecasts of income and expenditures. Sometimes the world changes so much that a budget cannot be achieved, but the usual situation is that budgets become self-confirming. If income or expenditures start to deviate from the plan, actions are taken to bring them back. If sales lag, new marketing efforts are initiated. If expenditures lag, new uses of funds are discovered. The prototype is the flurry of expenditures to exhaust a budget at the end of a budget period.

2.3.3 Capturing the Past: Experiential Learning

Although ideas of *future*-dependent adaptation of rules are common in social science, they are usually subsumed under the general rubric of rational action. In contrast, theories of identities, rules, and institutions tend to emphasize *history*-dependent adaptation. Ideas of history-based development have been used to understand the birth, death, and change of organizational forms and routines, cultures, institutions, or systems of knowledge. The past is seen as imposing itself on the present through retention of experience in routines. Rules are seen as a residue of the past.

Historical processes by which the present encapsulates the past are the mechanisms of theories of change, including theories of learning, culture, and natural selection. The theories differ in the way they imagine the informational consequences of history to be sustained and diffused within an evolving population, but they belong to a common family. In each case, the past is experienced through a combination of exploration and exploitation. Exploration produces variety in experience (experimentation, variation, diversity). Exploitation produces reliability in experience (selection, consistency, unity). The engines of development include mechanisms for interpreting, retaining, transmitting, and retrieving these lessons of the experienced past.

In this section *learning* processes, ideas about how rules change as a result of experience, are considered. In subsection 2.3.4 processes of environmental selection are considered. In a learning process, the rules change. In a selection process, the rules themselves do not change, but the mix of rules does. Despite this difference, the two perspectives share a number of common problems and ideas, and most modern students of decision making see the development of rules as an intertwining of these two history-dependent processes with processes of choice, bargaining, and imitation.

BASIC IDEAS OF EXPERIENTIAL LEARNING

The basic idea of experiential learning is that rules are modified on the basis of direct experience. Social systems create, suspend, and refine their rules in response to their own experiences. In that way, rules capture the past. Theories of direct experiential learning describe how inferences derived from historical experience are folded back into the actions that create subsequent history. Such theories normally postulate a cycle of four stages: (1) Action is taken using existing rules. (2) That action results in various kinds of outcomes. (3) Inferences are made from those outcomes. (4) Those inferences are used to modify the rules. The cycle is displayed in Figure 2.

The first step in this cycle has been discussed above in subsection 2.2.3. It depends on mechanisms that recognize situations, define identities, and retrieve and apply rules. Some aspects of the second step will be discussed below in subsection 2.3.5, particularly those associated with learning that occurs in the context of other learners. This subsection considers some features of the last two steps, the processes that convert feedback from outcomes into rules. Understanding how rules are modified by learning involves perceiving how small samples of ambiguous experience are converted into inferences about the world and how those inferences are used to change routines.

MAKING EXPERIENCE USEFUL FOR LEARNING

In order to shape learning, interpretations of experience must provide information about what happened, why it happened, and whether what happened was satisfactory or unsatisfactory. Ordinary experience, however, provides only a small sample of events on which to base an interpretation of a possibly complex

Figure 2
The Experiential Learning Cycle

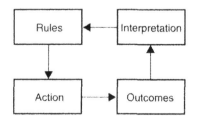

Source: James G. March and Johan P. Olsen, "The Uncertainty of the Past: Organizational Learning under Ambiguity," *European Journal of Political Research,* 3 (1975): 147–71.

world. Experience consists in a set of *observed* events (and interpretations of them). Observed events are a sample of actual *realized* events. Some of the events of history never enter experience because they are not observed. Realized events, in turn, are a sample of *potential* events. The realizations of history are draws from the set of all possible events that might be produced by historical processes.

This double sampling makes observed history a noisy representation of historical possibilities. Events are often difficult to observe precisely or to understand fully. Many interconnected things happen simultaneously, and information about them is incomplete and biased. Organizations are complex mixtures of individuals with different interests, competences, identities, and sentiments. Different individuals learn different things from the same ambiguous history. Those various learnings are combined to produce changes in rules. This subsection provides a brief introduction to the ways rules learn from experience, an introduction that focuses on a few basic features of how experience is recorded and recalled, interpreted, augmented, and evaluated.

Recalling Experience. In recalling experience, decision makers are likely to be affected by the *availability* of the event in memory. Among the many factors that make an event available, three are particularly relevant here:

First, personally experienced events are more available than events not personally experienced. Even though subsequent historians have considerably extended our collective knowledge about the Nazi era in Germany, events of German history from 1937 to 1945 are more available to people who were living in Germany during that period than they are to non-Germans or Germans born after 1945. The pains of failure and the joys of success are remembered more vividly and recalled more readily when they have been experienced in person than when they have been experienced vicariously. Individuals tend to recall their own experiences more readily than the experiences of others. Thus, the availability heuristic tends to lead successful decision makers (who have had generally good experiences with risk taking) to underestimate the risks they face, and to lead unsuccessful decision makers to overestimate them.

Availability biases are also observed in studies of how individuals assess individual contributions to joint projects. Asking partners in a marriage to asses independently the percentage of the housework they perform or asking participants in joint projects at work to estimate their percentage contribution to the success of a project almost always leads to responses totaling more than 100 percent. Since each individual recalls his or her contributions more easily than the contributions of others, the availability heuristic leads each individual to see his or her own contribution as greater than it is seen by others.

Second, the experiences of others with whom individuals share an identity are more readily available than are the experiences of more distant others. Women record and recall the reported experiences of other women more easily than do men. Physicians record and recall the reported experiences of other physicians more easily than do people who are not physicians. Reporters following a particular political candidate systematically overestimate the prospects of "their" candidate. When husbands are asked to estimate the contribution to housework of husbands in general (rather than just themselves), and wives are asked to estimate the contribution to housework of wives in general , the numbers still total more than 100 percent.

Third, people seem to record and recall vivid, concrete information more readily than pallid, abstract, statistical information. Television advertisements reflect awareness of this principle on the part of advertisers. They are more likely to tell a vivid story about one satisfied customer than to present tables of data about customer satisfaction. They are more likely to provide examples of the effects of a product's properties than data on those properties. Teachers report a distinctive feature of student examination answers: Relative to the frequency with which teachers present them, students recall stories and vivid slogans much more frequently than they recall abstract models or data.

Interpreting Experience. Learning processes do not reliably lead to valid interpretations of experience. Some fairly general biases exist in the interpretation of experience. For example, humans tend to attribute events to the intentions of human actors, even when such an attribution appears difficult to sustain. They are inclined to see historical events as necessary events, rather than as draws from a probability distribution of possibilities. They fail to take effective advantage of the information available in the world. They are insensitive to the quality and amount of data on which their inferences are based.

Three general features of the interpretation of experience are particularly relevant to learning: First, interpretations *conserve belief*. That is, experience is interpreted in ways that sustain prior understandings. Events that disconfirm prior theories or schemata are less likely to be recalled than those that support prior beliefs. Arguments that contradict prior conclusions are less likely to be considered relevant than those that reinforce them.

For example, individuals interpret relationships among variables according to their favorite theory instead of looking for other mediating factors that could also explain a relationship. Lower rates of heart attacks in Mediterranean countries are interpreted by the manufacturers of olive oil as a statement about the effectiveness of certain kinds of fats in the diet, by winemakers as testimony to the therapeutic values of wine, and by hedonists as a statement about the effectiveness of living in a culture with more family connections, a slower-paced lifestyle, and better weather.

Advocates of a particular decision can often use almost any outcome to confirm their belief in the decision's efficacy. If the outcomes are positive, the decision is seen as demonstrably effective. If the outcomes are negative, the results are seen as showing that the decision did not go far enough or was not implemented with enough vigor. This resilience of belief in the face of experience is an obvious feature of social movements, political and religious faiths, and equipment purchases.

Second, individuals use *simple causal theories* to interpret experience. They assume that most of the time causes will be found in the neighborhood of their effects. Thus, they associate actions and outcomes by their temporal and spatial proximity. If prices are raised today and sales fall tomorrow, decision makers are likely to think the two events are connected. If prices are raised today and ten years later the competition hires a new accounting firm, the two events are less likely to be connected.

The assumption that causes are to be found in the neighborhood of effects is not a foolish assumption. It is often true. Even when it is not true, the connection between nearby effects and distant causes is often mediated by a chain of proximate cause and effect links. Moreover, in an organizational context the assumption of proximity is a basis for organizational control. When a manager is held responsible for outcomes realized within his or her division, the organization acts as though it believes that causes lie in the organizational neighborhood of effects. By so acting, it perhaps increases the likelihood that the assumption will be made true.

Third, the interpretation of experience is a *social interpretation*. Ideas about the causes of events are developed and shared within a network of social connections. Individuals elaborate an understanding of history by following standard socially approved procedures for telling stories about events and by "sounding out" other individuals about ideas. They confirm their interpretations by establishing the credibility of those interpretations in the minds of others. Reality is certified by a shared confidence in it. For example, the spatial proximity that individuals often use to establish cause and effect relations is defined socially. Organization charts create a presumption that cause–effect distances are related to distances measured in organization charts, and organizational relations and resources are arranged through a negotiation in which managers seek to gain control over the outcomes that are to be viewed as "near" to them.

The classic socially validated outcome in a business setting is the income (or profit and loss) statement. Most decision makers construct such statements and use them to modify actions and rules. Ideas about outcomes found in income statements are developed and validated through interaction with others. The key actors in the construction of an income (profit and loss) statement are typically business firms and their associations, accounting firms and their associations, public agencies, and the courts. In the United States, some agencies are strictly governmental (e.g. the Securities Exchange Commission, the Congress). Others are public–private hybrids (e.g. the Financial Accounting Standards Board).

All the participants act within a mix of rules and incentives. Their roles demand certain actions. Their professional identities demand others. Their personal incentives include concerns about the consequences of having one kind of income statement or another for individual and organizational prosperity. For example, although accountants are presumed to be independent of management and are assumed to be accountable to the profession, to government officials, and to shareholders for painting an accurate picture of a client's performance, they are hired by management. They cannot help but be conscious that a continued relationship requires a certain delicacy in constructing an account.

Income statements are social combinations of problem solving, coalition formation, and imagination in the development of accounting conventions, and parallel combinations of problem solving, coalition formation, and imagination as decision makers try to live within the conventions and apply them to concrete situations to produce an income statement. The social understandings that are formed are continually being renegotiated, and both the rules of accounting and the specifics of a particular accounting statement gradually change.

Augmenting Experience. Since history ordinarily provides only small samples of experience, direct learning from experience involves assessing the validity of small samples, increasing them when possible, and augmenting the information in them. Small samples are often increased, but individuals tend to be insensitive to sample size, accepting small samples of information as being no less useful in their estimates than large samples. They place greater emphasis on assessing the quality of data drawn from experience than on the size of the sample.

In particular, individuals "overinterpret" experience, treating the events they have experienced as providing more information than standard theories of statistics would assume. The emphasis is on experiencing a limited history richly rather than on extending experience. For example, decision makers learn from the process of making a decision and taking an action as well as from its outcomes. Since learning from the process ordinarily occurs substantially before any possible learning from outcomes, it is frequently the former that makes a greater difference. Thus, if the process of making a particular kind of decision, or taking the resulting action, is painful, decision makers learn not to do such things. If the process is rewarding, they learn to make such decisions. These decision process effects are often independent of final decision outcomes. Because they are gained sooner, the lessons from the process of making a decision serve to frame later learning derived from its outcomes.

Similarly, decision makers learn from their expectations of outcomes before they learn from the outcomes themselves. Anticipations reinforce actions from which good things are expected and extinguish actions from which bad things are expected. Since decisions are ordinarily made with positive expectations, the immediate lessons of a decision tend to be positive. Because those prior anticipations have a positive bias, they will, on average, be more positive than actual realizations. As a result, in the absence of reinterpretation of aspirations or of experience, there is a tendency for the early lessons from a particular set of decisions to be more positive than the later ones.

Evaluating Experience. Learning from experience requires not only understanding how experience stems from actions but also evaluating the outcomes of action. Is the outcome positive or negative? Is the policy a success or a failure? Did the action improve performance or degrade it? Often there is ambiguity associated with determining "success" or "failure."

In general, people seem to learn to like what they get. This behavioral tendency to interpret outcomes in a positive light provides an important counterbalance to a statistical tendency toward postdecision disappointment stemming from exaggerated expectations (see subsection 4.3.2). More generally, the adaptation of desires to realizations is an important feature of learning. If the definition of what is desired is affected by what is received, the basic learning distinction between success and failure becomes endogenous to the process of decision.

This can be seen particularly by considering the way a satisficing decision maker distinguishes outcomes that are above an aspiration level from those that are below. It was noted in Chapter 1 that decision makers seem to have targets or aspiration levels for performance, and that they distinguish more sharply between being above and being below an aspiration level than they do among various degrees of success or failure. The same basic idea can be carried over to ideas about the evaluation of outcomes in experiential learning.

Suppose decision makers have (possibly changing) aspirations for their performance. Results that exceed their aspirations are treated as "successes," reinforcing their inclination to maintain the rules on which the actions were based. Results that fall short of their aspirations are treated as "failures," encouraging them to change the rules on which the actions were based. The learning process, then, depends critically not only on the association of outcomes to actions (and thereby to rules) but also on the aspirations for such outcomes.

If aspirations do not adjust to changes in performance produced by a changed environment, decision makers will experience long runs of success or failure, depending on whether the environmental change was positive or negative in its effects. On the other hand, if aspirations adjust instantaneously to changes in performance, decision makers will experience success and failure as essentially random events. In either case, the learning process will produce relatively little improvement.

"Success" and "failure" are also partly social constructions. Late in the history of the involvement of the United States in the Vietnam War, one U.S. Senator proposed that the army "declare a victory and come home." The response to the proposal demonstrated that there are limits to arbitrary unilateral evaluations of outcomes, but "success" and "failure" are not uniquely defined by the outcomes. Not only do decision makers adjust their aspiration levels, they also adjust their definitions of what is valuable. Typically, the adjustment is self-congratulatory in the sense that decision makers come to value what they achieve. If sales are up and market share is down, then sales are treated as the appropriate target. If overseas markets are unrewarding, they are devalued in subjective importance.

The social construction of success and failure may mirror the social structure of an organization or society, with different groups defining the same outcomes differently and learning different things from the same history. Internal conflict and competition provide a basis for persistent differences in the interpretation of events. The same outcomes will be seen as successes or failures, depending on whether they are attributed to one's own group or to a competitive group. When one product is successful and another is not, the advertising campaign that preceded the events is defined as a success by one product group and a failure by another. One faction's victories are another faction's defeats.

INCOMPLETE LEARNING CYCLES

The simple learning cycle displayed in Figure 2 is not necessarily achieved. One or more of the links portrayed in the figure may be broken, producing incomplete learning cycles with distinctive features. First, *rules are often rigid.* Individual inferences from experience are not immediately translated into changes in rules. This incomplete cycle is, of course, a very standard situation. Rules do not change to match every change in individual cognitions or beliefs. In many ways, that is the point of rules. The inhibition of rule adjustment to individual knowledge makes rule-based action predictable to others. It facilitates coordination. It makes rules capable of accumulating history across individuals.

Second, *learning is often superstitious.* That is, the link between past action and environmental response (outcomes) does not exist or is ambiguous. For example, imagine decision makers choosing among rules in a world in which almost any reasonable rule will lead to successful outcomes (an approximation to the situation in an expanding market or economy). Although decision makers will be successful regardless of what rules they use, learning is likely to lead them to believe in the efficacy of whatever rules they happen to follow. They are unlikely to notice that many other rules would also bring success. In such a superstitious world, successful decision makers are likely to publish books revealing their "secrets" of success; but other decision makers will have quite different perceptions of the right rules to follow. And few of them will notice that almost anything would work.

On the other hand, consider the case in which none of the available rules for action are followed by good results. A possible example would be a decision maker facing a contracting market or economy. In this case, decision makers are likely to find themselves oscillating among rules, looking for one that works, perhaps not noticing that nothing has. They would probably not publish books.

These two cases are examples of pure superstitious learning. The association between actions and outcomes is misunderstood, but learning takes place nevertheless. Rules are adopted and beliefs and actions are shaped by interpretations of experience. There is little chance of self-correction, because the learning and interpretations are internally consistent. They are wrong, but wrong in ways that do not easily reveal themselves and often may not make much difference. If a talented tennis player or a talented politician believes that the reason for her success is the bracelet she wears, the ritual of wearing the bracelet (or any number of other rules that decision makers may come to follow) will probably not affect the outcomes adversely, and its irrelevance may well be discovered slowly.

Although pure cases of superstitious learning are probably relatively rare, almost all learning from experience has elements of supersition. Beliefs in the effectiveness of various strategies, products, technologies, or rules are often learned in conditions that make it hard to determine causal relations. When individuals use simple models to learn about complex interacting worlds—which they ordinarily must do because of the limitations of information and experience—much of what is learned is likely to be based on associations between actions and outcomes that are more fortuitous than causal.

Third, *memory is often imperfect.* Rules do not reliably determine action. They must be conserved and retrieved. Memory is difficult to maintain. Transmission and socialization processes are not always perfect. Those responsible for socialization may have limits on their time. They may be more accepted by some groups than by others. Some rules may be overlooked or ignored because they conflict with rules imposed by subcultures or organizational subunits. Geographic or cultural distances may prohibit effective transmission of information and effective modeling of correct behavior.

Rules are also sometimes difficult to retrieve. The individual and organizational availability of a rule depends on the frequency and recency of use. Recently evoked rules are more likely to be retrieved than rules that have not been used for a while. This leads to flurries of rule use, like the flurries in application of particular criteria to the selection of political appointees. Rules "reside" in some part of a social or organizational structure and are more easily retrieved by parts of the structure that are near their location than parts that are far from them. Retrieval of home office rules is often difficult in a distant outpost.

Fourth, *history is often obscure*. It may be obscure at the time it occurs because of the small samples and causal complexity of experience. Even if it is clear at the time it occurs, history may become obscure with the passage of time. The primary form in which decision making memory is recorded is in the rules, procedures, and forms that encode experience. A characteristic feature of those memories is the way in which they record the lessons of history but not the history itself. As a result, uncertainty is absorbed by inferences, and the experiential basis for rules tends to disappear. To some extent the details of the history may be preserved by shared stories or individual memories, but both are subject to substantial distortion, social differentiation, and doubt.

2.3.4 Capturing the Past: Environmental Selection

Experiential learning is one procedure by which the past is encoded into rules, procedures, and forms. A second procedure is environmental selection. The two procedures represent parallel forms of adaptation, and they share many common features. However, they differ fundamentally in the mechanisms they

postulate for creating a match between environmental requirements and organizational rules.

The basic idea of environmental selection is that populations
adapt to their environment not by changing the attributes of
individual members of the population but by a changing mix
of fixed attributes. The distribution of rules and forms in a
population of decision makers or decision making organizations changes through differential births, deaths, and growth of
rules and of the institutions and individuals using them. In
short, the composition of the rule pool changes, not the individual rules.

THE EVOLUTIONARY ANALOGY

The vision of adaptation through selection is taken from evolutionary biology, and many contemporary discussions and issues
in population biology have direct analogs in the study of decision making forms and rules. In standard evolutionary theory,
evolution requires three things: (1) *variation:* some method for
producing variety in forms, (2) *selection:* some method for selecting the most appropriate forms, and (3) *retention:* some
method for retaining selected forms over time (generations).

In the classical Darwinian model of natural selection, variation occurs through mutations—rare, random changes in the
genetic endowment of the organism—and through the statistical combinations produced by sexual reproduction. Change in
the population comes through selection. Organisms increase
in numbers relative to their fellows because of higher fertility
or lower mortality (differential survival rates through reproduction age) produced by superior "fit" with their particular environment. Attributes that result in a survival advantage
are retained by being passed on to subsequent generations
through inheritance of genes (subject to mutations and statistical sampling).

The basic model can be complicated by factors that affect the
variation process, the selection process, or the retention
process. Mixes of types in an ecology are affected by migration
patterns that control who is geographically available to mate

with whom and by social hierarchies that control who is socially available to mate with whom. Mixes of types may also be affected by complementarities among types—symbiosis, predation, and competition—and by altruism, interactions in which the sacrifice of one organism's ability to contribute to the gene pool from which descendants are drawn preserves the genetic contributions of others.

Mutation and the statistical sampling of genes through reproduction give chance a powerful role in such a conception of adaptation. Because the models predict probability distributions of attributes, they have very little to say about the success of individuals. There is always some chance that a favorable mutant will be eliminated and an unfavorable mutant will be stabilized. The possibilities for combinations through reproduction are numerous. In addition, as chance accumulates over generations, persistent and irreversible genetic drift is likely, and accurate long-run predictions are extremely unlikely.

Subject to chance, the model is one of environmental control through competition for resources. As organisms compete for resources in the environment, the distribution of types in the gene pool comes to "match" the environment. Until fairly recently, the relevant environment has been treated as exogenous, its effects changing in response to changing competitive conditions but its basic resource structure and character given by some natural processes unaffected by evolution at the gene pool level.

VARIATION, SELECTION, AND RETENTION IN RULES

Students of the adaptation of rules through environmental selection focus not on the gene pool but on pools of rules, forms, and procedures within a population of decision makers or organizations. The biological metaphor is clearly useful, but the processes of variation, selection, and retention in rules differ in important ways from their analogs in the evolution of gene pools.

Consider first the process for varying forms and rules, since without variation, the adaptive power of selection is small. Fundamental innovations in rules, like mutations in genes, are comparatively rare and unlikely to be successful, but variation in rules is probably not as chance-like as the process in biological organisms. Variation is often goal-directed, it results from a process of problem solving by decision makers confronted with poor performance, and it tends to consist of refinements of current rules and technology more commonly than recombinations. Variation may come from imperfect imitation or from individual deviations from rules.

Variation in rules also comes from various kinds of "foolishness"—doing things for no good reason. Practices that stimulate variation include those that create arenas in which normal controls are relaxed, protecting playfulness from the usual pressures toward reliability and conformity. These "skunk works" generate ideas, most of which—like most mutations—are bad ones. But they are also a source of the occasional effective change. Thus variation is closely related to risk taking, a topic considered in Chapter 1, since risk taking is defined in terms of introducing or accepting variability. Ideas about how to stimulate (or retard) variation are implicit in the discussion there of how to stimulate or retard risk taking.

Most (but not all) theories of variation and selection in social institutions assume that inheritable changes in attributes can arise through experiential learning. In that sense, such theories are more Lamarckian than Darwinian. By consciously disseminating information and rules, social systems, including organizations, transmit learned attributes to generations of changing personnel. Organizations grow and spread their rules (e.g. a growth in the number of locations within a restaurant chain). Organizations merge and thereby allow one to transplant its rules to another. New firms and units copy old ones. Organizations imitate organizations that occupy more prestigious positions in the social hierarchies (e.g. state legislatures imitating the national legislature). Consultants and professional associations carry rules from well-established clients to newly founded ones.

Finally, consider differences in the selection mechanisms. In this case, there is somewhat more overlap between models of selection among genes and selection among rules. Most variation / selection models in the study of rules and organizations cite the importance of competition and differential survival as a selection mechanism. Organizations and rules die. Indeed, most new organizations seem to die relatively early, and the pattern of survival rates seems generally consistent with the idea that there is considerable heterogeneity among new starts. The birth, death, and transformation of rules has been less studied, but selection seems also likely to be a factor there.

Thus, special features of the process by which rules evolve through variation and selection include a reduced role of chance, an increased role of social diffusion, and a different role for the environment. Characteristics are not passed along through the Mendelian sampling of sexual reproduction (although something like that could be invented for a theory of imitation). In addition, mutations are less random. They are influenced by directed search and problem solving and by the conscious manipulation of slack. Forms spread through growth and social diffusion. The effects of migration and social hierarchy are more obvious, and traits can be acquired by learning. While the environment still determines survival, social systems appear to have power to enact their environments in some circumstances, to create a social reality. In addition, coevolution takes on a much greater role.

2.3.5 *The Ecological Basis of Rule Development*

A distinctive feature of rule development is its ecological, coevolutionary character. Ecologies of rules are tied together by links in almost every important aspect of learning and selection. Experiential learning depends on the link between actions and outcomes and on an evaluation of those outcomes. Each of those is affected by the interactions within an ecology of learning. Environmental selection depends on survival outcomes and on processes for reproducing or varying rules. Each of those is affected by interaction within an ecology of selection.

For example, as a decision maker learns a new set of lessons from experience, the learning of one lesson interacts with the learning of other sets of lessons by the same decision maker. Learning in one part of an organization interacts with learning in other parts. Learning in one organization interacts with learning in other organizations. These interactions make understanding and evaluating learning in a system of social institutions considerably more difficult than it would be in a simpler world.

As will be elaborated somewhat in Chapter 6, the coevolutionary features of rules complicate simple intuitions about the "survival of the fittest." They make the population of rules that are observed (and therefore the population of decisions observed) history-dependent. The rules followed today are not simply a solution to some kind of optimization problem involving the current environment but are an interactive, path-dependent representation of a history of coevolution among rules.

COMPETENCY TRAPS

One of the more common effects of the ecology of adaptation in rules is a phenomenon called the competency trap or lock-in. It arises in various forms in many adaptive systems and reflects the ways in which improving capabilities with one rule, technology, strategy, or practice interferes with changing that rule, technology, strategy, or practice to another that is potentially superior (but with which the decision maker has little current competence).

Decision makers learn from experience what rule to use and simultaneously learn how to improve any rule that they use. The two forms of learning interact. The more a particular rule is used, the better becomes the performance using that rule, so the more likely it is that that rule will be reinforced by experience. The more a rule is reinforced, the more likely it is to be used. This positive feedback loop produces considerable competence in using a current rule and makes substitution of another (potentially superior) rule difficult through a learning process. In this way, the natural processes of learning can easily lead to a competency trap, a stable suboptimal solution.

Competency traps are manifested in technological lock-ins at an individual, organizational, and societal level. Individuals find it difficult to shift from one computer or word processor to another (superior) one. In the short run, their performance would decline with such a shift. Organizations pursue and refine product and marketing strategies that work, gaining competence at them, and thereby exclude potentially superior strategies that involve new competencies. Societies sustain technologies (the QWERTY keyboard, the internal combustion engine) that are arguably inferior but on which competence has been developed to such a level that a shift to a new technology cannot easily be achieved.

INTERACTIVE EFFECTS ON OUTCOMES

The interactions among the lessons of learning are further complicated by interactions among learning decision makers. Each decision maker adapts to an environment comprising other learning decision makers, each embedded in organizations of interacting learning individuals and subgroups. Thus the dynamics of rule change cannot be understood simply by focusing on the development of rules by a single decision maker or decision making institution. The outcomes for any particular action depend on what other decision makers do.

This insight about the effects of an environment that is not only changing but changing endogenously is a recurrent theme in the study of decision making. When decision systems made up of multiple actors are considered, as in Chapters 3 and 4, the decisions by any individual actor become much more complex, because they have to take into account the preferences, identities, and likely actions of others. This ecological context of decision making is also significant to understanding the development of rules. As rules evolve, their interactions make their outcomes jointly determined. The rewards for the use of one rule are affected by the use of a second rule, and the rewards of the second are similarly affected by use of the first. Consider, for example, rules of the road, specifically rules about driving on one side of the road or another on a two-lane, two-way road. The interactive character of rule development is seen conspicuously in competition. The effectiveness of particular strategies, rules, or technologies depends on attributes of the competitors, the competition, and the environment. Consider a set of competitors each learning how to allocate resources to a set of alternative activities. The outcomes for any particular competitor will be a joint consequence of the potentials of the alternative activities, the changing capabilities of the various competitors within the various activities, and the allocations of effort by the various competitors to the various activities. Such a situation results in patterns of behavior that are strongly influenced by the ecological structure. The learning outcomes depend on the number of competitors, their learning rates, their rates of adjustment of their aspirations, the extent to which each competitor learns from the experience of others, and the differences among the potentials of the activities.

The relations among decision makers and their rules are not necessarily symmetrical. Some decision makers may interfere with or facilitate other decision makers while themselves remaining unaffected. Decision makers may also act as predators and prey (e.g. brokerage firms and investment innocents). Nor are they necessarily competitive. The interactive nature of rule development is seen conspicuously in cooperative activities. The evolution of communication rules, languages, and technologies is affected substantially by the cooperative, interactive character of communication. There are many different ways to communicate "yes," but (among people who want to talk to one another) language tends to coevolve so that all say "yes" in the same way. There are many different forms of communication technology, but the frequency with which one individual uses any particular technology will depend heavily on the frequency with which others do, and vice versa. These network externalities dictate important features of the learning process and make any theory of autonomous learning misleading.

ASPIRATIONS, DIFFUSION, LEGITIMACY

These interactive factors in outcomes are paralleled by interactive effects that affect other aspects of the adaptation of rules.

Consider three of those:

First, aspirations (and therefore definitions of subjective success and failure) are *social*. They are affected not only by a decision maker's own performance but also by the performance of others. When aspirations are tied to the performances of others, the evaluation of a given performance depends on the performances of others. This reduces the effects of self-referential indexing of performance, thus (on average) increases the chance that outcomes will deviate significantly from aspirations and decreases the likelihood of changing from success to failure or from failure to success. Both effects have consequences for learning. If aspirations in a population converge to the mean of the performances of the members of the population and there are structural reasons why some members of the population persistently do better than others, the population will tend to be partitioned into two groups, one that persistently achieves its aspirations and another that persistently fails to do so. In either case, learning tends to become superstitious.

Second, in both learning and environmental selection, rules "reproduce" by *diffusion*. Lessons gained from experience by one decision maker diffuse among other decision makers through the transfer of routines and the exchange of knowledge. As a result, theories of rule development need to attend to the structure of social networks and the ways in which knowledge is transferred through those networks. The structure includes associations (e.g. trade associations), networks of consultants and employees who move from one organization to another, and educational institutions and publications. Imitative diffusion can account for substantial elements of the spread of decision making rules, conventions, and technologies.

Third, in both learning and environmental selection, the *legitimacy* of rules is affected by the use of rules by others. Within a population of decision makers, the definition of appropriate behavior tends to be socially constructed by interpretations of observed behavior. What constitutes a proper decision maker? A decision maker who does what decision makers do. What constitutes a proper decision making rule? A rule that is used by proper decision makers. How does a decision maker know what a proper decision maker does or what decision making rule is proper? By observing what other decision makers do.

Practices, forms, and rules become more legitimate as more decision makers use them. Commonly used practices become institutionalized as myths defining legitimate decision making routines. Legitimacy is not, of course, determined entirely by use on the part of others. There are frequently official and semiofficial bodies responsible for legitimating particular practices. When a professional group defines standard operating procedures for engineers or professional standards for physicians, it makes those rules legitimate. This sometimes happens even before the practices are widely used, although professional certification of legitimacy is as likely to follow general acceptance as it is to precede it. Similarly, legal requirements may anticipate, or even seek explicitly to force, subsequent practice. The general point is that one of the main ways a rule becomes legitimate in one place is by being used in another.

2.4 Appropriate Rules or Consequential Choice?

As should be clear from comparing this chapter with Chapter 1, there is a substantial chasm between those students who see decisions as choices made in the name of consequences and preferences and those students who see decisions as rule following in the name of appropriateness. Some interpretations of the chasm have already been suggested and will not be repeated extensively here. However, it may be useful to note two versions of the interpretations and to reiterate the position reflected in this book.

2.4.1 Reason and Reasoning

Standard contemporary discourse, particularly in the traditions of decision theory, tends to equate reason with a logic of consequence. The idea is that a reasoning decision maker will consider alternatives in terms of their consequences for preferences. Thoughtful discussion about action is expected to illuminate a decision maker's expectations and preferences. Deviations from a logic of consequence are treated as deviations from reason. Within that tradition, the claims of duty, obligation, identity, and rules are inferior claims. Rule following is portrayed as unthinking and automatic, identities as arbitrary and imposed. The glory of choice is seen in its links to independence and thought. The shame of rules is seen in their links to dependence and thoughtlessness.

It should be clear that such judgments are not reflected here. A logic of appropriateness is different from a logic of consequence, but both logics are logics of reason. Just as a logic of consequence encourages thought, discussion, and personal judgment about preferences and expectations, a logic of appropriateness encourages thought, discussion, and personal judgment about situations, identities, and rules. Both processes organize an interaction between personal commitment and social justification.

The two logics are not distinguished by differences in their status as thoughtful action. They are distinguished by the demands they make on the abilities of individuals and institutions. One makes great demands on the abilities of individuals and institutions to anticipate the future and to form useful preferences. The other makes great demands on the abilities of individuals and institutions to learn from the past and to form useful identities. Both processes picture human beings and human institutions as having a relatively high order of reasoning skill. Each logic is consistent with the glorification of the human estate and with high hopes for human action. Both are plausible processes for reasoning, reasonable decision makers.

2.4.2 Mutual Subsumesmanship

In arguments between theorists of consequential choice and theorists of rule following, each group sees the other's perspective as a special case of its own. For theorists of consequential choice, rules are constraints derived from rational action at a higher level. For theorists of rule following, consequential choice is simply one of many possible rules that may be evoked and followed when deemed appropriate.

The approach here is conscious of, but largely indifferent to, these displays of subsumesmanship. Empirical observations of decisions provide ample examples of behaviors that are hard to understand without attention to both perspectives, and neither (at least in its present incarnation) explains enough of the phenomena to claim exclusive rights to truth. In the cultures and contexts (e.g. much of contemporary economics, psychology, and political science) where enthusiasts for consequential analysis and the pursuit of preferences are dominant, ordinary good sense probably calls for reminders of logics of appropriateness, identities, and rules. In cultures and contexts (e.g. much of contemporary sociology and anthropology) where enthusiasts for roles, rules, and institutions are dominant, ordinary good sense probably calls for reminders of logics of consequences, preferences, and calculation.

Since students of decision making straddle the standard disciplinary boundaries to some extent, it may be appropriate for them to try to fit these contentious cultures of disciplinary interpretation into a single world view. They also have incentives to do so. In this effort, they have allies among decision makers. Since most decision makers are more bemused by disciplinary disputes than inclined to join them, they are likely to find multiple visions complementary rather than contending..

CHAPTER THREE

Multiple Actors: Teams and Partners

I n Chapter 1 decision makers were portrayed as rational actors, searching for alternatives in a world of limited knowledge and evaluating those alternatives in terms of their preferences. The focus was on the ways incomplete knowledge of alternatives and consequences imposed limits on rationality, on how decision makers cope with those limitations through satisficing and problem solving heuristics, and on some of the consequences of those coping mechanisms for the accumulation of slack and the occasions of innovation in organizations.

In Chapter 2 decision makers appeared as rule followers, matching appropriate behavior to situations and trying to fulfill their identities. The focus was on the processes involved in creating, maintaining, and acting within conceptions of self that are multiple and sometimes unclear, on the ways in which rules encode history, and on some of the complications in capturing the past through experiential learning and environmental selection.

In both Chapter 1 and Chapter 2, the portrayal was implicitly of a single decision maker. In this chapter and the next, the focus shifts to processes involving multiple actors.

3.1 Interpersonal Consistency and Teams

The easiest transition from single-person to multiple-person decision making is one that treats the individuals involved as having consistent preferences or identities. That would mean every gain to one individual is a gain to others and there are no issues of allocating shares of the gain. It would mean every action mandated by one identity is consistent with the actions mandated by any other identity that is evoked in individuals who are involved. Such situations are rare in pure form, but they are sometimes approximated.

Where multiple consistent actors are involved in decision making, conflict is not a problem, but various issues of communication and coordination remain. Two individuals with consistent preferences may fail to achieve their best outcomes because they fail to act in concert. Similarly, two individuals with consistent identities may fail to fulfill those identities fully because they fail to fit their identities together. Many modern contributions of operations research and decision science are designed to improve the capabilities of consistent multiple actors to find and implement jointly desired strategies.

A convenient, and conventional, name for consistent multiple actors is "team." The name is useful, although many familiar teams—for example, most athletic teams—are not "teams" in the sense required. Individuals on the typical athletic team share some objectives, but they exhibit considerable internal conflict also. A team is a theoretical construct, a collection of individuals with problems of uncertainty but without conflict of interests or identities.

Although it is hard to find teams in the real world that meet a strict definition of internal consistency, it is fairly conventional to approach decision making in the large bureaucracies of business, government, military, or religious organizations by treating each bureaucracy as a team. Treating multiple actor decision making systems as teams has been justified in at least three ways:

1. *Teams as approximations.* Some multiple actor situations involve individuals with preferences and identities that are

close enough to being consistent that considering them as a team is a reasonable approximation.
2. *Teams as simplifications.* In some multiple actor situations individuals are organized into multiple groups (for example, in almost any large organization or system of organizations). In order to highlight the inconsistencies among groups, inconsistencies *within* groups are ignored, and the individual groups are treated as teams.
3. *Teams as contracts.* In some theories of multiple actor decision making, decision making is imagined to be divided into two stages. At the first stage, the inconsistencies are removed through various forms of bargaining, side payments, and agreements that define a contract binding the parties. At the second stage, the multiple actors operate as a team.

From the standpoint of theories of decision making, teams are essentially equivalent to single actors. They accentuate problems of communication and coordination, thus increase the relevance of concepts of information costs and uncertainty, but understanding decision making in teams involves using the ideas of limited rationality and rule following already discussed in Chapters 1 and 2. As a result, this chapter and Chapter 4 consider decision making involving multiple *inconsistent* actors.

3.2 Interpersonal Inconsistencies

Most theories of multiple actor decision making are not theories of teams. They consider situations where decisions must be made and action must be taken in the face of inconsistent preferences or identities. Such inconsistencies are palpable features of decision making. They may well characterize many decisions by individuals. They certainly characterize decisions involving multiple actors. Two Egyptian students of information systems describe their experiences and observations in designing a decision support system for the Egyptian cabinet. They found that the process is often murky; it is usually a group effort involving negotiation and consensus building; it involves a variety of stakeholders, with different assumptions and values; it takes place in an emergent fashion, exploiting serendipitous discovery; there is great deal of information, but much of it is qualitative, oral, or poorly recorded; the significance of the stakes involved leads both to political maneuvering and stress; top decision makers are short of time, resistant to change, comfortable with intuition, and powerful enough to enforce quick responses to their needs.[1]

The idea that decisions are made in groups and organizations despite inconsistency among individual actors is at the heart of social choice theory, most political conceptions of decision making, and modern game theory. The processes of multiple actor decision making described in this chapter and Chapter 4 are procedures for reaching a decision without necessarily resolving conflict of interest or identity. The procedures may include some effort to proclaim a common objective or shared identity, but they do not depend on that. Sometimes inconsistency is "removed," but more commonly it is accommodated.

3.2.1 Multiple Preferences, Multiple Identities

Decision making in groups, organizations, or societies confronts interpersonal inconsistencies. Different people want different things, and not everyone can have everything he or she desires. Different people have different identities, and their different definitions of appropriate behavior are mutually inconsistent.

Inconsistent preferences and identities are not pathologies. They are standard and predictable facts of social, economic, organizational, and political life. The level of interpersonal inconsistency varies with the mix of preferences and identities, with the level of available resources and with aspirations for resources. Scarce resources and high aspirations lead to more inconsistencies, as do noncomplementary preferences and identities. Attention plays an important role, because inconsistency depends on which preferences and which identities are salient at a particular time.

Although the rhetoric surrounding multiple actor decisions may sometimes invoke an aura of shared objectives or identities, and although conceptions of shared interests and destinies are actually quite common, many multiple-person situations cannot be understood easily within the frameworks presented in Chapters 1 and 2. Many decisions result neither from consequential calculations in terms of joint preference functions nor from joint awareness of consistent rules, but from decision making interactions among individuals and groups pursuing their own conceptions of appropriateness and interest.

Ideas of multiple actor decision making increase the theoretical possibilities. If there are multiple actors, each of those actors has to be characterized as a decision maker. As might be expected, theories differ in their assumptions about the individual actors—each of whom must be endowed with perfect knowledge or lesser degrees, with one identity or multiple identities, and with preferences. Moreover, they must be endowed with knowledge about each other, about each other's preferences, identities, and knowledge.

Classical versions of game theory assume that individual actors are pure rational agents with perfect knowledge. They emphasize the pursuit of strategies and contracts that structure incentives in a stabilizing way. That is, they try to identify "equilibria" where actors, all pursuing their own interests, have no incentive to deviate from their current actions. Exchange versions of decision making in sociology and psychology similarly assume that individuals are pure rational actors. They emphasize the advantage ("power") that accrues to those who either possess resources desired by others or desire resources that are not desired by others.

Behavioral versions of these processes emphasize the limitations on rationality and rule following that affect the actors, the ways in which their knowledge, identities, and preferences may be unclear and changing. These theories tend to emphasize the information complications in forming coalitions and bargaining, the processes of learning about others, the significance of trust and cultural understandings in discovering and sustaining stable coalitions, and the indeterminacy and stability of choices.

3.2.2 Core Assumptions of Multiple Actor Decision Making

The core assumptions of theories about multiple actor decision processes are simple. First, there are individual participants—individuals, groups, and organizations—each of whom is treated as having consistent preferences and identities. That is, each individual participant is a coherent, single-person actor or a coherent team. Second, preferences and identities differ among the participants. That is, not everyone wants the same thing or considers the same action appropriate. Third, the preferences and identities of participants are jointly inconsistent. That is, they cannot all be realized within existing environmental constraints.

Such a picture is, in fact, simpler than the world, where we often find internally inconsistent groups or organizations in conflict with others that are also not internally consistent. Some of the more interesting features of multiple actor decision making arise in these more complicated situations. Consider, for example, foreign policy conflict among countries within each of which there is internal political conflict over foreign policy. Or consider labor–management disagreements between organized groups that are themselves internally inconsistent. For the most part, decision systems involving inconsistencies at several nested levels are not explored in this book.

In multiple actor conceptions of decision making, each actor is assumed to consider a decision only from the perspective of his or her own identity or preferences and to expect others to consider it only from theirs. These considerations include second- and third-order effects: I assume that you assume that I assume you will be consistent to your own identity and values. In such a world of self-oriented cleverness or obligations, reaching mutually satisfactory and enforceable agreements can be difficult. Potential partners must find an agreement that is self-enforcing since each party anticipates that the others will fulfill their agreements only if it is consistent with their own conceptions of themselves, and each anticipates that the others will anticipate this.

As was noted in section 3.1, theorists of multiple actor decision making have often imagined decision processes to be separable into two stages. In the first stage—which could be called bargaining, negotiation, policy making, politics, or something similar—the initial conflict situation is converted into one in which there is agreement. A team is formed. In the second stage—which could be called administration, choice, implementation, execution, enforcement, or similar names—actions are taken consistent with the agreements and according to logics of consequence and appropriateness.

In this spirit, students of rational decision making often describe one process by which goals (joint preferences) are set and another, subsequent and independent, process for making decisions consistent with them. Students of rule-based decision making often describe one process for establishing a system of rules and another, subsequent and independent, process for making decisions that conform to them. Students of administrative decision making often describe one process for setting policy and another, subsequent and independent process for making the decisions required to administer the policy. Students of the cultural basis of decision making often describe one process by which conflicting norms and practices are reconciled and another, subsequent and independent, process by which actions are taken consistent with the reconciliation.

Numerous scholars in each of those traditions have noted that the division of decision making into these two stages is justified more by its analytical convenience than by its descriptive accuracy. The agreements negotiated in the first stage have a habit of transforming themselves in the second stage. Efforts to separate "politics" from "administration" are persistently frustrated by the tendency of political processes to creep into administrative processes. Often the solution of concrete problems stimulates the invention of principles of agreement, rather than the other way around. For example, competitors sometimes discover a basis for long-term collaborative agreements in the course of trying to negotiate a concrete deal.

Nevertheless, the distinction between multiple actor processes for making decisions *within* prior agreements and multiple actor processes for making decisions *about* such agreements is maintained to some extent here. The discussions of bounded rationality and rule following in Chapters 1 and 2 can be used as a basis for the latter processes. This chapter focuses particularly on the former processes, that is, on the political aspects of multiple actor decision making.

3.2.3 Implications of Interpersonal Inconsistency

Four important implications ensue from viewing decision making as involving inconsistencies in interests and identities.

1. *Action is strategic.* Actors are assumed to be clever and socially adept. They send and receive signals and create expectations. In their own actions, they anticipate the reactions of others, and they encourage others to anticipate them. In this world, information always serves a purpose. Depending on their strategies, actors may hide or make salient information about alternatives, consequences, identities, or rules. Honesty is not a virtue, though it may be a tactic.

2. *Beliefs are important,* particularly beliefs about who wants what, who has power, and who will act. As a result of the importance of such beliefs and the necessity of forming them in an ambiguous world, much decision making behavior is second-order. It is concerned with influencing beliefs, particularly reputations. Machiavelli, for example, recommended that princes build reputations that would lead their subjects both to love and to fear them (though he suggested that if a prince has to choose, fear is more reliable than love).

3. *Trust and loyalty* are both valued and scarce. The interaction of strategic action with the importance of beliefs makes it difficult to construct tight and binding agreements. Understandings with allies are inherently vague, and the behaviors the understandings are designed to control are in the future. There is a temptation for partners to defect. As a result, decision making in the face of inconsistency creates both an important role for trust and loyalty and, at the same time, a dynamic of maneuver that makes belief in the existence of such traits difficult to sustain.

4. *Attention is important.* To the earlier discussion of the importance of attention in models of limited rationality and models of rule following, this model adds the complicating factor of multiple participants. Decisions depend on who participates and to what degree. Actors with "power" and "resources" may fail because they are distracted, and actors with few resources and little power may succeed because they are alert or persistent. Decisions may be unstable in the face of shifting patterns of attention.

To develop ideas of decision making when preferences or identities are inconsistent, the next section begins with an exploration of the social bases for inconsistencies. The section after that considers a basic building block for theories of multiple actor decision making, the partnership between two individuals.

3.3 Social Bases of Inconsistencies

In most views of multiple actor decision making, individuals are pictured as having goals, values, wants, and identities that are well defined, stable, and exogenous. These stable but mutually inconsistent preferences and identities jointly create decision problems when confronted with the scarcity of resources in the environment. Like preferences and identities, environmental resources are assumed to be exogenous and stable (or to change only in a predictable way). Within such a framework, inconsistencies are imposed on the decision system by attributes of the individual participants and environments involved.

Such a view is incomplete if it ignores the ways in which inconsistencies are produced within the social and decision system itself. This section considers, in particular, three aspects of the cognitive and social bases of inconsistency:

1. First, decision processes depend on perceptions of preferences and identities. Those perceptions are subject to human error.
2. Second, preferences and identities are shaped within social institutions, particularly hierarchies. Those institu-

tions introduce systematic effects on the level and locus of inconsistency.

3. Third, inconsistencies are conserved by social processes of divergence. Conflict is sometimes sustained rather than reduced.

3.3.1 Misperceptions of Preferences and Identities

Individuals develop beliefs about their own and others' preferences and identities on the basis of incomplete information. They infer preferences and identities from actions, events, and communications that are susceptible to multiple interpretations. They guess values that are obscured by problems of interpersonal and intercultural communication, as well as by deliberate falsifications and strategic misinformation. Estimating preferences and identities is subject to all of the cognitive, information processing, and human inference limitations outlined in Chapters 1 and 2.

As a result, decision makers are likely to be inaccurately informed about what other people want, how they intend to get it, what they think is appropriate behavior, and how they feel about other people. Decision makers may also have incomplete information about their own preferences and identities. Depending on momentary impulses, the framing of a question, and the agenda on which it appears, individuals find themselves feeling differently about themselves on different occasions.

Since the perceived level of consistency is dependent on incomplete and misleading information, decision makers may easily come to believe that their own values and those of others are consistent when they are not. Or they may come to believe that their values are inconsistent with others when they are actually consistent. The former case leads to "unwarranted" trust. The latter leads to "unwarranted" distrust.

Erroneous perceptions of identities and preferences are sometimes corrected. Mistakes are revealed by the unfolding of history, particularly in repeated interactions among the same decision makers. Stable preferences and identities may reveal themselves through repeated exposure so that perceptions converge to reality. Such a result is not assured, however, and it is quite possible that biases in perceptions will persist. For example, ambitious junior managers try to determine the preferences of successful senior managers by interpreting their (mostly indifferent or unconscious) responses to the junior managers' behavior. The resulting misinterpretations of indifference as approval or disapproval are unlikely to be changed by repetitive experience.

Even more interesting perhaps are cases in which misperceptions lead to actions that make the misperceptions valid. Preferences and identities converge to beliefs about them, rather than the other way around. If Jake believes that Harry likes him, he behaves toward Harry in a way that increases the chance that Harry will, in fact, come to like him. If Jake believes that Harry does not like him, he behaves toward Harry in a way that increases the chance that Harry will, in fact, come to dislike him.

When preferences and identities are enacted from beliefs about them that are developed within the decision making system, inconsistencies are no longer exogenous to decision making but are created within the process of acting. The attitudes of individuals are shaped by the roles they are required to play and by the responses of others to those roles.

3.3.2 The Shaping of Inconsistencies in Hierarchies

The interaction between beliefs and values is not the only way preferences and identities are shaped. Decision structures themselves create the premises of decision. Among those structures, one of the more pervasive is hierarchy, a structure in which individuals are arranged by a cascade of authority and communication relations. Hierarchies not only organize individuals, they create them. Three aspects of hierarchical organizations and their effects on inconsistency are considered here: (1) the link between hierarchy and the careers of managers, (2) the process of co-optation within a hierarchy, and (3) the role of departmentalization and delegation in creating and buffering inconsistency.

HIERARCHY AND MANAGERIAL CAREERS

Many of the decision making systems observed in the modern world are hierarchies. Two functional explanations are commonly provided for the prevalence of hierarchical decision systems. The first is that hierarchy is an efficient structure for accomplishing instrumental tasks. The second is that hierarchy sustains and is sustained by strong normative beliefs, particularly those associated with a masculine conception of order based on relations of subordination/domination.

Both explanations are plausible, but they jointly obscure still a third functional interpretation: that hierarchy is a requirement for managerial careers. In order for a person to make "progress" in an organizational career, there must be opportunities for advancement, and advancement is defined in terms of hierarchical levels. From this perspective, hierarchies are primarily contexts for the pursuit of individual careers. This means:

> First, definitions of self—preferences and identities—are shaped by features of the hierarchical competition for getting ahead. Self-worth is defined by promotion and therefore by the qualities required for promotion. Individuals who are involved in competition for career advancement find their identities shaped by that competition. They conform in order to be acceptable. They differ in order to differentiate and distinguish themselves.
>
> Second, decisions in hierarchies have to be interpreted as confluences of careers. Any particular decision in a hierarchical organization involves several people. Each of those people fits any particular decision into his or her career. Thus, any decision results from a time-specific mosaic of individual lives that are themselves best understood by the way they are organized over time into careers.
>
> Third, decision making within hierarchies is organized in a way that serves the process of hierarchical advancement. The apparatus and process of decision making are affected by the necessity of justifying the hierarchical structure that allows careers. In order to decide who will be promoted, managers must be assessed on the quality of their performance and on

the sagacity of their decisions. This requires that reports be generated, information communicated, responsibilities assigned and clarified, and decisions evaluated. In short, a system of decision making serves a system of hierarchical careers as much as the other way around.

HIERARCHY AND CO-OPTATION

The development of inconsistencies in hierarchies is conditioned by interactions between those who occupy top-level positions ("the successful") and those who would like to do so ("the ambitious"). Both the successful and the ambitious are conscious of the fact that the latter might be able to overthrow the former and seize power, but such an outcome is not guaranteed. As a result, each of them has a choice: For the successful, the choice is between "sharing" and "resisting." They can offer to form a coalition with the ambitious that provides a sharing of the power in the future, or they can refuse to do so, gambling on their ability to defeat the challenge. For the ambitious, the choice is between "joining" and "fighting." They can agree to form a coalition with is promises of shared power in the future, or they can seek to gain complete power on their own immediately, gambling on their ability to do so.

The "join 'em or fight 'em" issue is a very general one in the development of social systems. It is evident in the development of political identities, oppositions, and regimes. It is evident in the development of scientific identities, oppositions, and paradigms. It is evident in the development of business identities, oppositions, and mergers.

Much of the stability of social regimes stems from their success in judicious co-optation—that is, from a willingness of the successful to form coalitions with certain of the ambitious and from the willingness of some ambitious actors to join forces rather than continue to fight. Such co-optation involves an exchange. The ambitious give up a possible ascension to full power in the future for an immediate commitment to a smaller share of the power. The successful give up part of their control in return for assuring its continuation.

The joint attractiveness of a coalition between the successful and the ambitious stems from some common differences in perceptions, some differences in time discounts, and some differences in risk preferences. In particular, co-optation is likely if both the successful and the ambitious are more pessimistic about their own chances of success without a coalition than their partners are; if the successful weigh future returns more heavily than do the ambitious, and if they are both risk-averse.

Such an analysis is, of course, incomplete without attending to the second-order effects of co-optation on the position of the successful. In particular, if co-optation is a route to success, then the system provides incentives for an ambitious person to organize a movement in opposition to the successful. Thus, co-optation stimulates opposition. The danger that such an incentive poses is somewhat mollified by the fact that the bargaining power of an ambitious individual in negotiating co-optation stems partly from that specific leader's indispensability to a group of dispossessed. Thus, ambitious leaders are likely to seek to maximize the dependence of supporters. As a result, while co-optation provides incentives for organizing the "masses," it also provides incentives for making them dependent on an individual leader. The latter incentives pave the way for the destruction of a movement through precise co-optation.

The rational analysis of co-optation casts some light on the situation, but it considerably exaggerates the consciousness of the process. Processes of co-optation are part of the day-by-day development of decision making systems. Preferences and identities are molded by efforts to get ahead and by efforts to maintain position, but those efforts and their link to co-optation are only partly deliberate. The successful sometimes fail to offer co-optation bribes when it would be in their narrow self-interest to do so, and the ambitious sometimes reject them.

Ambitious people set themselves in opposition to the establishment in order to increase their value, but in the course of doing so they transform their preferences and identities. They learn to take pleasure in the immediate glories of opposition. Successful people escalate their aspirations and are driven to disaster by their wish to preserve exclusive rights to power, or by their conception of authority as requiring rigidity and toughness. As a result, managing preferences and identities strategically is a relatively complicated game.

HIERARCHY AND THE ORGANIZATION OF INCONSISTENCY

Hierarchical organizations use delegation and departmentalization to mobilize diverse individuals into relatively coherent action. Delegation and departmentalization mold preferences and identities in the service of the organization. At the same time, however, delegation and departmentalization also produce inconsistencies. Hierarchical organizations locate any individual in a two dimensional space. The first dimension is the "vertical" one, the level in the organization. Where is this individual relative to the top and the bottom of the organization? The second dimension is the "horizontal" one. Where is this individual in the divisional or departmental structure of the organization? More complicated organizational forms, such as matrix organizations, add more dimensions.

Organizational subunits are important to the development of individual preferences and identities. They are collections of associations and friendships. They are a focus for the development of values, wants, and allegiances. They serve as information networks for development of common perceptions of resources and alternatives and for the development of a common sense of agenda and timing. Subunits are also collections of shared experiences. Members develop common interpretations of life and purpose, a sense of common fate, and shared frustrations with dependencies on others. They build barriers to contact, friendship, and loyalty with other departments, thus to the sharing of information and resources. They define their own group in opposition to other groups, other departments.

These horizontal cleavages tend to obscure the cleavages associated with the vertical dimension of organization. The sense of similarity and common destiny shared by vice presidents in different departments is undermined by their allegiances to their departments and the competition among them. The sense of similarity and common destiny shared by two unskilled workers in different departments is undermined by their allegiances to their departments. Hence the way in which the organization organizes has substantial impact on the kinds of inconsistencies that are evoked and maintained.

3.3.3 Conservation of Inconsistency

Many social processes are processes of convergence. Things become more like each other over time. People come closer to each other in attitudes and behavior through interaction. Disputants in a conflict find some middle ground on which they can agree. Imitation, compromising, and bargaining, for example, are all processes that tend to reduce differences among people.

These mechanisms of convergence affect the way inconsistencies in preferences and identities are viewed. Such inconsistencies are frequently defined as misfortunes, even abnormalities, that natural social processes will eliminate. Thus, it is common to talk about conflict reduction as both an objective of social policy and a natural consequence of social contact. Theories of social organization tend to make inconsistencies appear unusual and transitory.

In history, however, conflict appears more normal and permanent than abnormal and temporary. History suggests that inconsistencies in preferences and identities are fundamental in human systems and are maintained despite attempts to avoid or eliminate them. This leads to the speculation that conflict is conserved. That is, when inconsistency is reduced in one part of a social system, it is shifted to another, leading the overall level of inconsistency to be essentially constant over time. In this view, the only true limit on manifest inconsistency is scarcity of time, since one cannot be overtly inconsistent with everyone at all times.

In particular, three fundamental divergent processes in organizations should be noted:

1. *Differentiation of Identities.* When an individual creates a sense of self, it is a self that is different from others. While individuals often imitate others and often borrow parts of their

identity from others, they also attempt to be different. They choose to be a part of groups that are distinctive from the masses at large, and they choose to be distinctive relative to other members of their groups. Intra-group cohesiveness and unity are sustained by accentuating inter-group differences and conflict. Organizations encourage such differentiation.

2. *Insatiable Desires.* Satisfying current wants sows the seed of future dissatisfaction. The things achieved today become the starting point for tomorrow's aspirations. Satisfying the desires of individuals (e.g. by providing them more resources) may reduce conflict in the short run, but its longer-run effect is to stimulate desires and make it harder to reduce conflict in the future. These adjustments in aspirations serve to keep conflict at a fairly constant level in the face of fluctuations in resource levels and their distribution in the society.

3. *Competition for Primacy.* Organizations and individuals within organizations compete for relative position. In many respects, the true basis for human action is not avarice— the lust for personal gain and comfort, but envy—the lust for primacy. This competition over position converts non-zero sum games into zero sum games. With competition for primacy, trying to reduce conflict by increasing scarce resources is at best a short-run strategy. Competition for primacy emphasizes the distribution of resources, rather than the overall level of resources, as the main factor that determines the level of conflict. Decision makers seem less inclined to ask whether their own rewards satisfy their own wants than whether their rewards rank them higher than others.

To the extent that inconsistency is conserved, "managing conflict" means directing it rather than reducing it. Decision processes in organizations highlight some conflicts and ignore others. Organizational structures focus conflict along some lines of cleavage rather than others. This is particularly important in situations where there are some "natural" cleavages among members of an organization that threaten the effectiveness of a basic coalition or set of interests. Suppose a "natural" cleavage divides users of different kinds of technology, as you might find in a military establishment dividing the army, the navy, and the air force. Then organizational strategists would organize regionally if they wanted to focus attention along other dimensions of inconsistency, and would organize by technology if they want to accentuate the focus on technology.

Similarly, if differences in social class are a conspicuous basis for differentiation, then an organizational designer who wanted to reduce class-consciousness and conflict would emphasize departments rather than organizational levels as the fundamental basis of organizational structure. A designer who wanted to emphasize conflict across class lines would deemphasize departmentalization. The difference can be seen by looking at different colleges and universities. Where the organization of faculty and students is oriented to departments, institutes, and schools, cleavages and conflict tend to be between departments, with faculty and students divided by their departmental allegiances. Where the organization of faculty and students is oriented to the college or university as a whole, cleavages are more likely to be between faculty and students.

Similar observations can be made about the consequences of the organization of families for the mobilization of groups focused on ethnicity, gender, and age. Because family organization is much more segregated with respect to ethnicity than with respect to either gender or age, broader-scale conflict along ethnic lines is more easily produced and sustained than is conflict along either gender or age lines.

3.4 Uneasy Partners

Understanding decision making under conditions of value inconsistency begins with understanding the simple bilateral problems of relations between two partners whose preferences or identities are inconsistent. Suppose each of two partners would welcome collaboration with the other, provided the terms of that collaboration can be made favorable, but neither is certain to sustain that collaboration if the contending claims of individual preferences or identities conflict. Situations of this sort abound in decision making. There are frequently advantages to be gained by cooperation, but cooperation is threatened by other obligations of identity or by incentives to defect from collaboration.

3.4.1 The Prisoners' Dilemma

Within multiple actor theories of decision making, a partnership arises and is sustained because it serves the values of each partner. Possible partnerships have to be identified, and they have to be made feasible by making the inconsistent preferences or identities of the potential partners consistent. Approaches to thinking about those problems parallel our earlier contrast between consequence-based rational action and identity-based rule following.

Consider, for example, the most famous of modern examples of the difficulties of joint decision making—the prisoners' dilemma. Multiple actor decision making involves numerous complications not conspicuously present in the prisoners' dilemma, but the dilemma illustrates some canonical features of thinking about such decisions. The situation is called a "prisoners' dilemma" because of one simple storybook version of the problem. In this story, two prisoners are interviewed separately by the authorities. Each prisoner is assumed to be entirely self-regarding, acting only in consideration of his or her own preferences or identities. More specifically, in the classical prisoners' dilemma situation, each prisoner knows that if neither of them confesses to the crime of which they are accused, that is, if they "cooperate" with each other and maintain their innocence, each can expect to receive a prison sentence of a certain length, A1. If both confess, that is, if they do not "cooperate" with each other, each can expect a longer sentence, one of length A2. If only one confesses, the one who confesses (the one who breaks ranks) can expect a short prison sentence, one of length A3; but the one who does not confess (the one who remains loyal) can expect a long prison sentence, one of length A4. As long as the expectations for these sentences are such that A3 < A1 < A2 < A4, neither of the prisoners seems likely to risk staying silent. As a result, they are likely to end up with both confessing, an outcome that results in a term in prison, A2, for each of them that is longer than the term, A1, each would receive if they cooperated with each other and both resisted confessing.

Situations of this general type have been studied extensively. The studies have included two kinds of research. In the first kind, students of rational or rule-following decision making have tried to predict from a formal analysis of the situation what the two prisoners will do, imposing various assumptions in order to generate the prediction. In the second kind of research, students of decision making have tried to observe what kind of behavior actually occurs when two people are confronted with a prisoners' dilemma decision.

PRISONERS' DILEMMA THEORIES

The history of studies in the prisoners' dilemma tradition is a history of persistent problems in finding theories that predict the partnership behavior actually observed. Much of that history can be written in terms of two different perspectives on partnerships, derived from the two decision perspectives discussed in Chapters 1 and 2. Are partnerships to be seen as joining two actors each pursuing a logic of consequences? Or are partnerships to be seen as joining two actors each pursuing a logic of appropriateness?

The prisoners' dilemma was originally studied almost entirely from the standpoint of partnerships of rational decision makers. In this view, partners make individual decisions assessing possible consequences in terms of their own individual preferences. The complication is that since each partner decides independently and simultaneously, taking into account the situation faced by the other, neither can treat the other's behavior as characterized by a fixed probability distribution.

Game theory, developed to deal with such interactions of rational actors, generated a number of ideas about decision rules that would be followed and equilibria that would be achieved. The most common decision rule was one that involved considering for each possible action the worst payoff that could result from action of the other (the maximum "loss"). The decision rule was to select that action for which the worst possible payoff was best (that is, minimax, minimize the maximum loss). In the standard prisoners' dilemma situation, if each prisoner chooses that action for which the worst possible payoff was best, each would confess.

The prisoners' dilemma can also be considered from the point of view of partnerships of rule-following decision makers. When two individuals are placed in a situation in which each must choose an action that affects the returns to both parties, there are socially defined rules of proper behavior. From this point of view, rational action is simply one of many possible rules that might be evoked, probably by evoking an identity of "game player" or "competitive actor."

Such identities, however, are not the only ones that might be evoked. Perhaps someone in a prisoners' dilemma accepts the identity of friend, group member, or collaborator. Such identities are likely to evoke decision rules that are somewhat different from that of minimizing the maximum possible loss. One such rule that has been explored at some length is called "tit-for-tat." It calls for "cooperating" (that is, not confessing) the first time the game is played with any particular person and subsequently responding by mimicking the immediately previous response of the other person. This particular rule has a result quite different from the minimax loss rule. It leads to a stable equilibrium in which neither prisoner confesses.

Formal analysis of prisoners' dilemma partnerships has considerably enriched and deepened our understanding of partnerships of persons with differing preferences and identities. A comprehensive review of the analytical results would be beyond the scope of this section, but it may be useful to cite two fairly general clusters of results:

1. *Repeated trials.* It makes a good deal of difference whether the partnership is a continuing one with repeated experiences together in the same, or similar, situations, or a single-trial relationship. Partnerships that endure over repeated trials introduce considerations of reputation, trust, retaliation, and learning that are not present in single-trial

situations. Repeated trials allow for the development of mutually advantageous coordinated actions (e.g. tit-for-tat rules).

2. *Incomplete rationality.* It makes a good deal of difference whether the partnership involves (with certainty) two completely rational individuals with perfect knowledge and complete consistency, or whether each partner has to assume there is some small probability that the other person's actions are not completely rational. The equilibria in the former case are frequently quite different from the equilibria in the latter.

PRISONERS' DILEMMA BEHAVIOR

Studies of actual human behavior in prisoners' dilemma situations yield results that are too complicated to review here. In the aggregate, they suggest some mixture of the two perspectives on partnership. Partners often do become trapped in the jointly suboptimal outcome associated with both prisoners confessing. However, they often avoid that result, often successfully "cooperating" by not confessing, despite rational incentives for breaking ranks. They are inclined to feel some pressures of appropriateness, particularly if certain identities are evoked.

3.4.2 Information

As decision makers assess consequences and incentives, and as they evoke and fulfill identities, the information available to them is rarely "innocent." It is likely to have been collected and transmitted by people other than the decision maker. Since the providers of information have preferences and identities that differ from those of the decision maker, they have reasons for shaping the information. Since the decision maker has no direct way to check the accuracy of the information provided, there is an information problem for the partnership.

If decision information is generated or communicated by people with reasons for influencing decisions, it cannot be treated as having only random errors. Data then lose the properties of statistical independence and randomness on which statistical estimations are based. For example, multiple reports do not necessarily reflect multiple independent observations. One information provider who wants to lie can get ninety-nine others to do the same. In such a world, counting sample size becomes less important than determining credibility of information sources and the plausibility of their information.

STRATEGIC INFORMATION

Partnerships require information exchange at two stages: *Forming* a partnership involves information on possible partners and their attractiveness as partners. *Operating* within a partnership involves information on the extent to which the partnership agreements are fulfilled. Both types of information are subject to strategic misrepresentation, and much of information economics is devoted to identifying conditions for establishing valid information flows when preferences or identities are inconsistent. Most decision makers face many situations in which consistency is not achieved, thus in which the innocence of information is compromised.

Discussions in information economics distinguish two kinds of problems with strategic information: At the time a partnership is formed, there are risks of *hidden information.* Each party knows something relevant to the other party's decisions and may not report it accurately at the time an agreement is being negotiated. A potential partner may, for example, conceal unattractive properties. Those who purchase insurance may be those who have the greatest health problems, or those who offer used cars for sale may be those who have the lowest-quality automobiles.

Once a partnership is established and operating, there are risks of *hidden action.* For example, a partner might falsify reports of performance under a contract. If the contributions of the partners to an outcome are obscured by external factors (e.g. market conditions) or by luck, each partner might claim to be performing according to the terms of the contract when, in fact, he or she is not.

Each of these problems is well known to anyone who has dealt with partners. Decision makers need to be able to assess the validity of information provided them. Information providers need to devise ways of exposing their honesty. Partnership brokers need to design procedures that minimize the cost of maintaining a flow of valid information.

In the traditions of preference-based rational action, these procedures are largely procedures for soliciting or finding truth in a community of self-interested information providers. They include the use of signals that are more costly to (thus less likely to be used by) an impostor than to a truth-teller. Examples include expensive, nonreturnable engagement rings as signals of fidelity and college degrees as signals of intelligence. They include the use of competition among information providers. They include various forms of certification by outsiders or by cumulated reputation. They include guarantees that insure decision makers against false claims. Insofar as the procedures introduce third parties, of course, they raise such secondary issues as "Who monitors the monitors?"

In the traditions of identity-based rule following, procedures for improving the validity of information in partnerships rely less on incentives and more on associating information honesty with particular roles and identities. Modern students of rational partnerships have invented a variety of terms—strategic misrepresentation, self-disbelieved information, information impactedness—as euphemisms for lying. The euphemisms are not accidental. Within a theory of rational action, lying has no particular onus. One does it when it serves one's purposes. Within a theory of obligatory action, on the other hand, lying is lying. It is not appropriate under many circumstances. The validity of information is facilitated by identities (e.g. friend, professional, scientist) that have rules against lying.

LONG-RUN DYNAMICS OF STRATEGIC INFORMATION

In the short run, some people have advantages in a system of liars. For example, people who are facile with numbers have an advantage at lying with numbers. The advantage is limited by their difficulty in having numbers taken seriously by those who are disadvantaged by them. The glories of numbers are normally seen more clearly by people who are competent with and profit from numbers than by people who are not and do not. Since people who are not facile at numbers are normally intelligent enough to recognize their disadvantage, they often refuse to treat numbers as important to decisions.

These short-run advantages can be important, but their effects have to be viewed within a longer-run dynamic. One feature of the interactive dynamics of such information partnerships can be described in terms of the following morality tale:

> In the beginning there is innocence and cleverness. Innocence speaks without guile. Cleverness manipulates information in the service of self-interest. Before long, competition destroys innocence. Less clever people are eliminated from the competition, either by losing their innocence or by losing their livelihoods. But once innocence is gone, cleverness loses both victims and competitive advantage. The differential effect of cleverness on survival is nil when all engage in it, but none can abandon it without being eliminated. Since the energy devoted to cleverness is not devoted to other things, systems of cleverness are vulnerable to systems that have solved the problem of truthfulness without the costs of competition in cleverness.

In such a spirit, it is sometimes argued that, in the long run, truth will be discovered, either through the competitive actions of self-interested liars (e.g. the Anglo-Saxon legal traditions of justice through competition), through force of the environment (e.g. business firms must make enough money to survive), or through the revelation of truth in the simple unfolding of time.

The competitive version of the "truth will out" argument has, however, an important footnote that is implicit in the morality tale. As forces are mobilized and deployed in the battle of contending liars, the costs of truth rise substantially. Each additional lawyer on each side maintains the balance but increases the costs. Each additional element of self-interested cleverness on the part of information providers necessitates another element of cleverness on the part of information users, and so on. The "armaments" race that results from contending advocates and contending clevernesses seeking advantage may perhaps not affect the truth value of outcomes, though it will if the resources for competition are biased with respect to truth; but "armaments" races considerably increase the aggregate costs and thereby increase the vulnerability of the system to competing systems that do not bear similar costs.

Although the long-run evolutionary path of such a system is arguably one of cycles of cleverness and innocence, rather than the ultimate dominance of either, it seems clear that the dynamics of strategic misrepresentation are likely to make trust, reputation, and rule following important in information exchange. They are likely to provide competitive advantages to decision making systems that are successful in imposing identity-based obligations with respect to honest information.

3.4.3 Creating Partner Consistency

The most obvious strategy for building effective partnerships between individuals with inconsistent preferences or identities is to remove the inconsistencies. This involves either aligning the incentives pursued by rational actors or aligning the identities pursued by rule-following actors.

ALIGNING INCENTIVES

Insofar as the partners are acting on a basis of preferences and logics of consequence, removing inconsistencies means aligning the incentives of the partners. The relevant research is research on relations between principals and agents, on contracts, and on the design of deterrence and information systems.

Theories of Deterrence. One standard theory of aligning incentives in partnerships is a theory of threats and deterrence. Cooperation is sustained by mutually credible threats that sanctions will be imposed if the agreement is not fulfilled. The problems of designing and building effective systems of deterrence have been a central concern of students of international relations and peace. There are two conspicuous problems illuminated in their treatments.

First, systems of deterrence tend to be unstable unless they simultaneously deter both partners. Each partner's "second-strike" capabilities (measured in terms of the losses to the other) must be greater than the other partner's "first-strike" capabilities (measured in terms of the gains expected by the other). In a world of nuclear attack, this suggests that mutual deterrence is facilitated if each nation values preserving its own resources and lives more than it values inflicting loss on others. In more modest partnerships, it suggests that the first step in building a partnership is securing control over something of little value to yourself but much value to your partner—*and* giving your partner control over something of great value to yourself.

Second, systems of deterrence require credible threats. They are always imperiled by the possibility that a threat is, in fact, empty. A child assesses whether a parent will really go through with a threat. A manager assesses whether a supplier will really not send the part. The problem is particularly severe if the action threatened is draconian. The odds are very good that when it comes time to execute a drastic threat, it will, in fact, not be seen as rational to do so.

If a drastic threat fails, going through with it is likely to have more costs than benefits, at least in the short run. An engineer might threaten to leave an organization if he or she is not promoted by a certain date. If the date arrives without a promotion, it will not necessarily be in the engineer's best interest to implement the threat. A threat gains its intelligence from the response it elicits, not from its execution. But since, in the world of rational actors, this possibility will be anticipated by the organization, the threat does little to deter the action.

Since lack of credibility in a threat undermines its effectiveness, partners seek to make their commitments to threats irrevocable and known to be irrevocable. There are a number of mechanisms to solve the problem of sustaining credibility. Bridges may be burned. Decisions may be delegated to other people or to systems of rules or technologies that cannot be modified. Such mechanisms have the consequence, of course, of compelling actions that are, at the time they are executed, easily viewed as unwise.

Systems of revenge—though subject to other pathologies— provide credibility precisely because of their irrationality. Revenge is typically costly for the avenger as well as for the transgressor, so no rational person will take revenge for the transgressions of another. However, this may well leave both parties worse off, because agreements that cannot be enforced cannot be struck. A certain amount of irrational revenge may make cooperative action possible. People might try to cheat a rational person, knowing that a revengeful response would hurt the revenger and thus would be avoided, but the vengeance of an irrational person has to be anticipated even where it would be self-destructive.

One ancient use of deterrence to ensure implementation of an agreement was in the exchange of hostages. The basic idea of hostage exchange is that hostages will be forfeit if an agreement is not fulfilled. To help ensure that a hostage will be returned if the agreement is followed, it is generally useful if each hostage is of much greater direct value to the person whose action is guaranteed than to the person who needs to be reassured.

For example, according to some theories of wages, companies pay workers less than the value of their work early in their tenure, and more than the value of their work late in their tenure. Young workers work hard in anticipation of future rewards, and older workers continue to work hard because to do otherwise would forfeit their surplus payments. Thus young workers surrender part of their rightful payments as a hostage to ensure proper behavior in later periods.

Contracts. Rational models are concerned with incentives—anticipated consequences that induce action. A partnership involving rational actors needs to make the incentives of each partner consistent with the desires of the other. It does so basically by making exchanges among partners (side payments) contingent on desired action. Families and business organizations can be seen as webs of contracts. Mothers and daughters cooperate on the basis of expectations that if they cooperate each will receive benefits that the other controls. Bosses and subordinates cooperate for the same reason.

Partnerships require some mechanisms for arranging and enforcing such incentive-aligning agreements. Particularly in situations where a partnership is expected to be short-lived, each partner is likely to be uneasy about the other. The partners cope with the uneasiness by trying to negotiate explicit contracts that specify the duties of each partner and the exchanges that will follow if the duties are fulfilled. However, since each partner anticipates that the other will fulfill agreements only if it is in his or her own self-interest to do so, and each anticipates that the other will anticipate this also, a partnership faces some standard problems in assuring compliance with an agreement:

Problems of verifiability. If actions can be observed, the two parties can write a contract that specifies actions expected from each partner and arranges appropriate side payments so that both parties are satisfied to take appropriate actions. When actions cannot be observed directly, conformance to the contract must be inferred from observing outcomes. The quality of the inferences that are possible is limited by the complexity of the relation between outcomes and action. For example, performance outcomes are often used to estimate the amount of effort or competence being provided by a partner; but outcomes may be influenced by many unobservables (e.g. environmental munificence, technological possibilities) that obscure the relation between them and a partner's effort or competence.

Problems of incompleteness. Partnerships are often expected to extend over many different situations and over time. Many of those future situations cannot be specified precisely in advance. Each partner might prefer to wait until the unknown contingencies arise and then negotiate the precise terms of an agreement, but such a strategy severely limits the kinds of partnerships that are possible. As a result, contracts mandating future commitments are made, but they are necessarily incomplete. They commit the partners to actions that cannot be determined in advance, thus cannot be explicitly enumerated in the contract. Each partner has to be concerned about interpreting and enforcing such incomplete contracts and has to anticipate that the other partner will also be concerned.

Problems of misplaced specificity. One common solution to problems of verifiability and incompleteness is to write contracts in terms of observable performance. For example, a teacher might contract with a student that a certain score be achieved on a future test. An employer might contract with an employee that a certain level of performance be achieved on a profit and loss statement. Those efforts to tie contracts to performance are frequently useful, but they pose a clear risk. Typically, the performance measure is an *indicator* of the desired behavior rather than the behavior itself.

For example, a teacher who gives a test wants students to learn the subject matter. A test is simply an indicator of that learning. Often, however, students, and other partners, can discover easier or cheaper ways to satisfy the indicator than to do what is really desired. A student learns to cheat on a test or to study specifically for a test, thereby improving test scores but not learning. A manager learns how to manage *accounts* of performance rather than the performance itself.

So one of the great puzzles in designing systems of control among partners is how to give direction without encouraging clever manipulations of performance indicators. Partners wish to exercise control by providing as much specificity as possible, but such precision is also a guide to manipulation. The dilemma is complicated by modern pressures toward clear numbers as an issue of intelligence and "fairness."

Reputations. When partnerships involve repeated interactions, the opportunities for crafting cooperative agreements are increased. Since repeated games have both a history and a future, participants can take action contingent on things that have been observed in the past (reducing problems of information) and can promise retaliation or reward in the future, depending on how well behavior conforms to standards in the present period. This combination of greater information and greater opportunities for retribution makes partnerships involving repeated interactions quite different from single-play partnerships.

The differences are usually summarized by talking about the accumulation of a "reputation." A partner's reputation for acting cooperatively, fulfilling promises, or interpreting agreements in a fair way makes it possible to build joint confidence within a partnership. Joint confidence greatly extends the possibilities for mutually advantageous self-interested cooperation. Notice that, in this conception, a reputation for integrity is pursued only when it yields personal advantage. Reliability in fulfilling promises is a practical tactic, not a moral imperative.

Reputations ("good names") function as hostages. Because those who are reliable in fulfilling their agreements are more valued exchange partners than those who are not, "reputation" is a valuable personal asset. Because reputation is valuable to individuals, it can serve as a hostage in any exchange. And because it can serve as a hostage, it facilitates the maintenance of cooperative relations. Libel and slander are crimes partly because personal reputations are treasured by individuals and partly because personal reputations are vital to a social system of bilateral cooperation.

Reputation is even more important when there are many interacting partners. If the reputation of one partner in one autonomous partnership is compromised, that partnership will be hard to sustain. But if a partner's failure to fulfill expectations in one partnership damages a reputation that is relevant in many relationships, the effects extend throughout the social system and over time. Families, professions, and communities provide networks of reputational information that help sustain each of the partnerships within them.

This discussion of reputation is generally consistent with the usage of the term in game theory and with the results of the many game theoretic analyses of game equilibria. However, the discussion understates the problems in understanding such games. For example, the positive effects of reputation on cooperation in games appears in theorems about infinite games, but not in theorems about very, very long finite games. Cooperation in any relationship of less than infinite duration tends to unravel as the ending of the game (and thus the final irrelevance of reputation) is anticipated.

ALIGNING IDENTITIES AND RULES

Insofar as partners are acting on a basis of identities and logics of appropriateness, removing inconsistencies means aligning the way partners define the situation and their identities, as well as the action implied by their identities. The relevant research is research on the development of rules and roles and on socialization into conformity with them. Most theories of rules and identities see them as coevolving. The identity of parent coevolves with the identity of child; the identity of buyer coevolves with the identity of seller. Indeed, it is hard to conceive of a parent without simultaneously conceiving of a child, or a buyer without a seller. The process by which rules and identities develop tends to align them with each other.

This tendency toward alignment extends even to identities that are defined in opposition to one another. Political opponents or business competitors follow rules of engagement that have coevolved. Conservative doctrine "fits" radical doctrine in the sense of being consistently developed to oppose it. The problems for these traditional opponents of political engagement or business competition lie not in their opposition but in the occasional instances where they find themselves in agreement.

However, long-run processes of alignment leave frequent short-run cases in which identities and rules are not aligned. The processes of identity coevolution are slow, and there are numerous occasions on which identities and rules threaten to be inconsistent with each other. Decision making systems deal with these threats through selection, socialization, attention, and interpretation.

Selection. Individuals are collections of identities and rules. By selecting some individuals as partners and not selecting others, a decision maker creates identity alignment. When decision makers choose persons of similar background, ethnicity, or education in forming partnerships, they adopt a strategy of selection. They do not attempt to mold partners to the collaboration but seek to exploit preexisting molds.

There are two problems with selection as a strategy for aligning identities and rules: First, it tends to limit the formation of partnerships between individuals of differing talents and styles to those partnerships that are already recognized within the society. For example, a neurosurgeon and an anesthesiologist are identities characterized not only by certain competencies but also by interlocking, consistent rules. As a result of the joint development of the two identities, the practices of one match the practices of the other. Either partner can presume a substantial amount of consistency in choosing the other simply by knowing his or her specialty. But where the desired combinations of talents and styles are novel or are less recognized by social experience, it is harder to use selection. The partnerships that emerge either are internally consistent but lack necessary talents or have the talents but are internally inconsistent.

Second, reliance on selection tends to limit partnerships to preprogrammed collaboration that is likely to fail in the face of surprises. For example, commercial airlines traditionally have created aircraft crews through selection, by assigning each crew member independently to a particular flight. Each flight involves a different combination of crew members. In this procedure, each pilot, copilot, and flight engineer is assumed to know his or her job, and the jobs are assumed to fit together regardless of the individuals involved. Such a procedure has some obvious scheduling advantages for the airline and it tends to enforce standardization in the execution of the individual crew tasks. At the same time, however, it tends to reduce the capabilities of the crew to meet novel situations as a team.* That is perhaps one of the reasons why contests between all-star teams

---

*The example is taken from a talk by Richard Hackman.

in games such as American football often place limits on the variety of offensive and defensive maneuvers allowed.

Socialization. Partners socialize each other. Studies of the relation between jobs and workers, between bridge-playing partners, and between spouses indicate that partners coevolve skills and procedures so that each becomes well adapted to a familiar partner and (comparatively) poorly adapted to others. Each partner develops identities and rules that mesh with those of the other. The resulting bilateral interdependence simultaneously makes the partnership relatively stable in the face of alternative possible partners and relatively contentious about internal divisions of effort and gains.

The convergence produced by mutual learning shapes decision making. For example, as is well known in the negotiation literature, the outcomes of mutual learning are affected by the relative rate of learning of the two partners. Fast learners move more. Partnerships end up at solutions close to the initial positions of the slower learner. Fast-learning wives make slow-moving husbands. Fast-learning parents make children who do not change. Fast-learning manufacturers make rigid customers.

On the other hand, mutual socialization provides considerable stability to a system of partnerships. Studies of the stability of matches between women and men, workers and jobs, and products and customers all indicate that the durability of a match tends to increase with its duration. Part of that result can be attributed to heterogeneity in some fixed properties of matches that lead poorly matched pairs to break earlier, but part of it is attributable to mutual adaptation. Women and men, workers and jobs, and products and customers all adapt to each other over time. As they do so, they reduce the likelihood of ending the partnership.

Attention and Interpretation. Any individual is a collection of identities. Research on role conflict has long considered the effects of attention and interpretation when individuals associate themselves with multiple identities. When do biologists reared in a fundamentalist Christian religion interpret those identities as being in conflict? When do they attend to the identity demands of their training as biologists, and when to those of their religious training? When do police officers, facing a cataclysm that threatens the well-being of their communities as well as their families, interpret the demands of their police officer identities as being in conflict with the identities associated with being spouses and parents? What do they do?

In any particular situation, identities have to be evoked. They also have to be interpreted. Situations and behaviors appropriate to them are ambiguous. As a result, the art of partnership often involves managing the evocation and interpretation of the identities of the partners to reduce attention to inconsistent identities. Standard folkloric recommendations to avoid topics of politics and religion in casual conversations are rules that reduce the amount of attention given to inconsistent identities. In a similar spirit, organizations characteristically buffer task-related identities from potentially inconsistent family identities.

CHAPTER FOUR

Multiple Actors: Conflict and Politics

C hapter 3 looked at decision making when partners do not have consistent preferences or identities. As was suggested there, inconsistencies lead to complications, and one common instinct of theorists of multiple actor decision making is to see the decision making problem as that of converting inconsistent partnerships into teams by aligning preferences and identities. That leads to concerns with contracts, incentives, selection, socialization, and attention that seek to remove or reduce inconsistencies. Studies of collaboration between two uneasy partners form the background for examining broader social systems and enduring social institutions involving mutually inconsistent decision makers.

This chapter shifts attention to those larger systems and considers a set of ideas about decision making involving multiple inconsistent actors that are less inclined to emphasize eliminating conflict in preferences or identities. It examines two classic metaphors of decision making in the face of inconsistent preferences and identities. The first metaphor pictures decision making as based on a power struggle. It asks: Who gets what, when, and how? The second metaphor pictures decision making as coalition formation. It asks: How are partners found, how are agreements negotiated and enforced? Finally, the chapter considers some effects of attention and other factors on decision instability.

When multiple actor decisions are considered in this way, they are often called "political" or "conflictual," not because the process necessarily involves the institutions or practices of government, nor because it is necessarily characterized by violence or outbursts of emotionality, but because decision makers sustain inconsistent preferences or identities. Many familiar systems for collective decision making, including free markets and systems of governance, are political in the sense that they create mechanisms for decisions without agreement on either preferences or identities. Market mechanisms use prices and coercively enforced contracts. Systems of democratic governance use voting, constitutions, political parties, and coercively enforced legislation.

The resulting decisions are sometimes confusing if considered from the perspective of a single, coherent decision maker or a team. They sometimes seem to bring together people who share nothing beyond indifference toward each other's wishes. They sometimes seem to reflect everyone's second choice and no one's first choice. They sometimes seem not to be implemented, or to be implemented in ways that change the original decision. They involve complicated combinations of trust and distrust and substantial uncertainties that are only partially resolved by the process of decision.

4.1 Decisions and Power

One of the ideas most commonly invoked to talk about decision making when interests and identities are inconsistent is the idea of power. The concept of power reflects the intuitive notion of struggle, with outcomes determined by the relative strengths of contending forces. Some people seem to get more of what they want than do others. Individuals and groups consciously pursue power and knowledge about power. Hierarchy, one of the most pervasive design features of organizations, presumes and imposes differences in power.

The metaphor of power is a part of ordinary language, easily understood by ordinary actors. It is used in everyday conversations and in storytelling. It fills the professional literature and the self-help books of airport bookstores. The familiarity of power and the ease with which the term is used in daily discourse are great assets. People usually have no difficulty answering questions about who has power, and they often agree with each other. Discussions of power have a ring of reality to them. They sound right. At the same time, the familiarity of the idea also makes it difficult to use in understanding decisions. It needs to be defined carefully and developed precisely. When that is done, power loses some of its charm as a general-purpose explanation of decision making.

4.1.1 Power as Getting What You Want

The basic idea of decision making in the face of inconsistency is that different people want to have different things or to fulfill different identities, and not everyone can have everything desired. As a result, individuals (and groups) struggle, competing and cooperating with each other, trying to satisfy their individual preferences and identities. Power is the capability to get what you want or to fulfill your identity.

Although the assumption can be misleading, most theories of decision making assume that power is desired, that each individual wants to have decisions made that are consistent with his or her preferences and identities. The distribution of power in a society, therefore, is a distribution of advantage in the pursuit of a life consistent with personal values. The standard presumption of democracy is equality of power. The standard presumption of personal ambition is the pursuit of power. The standard presumption of decision making is the struggle for power and, through power, for desired outcomes.

Students of power use two kinds of models in examining decision making. *Force* models of power portray decisions as being weighted combinations of the wishes of participants. *Exchange* models of power see choices as being produced by voluntary exchanges. They use "power" as another word for "trading advantage."

4.1.2 Force Models of Power

In a force vision of power, decisions by a collectivity are portrayed as the result of various kinds of social "averaging" processes. Those processes consolidate conflicting wishes into a compromise decision. The exact compromise that will be realized depends on the relative powers of the parties. There are many variants on the details of such processes, but the central idea is that conflicting desires are pooled to arrive at a joint decision.

THE SIMPLE FORCE MODEL

The simplest force model is one that assumes that decisions are the weighted average of the wishes of individual participants, where the weights are the relative power of the various individuals involved. The vision of the decision process is one in which each individual participant has a wish that can be represented by a number and some amount of power. As the individuals apply their powers in support of their wishes, the system records a decision that reflects the net effects.

This model is a simple and elegant variation on standard notions of force. If a particular decision outcome and the prior wishes of decision makers are known, the power of specific decision makers can be estimated. Alternatively, if the powers and the wishes are known, the decision outcome can be predicted; or if the powers and outcomes are known, the wishes can be estimated.

For the simple force model to be useful as a basis for understanding decision making, the wishes of participants must be observable, and power estimates must be stable over repeated observations of outcomes. The main problem with the model is its clear inability to fit data on multiple person decision making. If power indices are estimated from two different decisions, the indices do not agree.

COMPLICATING THE MODEL

There are numerous reasons why estimates of power are not reliable across decisions, and each of them defines a possible elaboration of the basic model:

1. Power is both *positional* and *behavioral.* Effectiveness due to being in a particular position or having a particular role is confounded with effectiveness that stems from a particular style or cleverness of action. The two aspects are unlikely to be well correlated and will, in any event, have to be estimated separately.

2. Power is *domain specific.* A person powerful in one domain is not necessarily powerful in another. There is not a single index of power for an individual decision maker, but different powers for different decision arenas. The domain specificity of power is observed not only in government but also in business firms, families, and churches. A force model has to have subscripts to reflect the domain involved.

3. Potential actors in a decision process have to be *activated.* Potential power is not always exercised. Attention is uncertain. Energy may be deflected to other concerns. As a result, a force model of power should decompose power into potential power and activation, with realized power being their product. But once this done, the model requires an independent estimate of either power or activation in order to use data on decisions to estimate the other. And since attention is not constant over time, the model requires time subscripts on attention.

4. The use of power affects power. There is evidence for force *depletion*: A frequent observation is that power is "wasted," used up. The usual presumed mechanism is that the exercise of power expends good will or past favors that must be renewed if power is not to decline. Power is a fixed resource, which the exercise of power decreases. There is also evidence for force *conditioning*: Power acts like a skill that increases with exercise. The mechanism may be a gain in competence or it may be a gain in reputation. In particular, the exercise of power leads others to concede power.

All these additions to the basic model are plausible. Each has some basis in observations of real decision processes. Unfortunately, as the model becomes increasingly realistic, it becomes more difficult to use empirically. In particular, using empirical data to estimate the various factors becomes impossible. The amount of data required is several orders of magnitude greater than the amount of data imaginable.

The result is that force models and metaphors are very general, but they do not lend themselves to empirical confirmation or disconfirmation. Power can be conceived as a force that weights wishes to determine an outcome, but such a conception is not particularly useful unless there are independent ways of estimating power.

THE ROLE OF WISHES IN INDIVIDUAL POWER

Despite those empirical difficulties, force models of power are useful in suggesting a source of power that might easily be overlooked. A conspicuous feature of such models is that power comes from the relation between one's own wishes and the wishes of others. There are advantages to having preferences and identities that are consistent with those of powerful people. This advantage is sometimes decried as a complication in measuring power (distinguishing the chameleon from the "genuinely" powerful), but it is a real phenomenon also. If decision makers want what other people want, they are more likely to get what they want.

More generally, considerable advantage comes from having wishes that lie close to the "center of gravity" of the rest of the system. Conversely, individuals who have wishes that lie far from the "center of gravity" will experience persistent powerlessness. Interestingly enough, from the perspective of theories of democracy, such powerlessness will not be particularly reduced by giving citizens who are thus disadvantaged more control over resources or access to decisions.

Consider, for example, how perceptions of power (and thus power) are influenced by the distribution of preferences or identities as translated into wishes. Suppose the power of an individual is the power he or she is perceived by others to have. Suppose further that each actor estimates the power of each other actor by observing individual wishes and resulting outcomes and inferring individual power indices (by assuming that those who get what they want have more power). Although it might be imagined that initial reputations for power would be augmented by the processes of reputation formation, under fairly general conditions a different result is produced. If perceived power determines actual outcomes, a process of updating perceptions by observing outcomes actually converges to a stable distribution of perceived power that depends not at all on the initial distribution of perceived power but only on the distribution of wishes.

These features of force models are of some significance in thinking about ways of equalizing power in a social system. They suggest, for example, that strategies for reducing disparities in power probably should include not only redistribution of resources but also redistribution of personal preferences and identities. That result has implications for democratic governance. It indicates that a theory of democratic governance that emphasizes the role of democratically elected officials in reflecting the wishes of citizens may encounter intractable difficulties in achieving political equality. Political equality may require not only efforts to make government responsive to wishes but also efforts to affect the wishes.

DISAPPOINTMENTS IN FORCE CONCEPTIONS OF POWER

The idea of power as force yields some interesting nonintuitive ideas, particularly those that consider dynamic changes of power over time and the role of wishes in reputations for power. However, it is also an idea that has a history of disappointment as a concept for interpreting decision making.

Power as Tautology. "Power" tends to become a *post hoc* label for the unexplained variance of students of multiple person decision making. *Post hoc* labels for unexplained variances have a long tradition in social and behavioral science. They creep into the economics literature, using words like "utility" or "risk"; into the sociology literature, using words like "norms" or "legitimacy"; into the anthropology literature, using words like "culture" or "tradition"; and into the psychology literature, using words like "personality" or "habit."

In each case, there is nothing intrinsically wrong with the label or the intuitive idea behind it. The labels become problematic, however, when they are used as generic after-the-fact explanations of events. That is the frequent fate of the concept of power. If it is determined that someone has "power" by observing that they get what they want, using power as an "explanation" of why they get what they want is an exercise in tautology.

The Symbolic Significance of Talking about Power. Power is also linked to important personal and social beliefs. It is part of the grammar of modern political and social realism that contrasts itself with grammars of idealism, with its hopes for civic duty and the integrity of office. Power is tied to beliefs in the importance of individuals. Ideologies of individualism are couched in terms of self-esteem and empowerment. Power is tied to concepts about the proper relationships among individuals, for example, democratic beliefs in equality. Many societies seek to reduce disparities in power.

As a result of those connections to beliefs that are deeply held, the term "power" mobilizes considerable emotional force. Its use protects a person from being considered naïve, and shows attention to concerns over disparities in power. Thus, the term is often a signal by which individuals (including students of decision making) proclaim both their sophistication about the world and their concern for the position of the weak.

Images of power are symbolically significant in another sense. They evoke conceptions of life as struggle and conquest, domination and subordination. They link "power" to ideas of forcefulness and traditional conceptions of masculinity, thus tend to define decisions (as well as the study of decision making) as being domains for establishing "manliness." Those associations of the concept of power have consequences both for making decisions and for interpreting decision processes.

Difficulties in Measuring Power. If differences in power are enormous, as they are sometimes when the power of dominant groups is compared with the power of weak groups in large social or political systems, measures of power appear to be fairly useful. The power measures taken from one situation extend to a number of others, and broad predictions can be made. For example, by almost any measure of power, poor people are systematically weaker politically than other citizens in almost all political systems.

On the other hand, when measures of relative power among active participants in a smaller political system, for example in an organization, are used to predict decisions, the results are usually disappointing. It does not appear to be possible to predict future outcomes reliably by estimating power from previous outcomes. Our restricted ability to measure power combines with the complexity of power to lose whatever "signal" there may be in "power" in the "noise" of other factors.

One reason the effort is unrewarding lies in the elusive nature of fundamental ideas about power. Consider, for example, the following three problems:

1. *Interpersonal comparisons of wish fulfillment.* If power is to be measured by the ability of individuals to get what they want, how can comparative statements about relative power be made? Power comparisons require that the extent to which one person's wishes are realized be compared with the extent to which another's are. This presents a number of problems. A measure based on wish fulfillment requires us to determine whether some people came closer to their desired preferences or identities than others. For a variety of reasons, interpersonal comparisons of subjective utilities are viewed with doubt and are usually rejected in theories of choice.

2. *Strategic expression of wishes.* The expression of preferences and the declaration of identities are strategic weapons of negotiation. Those who want to assess them accurately must therefore solve the problem of measuring things that are being consciously and strategically manipulated.

3. *Pliability of wishes.* The usual treatment of power implicitly

considers wishes to be fixed and measures how well the world conforms to them. In reality, preferences and identities adapt at least as much as the world does, and measures of their fulfillment are, at least to some extent, measures of their flexibility.

For these reasons, as well as others, the search for a good empirical measure of power seems to be endless and largely fruitless.

4.1.3 Exchange Models of Power

The crucial difficulty in using force conceptions of power is the fact that power weights cannot be independently observed but must usually be estimated from their consequences. Exchange models of power address that problem by focusing on a small number of factors that provide a trading advantage in a system of voluntary exchange.

THE SIMPLE MODEL OF EXCHANGE

The fundamental idea in an exchange model is that participants (individuals, groups, organizations) enter into voluntary exchange relationships regulated by some system of rules. Each participant brings resources to the arena. Those resources include such things as money, property, knowledge, competence, access to others, rights and authorities, and information. The process of choice is one of arranging mutually acceptable trades within the rules. Each individual seeks to improve his or her own position by trading with other individuals. When the exchanges reach a place where no more legal and mutually acceptable trades are possible, the process stops.

FACTORS IN TRADING ADVANTAGE

In an exchange model, it is imagined that people improve their positions by trading money, status, affection, or any other resource that they control and another wants. The word "power" is superfluous to such theories. The theories could be presented, understood, and used as theories of exchange without recourse to the word. Within an exchange model, the ability to pursue one's preferences or fulfill one's identity (i.e., power) depends on three things: control over the rules, control over resources, and control over preferences and identities. So any exchange theory of power considers the ways in which these three are determined.

Control over Rules. Exchanges, like all social interactions, take place within a social structure of rules. Social rules set the playing field for decisions and constrain them. Social rules specify proper decision procedures and proper justifications for decisions. Some things are taken as given, some questions remain unasked, and some alternatives are unexamined. The ability to affect those constraints is a fundamental source of power.

One of the principal forms of contention in the study of decision making is the claim that theories of choice systematically ignore questions of how the rules of decision making are specified while devoting enormous attention to the ways individuals operate within the rules provided to them. Theories of power that consider only the exercise of power within a taken-for-given set of rules may overlook the effects of these social "constitutions" on decisions. As generations of legislators have discovered, the rules of legislative procedure are not neutral.

Control over Resources. Power in an exchange model comes from control over resources desired by others. Whatever is required to satisfy one's own preferences or to fulfill one's own identity is obtained by exchanging resources. When decision makers have something others want, they can exchange it for something that they want. Most studies of power in the exchange tradition emphasize the simple point that possession of desired resources gives power. In order to be powerful, decision makers seek control over resources.

Such ideas have been used in studies of decision making to yield predictions associated with resource dependency theories: that individuals and organizations will respond to internal and external forces that control vital resources, and that individuals and organizations will seek to limit their dependence on such resources. Control over resources empowers individuals and groups. Thus, the standard advice for becoming powerful: Become rich; seize a hostage; build a better mousetrap.

Control over Preferences and Identities. As parents and advertising agencies have repeatedly demonstrated, a possible way of gaining power within an exchange model is to transform the wants of others so that they demand goods you can provide. Instead of seeking to provide the things that others want, a power-seeker tries to induce others to want the things he or she can provide. In the literature on leadership, this is called transformational leadership. In some other literatures it leads to the "problem of the happy slave," for power comes from making people happy with what is given to them.

Changing others is not the only way to change preferences and identities. It is also possible to imagine changing one's own self. In particular, notice the other side of the proposition that trading advantage is well served by having things that others want. Trading advantage is also well served by wanting things that others do not. With some exceptions, it is deviant tastes and identities that are more easily satisfied through voluntary exchange. A person who craves Swedish licorice will generally do well in a world of chocolate lovers.

This proposition differs substantially from the comparable proposition derived from force models of power. When the decision process produces decisions by "averaging" over participant wishes, participants with deviant wishes will be persistently disadvantaged. When the decision process arranges voluntary trades among participants, participants with deviant preferences will be persistently favored. One relatively pure form of exchange decision making is the "logroll." Logroll processes tend to improve the relative position of deviants (e.g. people with strong values or identities unrelated to the values or identities of others). This is, perhaps, one of the reasons why such a procedure strikes some people as essential and strikes others as perverse.

LIFE AS AN INSURANCE SCHEME

Exchange theories of power suggest that decision making can be seen as a grand insurance scheme in which favors are offered today in return for an option on reciprocal favors in the future. Actions are taken in the expectation of future favors, but the process of exchange is complicated by the uncertainty of the future. Decision makers know that they may need help in the future but rarely know what kind of help, or when, or from whom. Thus, they spread favors broadly, hoping thereby to buy "insurance" against future needs.

Favors are done with some expectation of return, but risk aversion leads most actors in a social system to give much more than they demand in return. This imbalance is accentuated by the tendency of recipients to discount past favors heavily: "What have you done for me lately?" This structure of reciprocal insurance in favors, like rules of politeness in social interaction, strengthens the system and builds a community in which the level of unsolicited favor-giving is quite a bit higher than the demands for reciprocity.

4.2 Decisions and Coalitions

A second political metaphor for decision processes in multiple actor systems is one that highlights bargaining and coalition formation. The distinction between bargaining and coalitions on the one hand and power on the other is somewhat arbitrary. Force models of power, for example, presume some process by which wishes are combined, and coalition formation is a prime candidate for such a process. Exchange models of power presume a process by which exchanges are negotiated, and bargaining is a prime candidate for such a process. Bargaining and coalition formation, however, provide foci that put greater emphasis on the interactive social aspects of exercising control over decision making. Within this view, decision making involves horse-trading and logrolling, associations and alliances.

4.2.1 The Idea of Coalition

Ideas of bargaining and coalition formation, like ideas of power, are organized around an assumption of preference and identity inconsistency. Decisions are made and cooperative programs are pursued within a context of potential conflict. Theories of bargaining and coalition formation emphasize two important aspects of multiple actor decision making:

> First, they emphasize the structure of the formal decision making system, the rules that are (at least implicitly) treated as inviolate by participants. Those constitutive rules define the resources available to persons occupying particular roles (e.g. citizen, legislator, director, executive) and specify the combinations of roles that constitute a winning coalition capable of declaring a legitimate decision. For example, standard legislative rules for voting specify that any coalition containing more than half of the votes can legitimately make decisions for the entire community. Sometimes such rules are themselves imagined to be the result of decisions negotiated within a supergame, but they are considered as given.

> Second, ideas of bargaining and coalition formation emphasize the ways in which individual decision makers pursue their objectives by making deals. The primary objective is to form a coalition capable (within the rules) of making decisions favorable to its members. Coalitions are formed by entering into agreements with others that specify the decisions that will be made by the coalition. Those decisions simultaneously extract resources from the system through coordinated action among coalition members and distribute those resources within the coalition through competition among coalition members.

4.2.2 Building Coalitions

Most theories of coalition building presume that individual actors have well-defined preferences or identities and that they enter into coalitions to satisfy those preferences and fulfill those identities. The actors are assumed to do the best they can, given the rules of the game and the demands of other participants.

OBJECTIVES AND RULES

In the resulting bargaining process, there are two key decisions to be made: Who will be in a coalition, and how will the spoils be divided among coalition members? Actors attempt to affect their personal shares of the spoils, deciding what coalition to join based on an estimation of the way those allocations serve their preferences or help fulfill their identities. Within a particular constitutional order, *rational actors* generally desire to belong to a winning coalition, to which end they seek allies. However, they do not want to have too many allies, for each ally makes a claim on coalition winnings. They like to be members of a coalition that is large enough to gain control of the system, but no larger. The "minimal winning coalition," if it can be identified and achieved, will maximize individual payoffs. In a world of uncertainty, subcoalitions, and maneuver, however, somewhat larger coalitions are likely. *Rule-following actors,* on the other hand, seek coalitions and distributions that will satisfy the norms of proper behavior they accept. They have standards of "fairness" and expectations about legitimate coalitions and legitimate coalition actions.

Conventional theories typically assume the existence of a monetary prize that goes to the winning coalition and is then distributed among the coalition members. In such cases, the distribution of winnings has the rather special limitation that one person's gains are another person's losses. The demands of one coalition member are strictly conflicting with the demands of another.

There are winning coalitions that involve fewer than all participants and winning coalitions have broad rights of decision making. Theories of coalition formation within such rule structures are redistributive in appearance. They allow members of a winning coalition to redistribute the resources of the organization or social system in their own favor. Subject to limitations imposed by the rules, winners can "tax" losers and claim the resulting "revenue." There is ample evidence that the redistributive appearance of "winner-take-all" rule structures is not misleading, since such systems have often produced significant redistributions.

There are, however, some restrictions on redistribution. The most obvious restriction is the ability of the system to ensure that losers will be bound by the decisions of winners. Standard theories of decision making through coalition formation presume a constitutional order that enforces the rules and decisions within the rules. The conditions for sustaining that order among *rational actors* require that participants be able to calculate that, even if those rules currently place them in a disadvantaged position, in the long run their interests will be better served by accepting the rules of the game than by moving to another game. Similarly, *identity-fulfilling actors* must presume that participation in the present decision system will be, in the long run, be more consistent with their unfolding identities than undertaking a different system.

Although it typically pays to join the winning coalition, there are exceptions: The more you demand of the spoils, the less attractive you become as a member; and there is always the possibility that a particular individual may be better off in a "losing" than in a winning coalition. As in the case of simple partnerships, effective strategies depend, among other things, on whether the process occurs only once or many times, and whether everyone can be assumed to be "rational" or whether a small number act irrationally.

LIMITS TO IDEAS ABOUT COALITION FORMATION

The central problem with many ideas about coalition building that are found in the literature is that they adopt relatively pure forms of uncomplicated rationality or rule following. Rational theories of coalition formation tend to make heroic information assumptions, often assuming that all participants have perfect knowledge of all other participants' preferences and information. Simple theories of rule following tend to assume that rules are obvious, shared, and always evoked. These pure forms seem not to capture coalition formation in multi-person, multi-goal, multi-identity, multi-arena situations in conditions of limited rationality, limited attention, and limited consistency.

Behavioral students of coalition formation suggest that there are a large number of difficult assessments that need to be made (at least implicitly) in this kind of process. Which of the impossibly large number of possible coalitions will be considered? What is the nature of coalition contracts? How can partners to a coalition enforce their agreements when they are not effected simultaneously? How do variations in mobilization of participants affect the operation of the formal rules specifying winning coalitions? How are particular identities called to attention or forgotten? How are inconsistent rules applied in forming coalitions?

4.2.3 Complementarity in Demands

The imagery of coalition formation used so far centers on the idea that a winning coalition gains a certain amount of resources which it then can distribute among its members. The idea is borrowed from theories of games in which there is some collective payoff associated with a coalition. It is useful imagery, but it fails to capture an important aspect of coalition formation in decision making: the role of demand complementarity.

CONGRUENCE AND INDIFFERENCE

When a coalition is built in order to secure and distribute monetary winnings, it is usually assumed that the demands of coalition members are strictly opposing. Although different coalitions may receive different payoffs, the share of the payoff given one member of any coalition reduces the share that can be given to other members. It is this feature of the demands that leads to the theorem about the "minimum winning coalition."

Decision making, however, often involves the crafting of a policy decision, such as a decision to purchase an array of equipment, to approve a budget, to pursue a particular set of advertising strategies, or to enact a piece of legislation. In these cases, the demands of potential coalition members are ordinarily not strictly opposing. A demand that an organization purchase a new piece of equipment and a demand that it exhibit "modernity" are complementary. A policy that meets one demand reduces the marginal cost of meeting the other.

Complementarities of demands come in many forms, but two extreme cases illustrate the importance of demand complementarity to policy formation. The first is the case of *congruence*—coalition members who want policies that are mutually supportive. The most natural coalition imaginable in decision making is a coalition of persons all of whom want the same policy. Each additional coalition member adds strength to the coalition without exacting any "cost." Sales agents whose customers all desire precisely the product being sold are involved in such a coalition. Each additional customer requires no change in the design of the product. In a like manner, a coalition of advocates of a particular tax reform can add additional advocates without cost. Similarly, individuals with congruent identities form coalitions more easily than individuals with incongruent identities. Parent/child, boss/subordinate, or buyer/seller pairs are more easily formed than are combinations of roles that do not fit together.

The second extreme case of complementarity in demands is the case of mutual *indifference*. Two individuals who are indifferent to each other's demands can form a policy coalition to satisfy both. In effect, indifference provides another form of congruence. Policies that do not affect one another and identities that do not touch one another are natural allies in situations in which coalition size makes a difference.

In practice, neither complete congruence nor complete indifference is common, but the principle extends to demands that overlap without being identical. Customers who want similar products are more easily accommodated by a single supplier than customers who want radically different ones. Advocates of related tax policies can form a coalition more readily than advocates of conflicting tax policies. Rule followers with consistent rule sets can form coalitions more easily than those with inconsistent sets.

The propositions are intuitively obvious, but they lead to some features of coalition formation that are sometimes overlooked. For example, demand complementarity makes it likely that *winning coalitions will contain more members than the minimum required to win.* The policy cost of additional members is less than the increased security they provide against misestimates of strength or random fluctuations in decision outcomes.

These features of coalition formation also lead to some propositions about bargaining advantage. In particular, the likelihood of any particular individual being on a winning coalition depends on the degree of complementarity between his or her own preferences and identities and those of others. Complementarity may come from either congruence of demands or mutual indifference. Thus, being on a winning coalition is facilitated by having preferences and identities that either mesh completely with the preferences and identities of others or by having preferences and identities that do not connect at all.

The advantage produced by mutual indifference is illustrated by a stylized story of traditional politics involving three contesting groups: capitalists, workers, and farmers. In this stylized portrait, it may be plausible to assume that a winning coalition consists of any two of these groups. From the present point of view, the traditional coalition advantage of farmers has been that their demands were more consistent with the demands of either workers or capitalists than either of the others were with each other. While workers and capitalists often tended to have opposing interests, farmers tended to want things that were relatively unimportant to the other two groups.

Since farmers were able to contribute votes to the coalition of which they were a member and were relatively "low-cost" coalition members, the only two winning coalitions that were likely were between capitalists and farmers and between workers and farmers. Thus, farmers should always be found on the winning side. A casual historical observation is that, for many years, farmers tended to wind up in the winning coalition with one of the other groups (either workers or capitalists). The historical story is excessively simple, but the point is clear: Having demands that are complementary with others makes one a preferred coalition member.

POLICY LOGROLLS AS COALITIONS

Complementarity is a key feature of coalition formation through policy "logrolls." A logroll is a coalition of individuals or groups who are largely indifferent to each other's demands but agree jointly to support each other so that each can have what he or she wants. One decision maker agrees to support the pet project of another (about which the former decision maker is indifferent), receiving in return similarly indifferent support for a favorite project.

The usual example of a preference-based logroll is the annual "Rivers and Harbors Act" of the United States Congress, a collection of local projects that collectively command a majority vote, although any one of them alone would probably not be supported by more than a handful of legislators. The usual example of an identity-based logroll is the mutual tolerance of personal identities traditionally found in liberal democracies.

Logroll coalitions are particularly attractive in a world of single-issue participants, participants who have passionate demands on a few issues and much weaker feelings on most. For example, contemporary democratic political systems seem particularly attracted to logrolls among single-issue participants committed to protecting their claims on public support, and contemporary business decision systems seem particularly attracted to budget logrolls among single-issue participants committed to protecting their claims to budgetary support. A more apocryphal example would be a marriage in which a wife makes the decisions about where to live, what to eat, how to dress, and how to raise the children; while her husband makes decisions about the family's policy toward foreign nations, international trade, and military strategy.

As the example of liberal democracy suggests, there is a sense in which both modern democracy and modern organizations are designed as logrolls. Individual freedom, delegation, and division of labor can all be seen as ways of forming coalitions in order to make decisions. Each of those seems to be adopted more readily and to function more smoothly when there is a substantial area of mutual indifference. Political systems and organizations contribute to mutual indifference by building information barriers that promote mutual ignorance.

Policy logrolls are ways of making decisions that are easily overlooked when decision processes are framed as either problem solving, rule following, or exercises of force. The idea of forming coalitions among mutually indifferent coalition members is an important part both of theories of multi-actor decision making and of observed decision making. Logrolls are found not only in the United States Congress but also in business firms, military organizations, and universities.

It must be observed, however, that logrolls do not appear to occur as frequently as might be expected from an analysis of the coalition building advantages they offer. One clear reason for the relative infrequency of logrolls is that they require tolerance—even encouragement—of differences. If the first instinct of decision makers is to try to convert others with tastes or conceptions of self different from their own, they are unlikely to form logrolls with them.

There are also practical problems in organizing coalitions based on mutual indifference:

1. *Problems of discovering partners.* Most people find it easier to identify people who agree or disagree with them than people who are indifferent to them. Similar or opposing preferences lead people to attend the same meetings and to be engaged with each other. As a result, it is ordinarily more difficult for decision makers to identify people who are indifferent to the things they value than to identify people with attitudes or identities that do not touch the same dimensions.

2. *Problems of organization.* A coalition of mutually indifferent people is more likely than a coalition of similar thinking people to require conscious planning and strategic action, rather than gradual social commitment. Since participants in such coalitions do not speak the same language or share the same expectations, and are not linked in interconnected identities, coalition formation does not arise naturally from social interaction. In throwing together unfamiliar bedfellows, such coalitions are confusing not only to observers but also to participants.

3. *Problems of trust.* Logrolls are difficult to sustain if their agreements require exchanges over time. Since bargains often

unfold over time, and there are only weak mechanisms for enforcing agreements, logrolls tend to require a certain amount of trust. But trust is hard to maintain among mutually indifferent partners.

4. *Problems of strategic falsification.* The logic of logrolling invites falsification of preferences and identities. A decision maker who agrees with a potential partner on one issue and knows that that individual is indifferent about a second issue may be tempted to act strategically. Instead of revealing the agreement on the first issue, the decision maker claims indifference in order to arrange a logroll on the second issue. Since this strategic opportunity is known to everyone, it undermines the already tenuous basis for negotiation among the mutually indifferent.

These difficulties do not prevent logrolls, in either political or business alliances. They do, however, suggest some reasons why some of the coalitions that offer the highest payoffs are also the hardest to organize and sustain. In a world of exchange, mutual indifference is a source of power and a basis for coalition. In a world of cooperative joint action, mutual indifference is a source of difficulty and lack of solidarity. Since mutual indifference and mutual support are difficult to achieve simultaneously, winning coalitions tend to be internally ineffective, whereas internally effective coalitions tend to be unable to gain support broad enough to win.

4.3 Participation and Decision Instabilities

As was discussed in Chapter 1 and 2, modern theories of limited rationality and of rule following emphasize factors of attention: Which alternatives are considered? Which consequences? Which preferences? Which identities are considered? Which rules? In a similar fashion, multiple actor theories of decision making focus on the question of which potential interpersonal inconsistencies are evoked, thus on who participates, when, and where.

The demands of time and the constraints of rules assure that different combinations of participants will be activated in different places. As a result, not all the potential contradictions in preferences and identities come into play, and there is less immediate conflict. At the same time, outcomes depend on which individuals are activated. Actors move in and out of the arena in response to various claims on their attention. Since demands on attention are constantly shifting, the climate of decision is unstable in many small ways that cumulatively affect the course of events. Decision makers are pressed to meet the inconsistent demands of a changing group of actors. Consequently, decisions are likely to be unstable over time and space. For example, the interests and identities activated during the adoption of a policy will often be different from those activated during its implementation.

The instabilities may conceal regularities that should also be noted. Although any particular decision is subject to idiosyncratic flows of attention from possible participants, the statistical distribution of attention imposes a certain amount of aggregate consistency on the processes. Some people are disadvantaged by the rules of participation, by other claims on their attention, and by inadequate resources to exchange for direct involvement. In any particular situation they may be able to overcome those disadvantages, but not on a regular basis.

4.3.1 Participation in Multiple Actor Decision Making

Participation patterns affect decision efficiency, decision outcomes, and decision acceptance. To interpret the shifting mix of participants in multiperson decisions, consider two aspects of the activation of participants in decision making. First, what are the constraints on participation? What are the rules that regulate the involvement of potential decision makers in decision arenas? Rules specify the rights and responsibilities of actors: Who can participate? Who must participate? Who cannot participate? Second, how do decision makers allocate attention to decisions within the rules? How do the other claims of life impinge on decision participation?

RULES OF PARTICIPATION

Insofar as preferences and identities are shared or consistent, the pattern of participation makes little difference. In ancient

Athens it was possible to imagine choosing leaders by lot, since citizens could be assumed to be essentially equivalent. In an organization with consistent preferences and identities, individuals often enjoy broad authority to act on the behalf of the collective because they are presumed to share common goals and desires.

If preferences and identities are inconsistent, however, the decisions made will depend on who participates. Left to themselves, some individuals would participate too much (from the point of view of the system), and some too little. For example, effective and talented participants may exit from the process, because they bear the costs of participation themselves, while gains from their participation flow primarily to others. This collective flight of the talented leads to decisions unattractive to most. Conversely, some individuals are, for personal reasons, more eager to participate than their contributions justify from the point of view of others. Their disproportionate activation also leads to decisions unattractive to most.

As a result, every social system has rules of participation with respect to every decision, rules that require some people to participate, allow others to participate, and forbid the participation of still others. Justifying such rules is an important part of political and decision philosophy. Who should participate in decisions on the allocation of water rights in a watershed? Who should participate in decisions about the closing of an industrial facility?

Although a detailed discussion of participation rules and their justifications is beyond the scope of this book, it may be helpful to note that participation rules typically reflect three important concerns:

1. *Personal consequences.* Any particular decision has more important consequences for some individuals than for others. Participation rights are often made contingent on the extent to which the individual is personally affected. In democratic theory, it is generally argued that a proper decision system will provide greater access to those who are affected by a decision than to those who are not. Early colonists in America campaigned

for access under the slogan "no taxation without representation." On the other hand, in some theories of judicial and bureaucratic decision making, personal consequences are bases for forbidding participation. Judges are expected to disqualify themselves from participating in decisions that affect their personal interests. In both cases, the magnitude of personal consequences from a decision is a factor affecting the right to participate.

2. *Social benefits.* Some individuals are seen as having made, or as being able to make, greater contributions to a society than other individuals. Those contributions are generally used to justify greater access to decision making. The arguments are of two kinds. First, there is an argument of competence. It seems appropriate to arrange that individuals with greater relevant competence be more active in making a decision than individuals with less competence. Second, there is an argument of compensation. It seems appropriate that individuals who are more valuable to a society—in the sense that they have contributed to the society—should be compensated by being allowed and encouraged to participate more than those individuals who are less valuable.

3. *Creating community.* Participation rules are not just devices for regulating the substantive content of decisions. They are also symbols of and instruments for the creation of a community. Rights and obligations to participate are linked to acceptance as colleagues or members of a community. They symbolize individual significance and the existence of a meaningful collective. Participating, or not participating, in decision making is an important certification of "citizenship," of being a person of importance and recognizing the responsibilities of importance. A personal sense of efficacy (or alternatively a personal sense of alienation) depends on participation in decision making.

Because these considerations are not necessarily clear in their joint implications, and because different people may differ with respect to how they interpret them, the contention over participation rules in decision systems is a critical constitutional struggle. It often leads individuals to fight for participation rights that, once acquired, they will scarcely exercise; it causes frequent inconsistencies between the participation indicated by personal preferences and identities and the participation demanded or permitted by others.

PARTICIPATION PATTERNS WITHIN THE RULES

Much of the structure of participation is found in the rules. Most decisions carry with them rules mandating, allowing, or prohibiting the involvement of particular individuals or roles. Nevertheless, there is room for some behavioral variation within the rules. Some decisions happen because particular individuals who might well have been present actually were not, or because some individuals who might well have been absent actually were present.

Participation decisions can be seen as conscious actions taken by either a rational actor or a rule-following actor. Three relatively conscious factors make participation attractive:

1. *Salience.* Decisions are perceived to be important to preferences or identities.
2. *Efficacy.* Participation is seen to have an effect on the outcomes of decisions.
3. *Efficiency.* There are no better alternatives for achieving preferences or fulfilling identities.

It is not surprising, perhaps, to find that individuals are more likely to participate in decisions when their own interests or identities are affected than when they are not, more likely to participate when they think they can affect decision outcomes than when they think they cannot, and more likely to participate when they think they have no alternative ways of acting appropriately or accomplishing what they want than when they think there are other ways.

The principal issues associated with the allocation of attention have already been considered (subsections 1.3.1 and 2.2.3) and will not be reviewed here. It may be useful, however, to note three special features of participation behavior: the ways in which participation can be indirect as well as direct, the ways in which future participation is affected by past participation, and the ways in which patterns of participation affect the legitimacy of decisions.

Indirect Participation. Theories of limited attention typically assume that a fixed amount of time and energy is allocated among contending claims. Attending to one set of problems, preferences, choice situations, or identities precludes attending to others. Individuals enter a decision arena directly with their voices and physical energies. They complain, protest, organize, and argue. Direct participation in one decision arena makes simultaneous direct participation in another difficult or impossible.

The assumption is useful, but it clearly is not quite correct. In particular, it underestimates the importance of indirect attention, or in this case, indirect participation. People often delegate their concerns to an appropriate agent (a representative, leader, lawyer, or lobbyist). By using representatives, decision participants circumvent the limits on attention. In effect, by substituting monetary resources (in the case of a hired representative), social capital (in the case of a volunteer representative), or threats of future retaliation (in the case of a partner) for time, participants are able to be in several places at the same time. The complication, of course, is that agents are imperfect representatives.

The example of retaliation is a reminder of a second important form of indirect participation. Absent participants are represented by the consciousness of others that if they act sufficiently at variance with the wishes of those who are absent, they will mobilize the absent to be present. Customers are "present" by virtue of their threats to switch their allegiance to other brands. Employees are "present" by virtue of their threats to leave for other employment. Citizens are "present" by virtue of their threats to emigrate to other political parties or other lands.

Threats of participation need not be overt. They are implicit in any social relationship. Decision makers consider the possible effects of their deliberations and their actions on the mobilization of potential participants. As they do so, they make guesses about the wishes of others and about the likelihood that those wishes will lead to a change in participation. Those guesses affect actions, but they are clearly subject to substantial uncertainty. Exactly what the threat is and whether it will, in fact, be executed is likely to be unclear. As a result, the efficiency of threats is balanced by their imprecision. This, in turn, periodically leads threat-givers to execute threats to participate in order to confirm the genuineness of the threats—even though they would otherwise be happy to stay away and allow minor deviations from their most desired courses of action.

That dynamic makes mobilization of the weak a two-edged sword. Because participation makes a difference, mobilizing the weak increases their influence. But if mobilization of the weak stimulates policies that encroach too much on the prerogatives of the absent strong, the strong will be activated and act to restore their position. The difference between the policy point at which they withdraw from direct participation and the policy point at which they reenter defines both the possibilities for strengthening the weak through mobilization and the dangers of doing so.

Effects of Participation on Participation. Participation in decision making has two important effects on subsequent participation. On the one hand, participation is very likely to be frustrating. Although there are some tendencies to develop illusions of decision effectiveness in order to confirm the expectations that originally stimulated participation, the observable consequences of participating in a decision process are likely to be less than anticipated. The social nature of decision making renders personal influence hard to determine, and the complexities of social causation make the ultimate effects of a decision hard to predict. Circulation among decision makers is often driven by outsiders believing they can do better than current decision makers, fighting for the right to participate, becoming disabused of their ambitions as a result of experience at the frustrations of decision making, and abandoning the field to the next wave of crusaders seeking access to the process.

On the other hand, participation has numerous positive side consequences. It provides social certification of position and opportunities for interaction. It sometimes occurs in the stimulating circumstances of time pressure and social excitement. It offers explicit confirmation of human importance in general and of the importance of particular individuals. Decision makers often complain about the pressures of the role, the unreasonable demands made of them, and the stresses of being responsible; but those pressures lend an excitement to decision making that enhances its attractiveness.

The net effect of these countervailing effects is not easy to predict in every case, but it seems likely that in most cases frustration is slow in onset but increases with time, while excitement is immediate but wanes with time. As a result, a natural sequence to be expected is one in which participation first increases the attraction to decision making and then gradually decreases it.

Effects of Participation on Decision Legitimacy. Participation also affects satisfaction with the process and outcome. The most common assumption in discussions of participation in decision making is that acceptance of a decision depends on the pattern of participation in a decision process. In introducing a new technology or changing a standard operating procedure, those who participated in the decision are more likely than nonparticipants to believe in the correctness and efficacy of the new technology or procedure.

The argument extends to the more general legitimacy of decision processes. At least within the ethos of Western democracy, decision processes gain legitimacy through a sense of involvement in them. The involvement need not be formally democratic, indeed it normally is not, but it includes a sense of being consulted, of having one's opinion's heard, and of confidence that the decisions, in some sense, "represent" attention to one's concerns.

The link between participation and decision legitimacy has led to a host of managerial tactics for providing the illusion of involvement in decision making without genuine influence. Meetings are held to "solicit input" on decisions already made, or long before any issues are clear enough to frame meaningful alternatives. Personal interactions are laced with comments confirming the importance of suggestions made. This tactical corruption of participation has, in turn, led to considerable suspicion of participation initiatives. Whatever attraction there might be in involvement is compromised by doubt that the involvement is genuine.

The general consequence is likely to be a considerable devaluation of participation. For the reasons outlined above, decision impact is difficult to establish in the best of circumstances. One person's effects on a decision are lost in the effects of others, and one decision's effects are lost in the general confusions of history. When those ambiguities are increased by suspicions of the process, experience is likely to teach that participation is a fraud and a waste.

4.3.2 The Implementation of Decisions

One of the more persistent problems in multiple-actor decision making is the problem of implementation. For decisions to have effects, they must be implemented. The study of organizations has repeatedly examined the way policies and programs adopted by boards of directors, legislatures, or top managements are subsequently executed, modified, and elaborated by those who implement them. Decision histories abound with cases of unimplemented, partially implemented, or exotically implemented actions.

INCONSISTENCIES, MULTIPLE ACTORS, AND IMPLEMENTATION

Constructing appropriate mechanisms to induce administrators to execute policy decisions is one of the central concerns of organization theory. How can administrative identities be constructed so that the personal preferences of an administrator do not twist a policy decision? How can a decision process first stimulate disagreement and factionalism through open debate over policies and then, using the same personnel, achieve an effective implementation of a policy that earlier was vigorously opposed by a substantial minority?

Implementation difficulties can be explained partly by problems of incomplete and unshared information. Most decision makers are neither omnipresent nor omniscient; they have limited abilities to attend to all events and limited knowledge by which to interpret observable actions. Because of these limitations, differences might be expected between the decisions of policy makers and the decisions taken by those responsible for implementing the policy, even in the absence of inconsistencies in preferences and identities.

Inconsistencies complicate the story by introducing conflict. Decision makers, their allies, and their opponents seek to renegotiate policies and practices after they are "decided." Policies announced by policy makers are opportunities for others to pursue their own visions, and those responsible for implementing policy will usually have reasons for pursuing preferences or identities that are different from those pursued by policy makers.

The problems are endemic and have been extensively discussed in the literature on organizations, as well as in treatises on optimal contracts, incentive schemes, and theories of agency. Decision processes are particularly vulnerable to implementation problems when it is not possible to specify complete coalition agreements at the time of making a decision. Policy makers cannot anticipate all of the contingencies that will occur in the course of implementation. Without discretion on the part of administrators, implementation is likely to sacrifice intelligence to standardization. Decision makers know this and accept that implementation of decisions calls for local information and local expertise. However, most of the procedures that facilitate intelligent administrative elaboration of policy also invite creative administrative deviations.

INSTABILITIES OF COALITIONS

In order to implement policies, coalitions require stability across time. Temporal stability is continually undermined by problems of attention—it is not easy to sustain the attention of all coalition members against alternative claims on their time and energy. Decision making often elicits attention that is not sustained once a choice is made. Implementation also requires stability across institutions. Since the political forces active in decision making are not always the same as the political forces active in implementation, institutional stability is problematic. The political forces active in one part of an organization are different from the political forces active in another part. The political reality facing a police officer on the street during a riot is different from the political reality facing a city council debating police policy. These complications of coalitions across time and space are not simply pathologies of social systems. They reflect some important aspects of how those systems manage to survive and thrive.

Forming a coalition in order to support a policy, whether in a legislature or in a board room, involves standard techniques of horsetrading, persuasion, bribes, threats, and management of information. Those are the conventional procedures of discussion, politics, and policy formation. They are well conceived to help participants form coalitions, explore support for alternative policies, and develop a viable policy. Much of the genius of modern organizational leadership lies in skills at producing policy from the conflicting and inchoate ideas, demands, preconceptions, and prejudices of the groups to which organizational leadership must attend.

At the heart of several of these techniques for achieving policies, however, are three features of decision making that make coalitions unstable and thereby make implementation particularly problematic:

1. *Decision ambiguity.* Ambiguity is frequently an advantage in the development of a coalition to support a decision. It is easier to conceal or ignore disagreements if policies are written with provisions or terminology that can be interpreted differently by different people. In assembling a coalition to support a policy, it is often necessary to make the terms of the agreement unclear in order to hide or suppress conflicts. The effort to

achieve consensus or mutual indifference leads to ambiguous policies (e.g. party platforms in national elections). Ambiguous policies allow for a healthy level of selective interpretation on the part of not-quite-natural allies. When ambiguities are clarified in the course of implementation, the coalition tends to fall apart.

2. *Outcome optimism.* Forming a winning coalition almost always leads coalition members to overestimate the positive consequences to be expected. There are both motivational and structural reasons for this. Structurally, since programs are rarely adopted when expectations are erroneously pessimistic, the sample of programs actually adopted is more likely to exhibit errors of overoptimism than of overpessimism. Winning coalitions will suffer from the winner's curse. Policies are adopted because their probable return has been exaggerated. This is not because decisions are made foolishly, but precisely because decision makers estimate expected return under conditions of uncertainty, and expectations for the alternative with the highest expected return will (on average) be unduly optimistic.

The structural exaggeration of expectations is exacerbated by the social dynamics of coalition formation. In order to build a coalition, coalition members will systematically exaggerate the probable good effects of the policy and will systematically underestimate the probable negative effects. Policies will, on average, be oversold.

Both structural and social sources of overestimation lead, on average, to post decision disappointment on the part of at least some coalition members. Thus, great hopes lead to action, but great hopes are invitations to disappointment. This in turn leads both to an erosion of support and to an awareness of "failures of implementation." As the policy is revealed to provide fewer payoffs to coalition members than they anticipated, the coalition tends to fall apart.

3. *Support exaggeration.* Few major policies could be adopted without some supporters for whom the policy is relatively unimportant except as a political bargain. They may be persuaded to join a coalition by claims of loyalty or friendship, or by a logroll

in which their support is traded for support on other issues. In addition, a prominent feature of decision making is that individuals and groups enter a decision arena for a variety of reasons, only some of which are concerned with the content of the decision. A typical coalition includes members who support the decision primarily so that they will be recorded as a supporter. For them, the decision has symbolic significance, but its implementation does not. As history moves from the adoption of a decision to its implementation, the coalition tends to fall apart.

4.4 Single Actors and Multiple Actors

Students of decision making usually insist on a distinction between single-actor, or individual, decision making, on the one hand, and multiple-actor, or organizational, decision making, on the other. The distinctions are reflected in the differences between Chapters 3 and 4, on the one hand, and the two chapters preceding them, on the other. They stem from some understandable resistance on the part of students of organizations to characterizing organizations as having the kinds of preference and identity consistency assumed in most theories of individual decision making.

There is a history. Economic theories of markets and political theories of international relations, for example, were originally theories of individuals. Individual entrepreneurs met individual workers and customers in markets. Individual sovereigns, or their agents, met other sovereigns in international interactions. It seemed natural to treat such decision makers as individuals. As those decision makers grew into large, complicated corporations, in one case, and large, complicated political institutions, in the other, that framework was retained, a fiction reinforced by a parallel legal fiction transforming such corporate bodies into imaginary beings with many of the legal rights and properties of individuals.

Ultimately, it was inevitable that the internal coherence of corporate actors would be challenged, as it has been in several domains of thought, including theories of decision making. Although popular journalism sometimes presents a more consistent portrait, most students of decision making in economic, political, military, educational, religious, and other social institutions see them as involving multiple actors with inconsistent preferences and identities. A theory designed for situations involving consistent individual preferences and identities has seemed less than adequate for dealing with such situations.

Students of decision making have recognized the difficulties, though many of them have preferred to maintain a theory of multiple actors that consists largely of ideas about how multiple actors could be induced to form consistent preferences and identities, to be a "team." With increasing awareness of the extent to which multiple-actor decision making proceeds without consistency—through more "political" processes for making decisions without achieving agreement on preferences or consistency in identities—has come increased reluctance to use single-actor theories to comprehend multiple-actor situations.

What has become somewhat less clear is whether a theory designed for multiple actors might, in fact, come to comprehend individual decision making better than theories based on individual consistency. It is a sometimes convenient to portray individuals as having consistent preferences and identities, but clearly such a portrayal is often a substantial fiction. The processes of individual choice often seem to be as filled with incoherence as the processes of collective choice. Insofar as that is true, it is possible (though by no means assured) that individual processes of choice can be understood in organizational terms better than they can be understood in the classic individualistic terms.

Such an argument, however, is somewhat beyond predominant current thinking. It is clear that many ideas that have come from observations of organizational decision making have become standard in treatments of individual decision making, but the converse is also clear. As this book perhaps serves to confirm, many of the ideas about decision making found in discussions of individual choice are also found in discussions of organizational choice. Ideas are borrowed back and forth with considerable ease and, on the whole, effectiveness. Many of the concepts and processes discussed in Chapters 1 and 2 of this book can be slid into Chapters 3 and 4, and vice versa. Inconsistency of preferences and identities has turned out to be an important factor in decision making, but it appears not to be reliably connected to the distinction between single actors and multiple actors.

CHAPTER FIVE

Ambiguity
and Interpretation

Chapters 1 and 2 developed two basic conceptions of how decisions happen, one based on a logic of consequence, the other based on a logic of appropriateness. Chapters 3 and 4 complicated those conceptions by imagining that decisions involve multiple actors with inconsistent preferences or inconsistent identities and considered some ways in which collections of individuals make decisions in the face of those inconsistencies. This chapter complicates things further by examining the effects of ambiguity in the decision calculus—the many ways in which there is both interpersonal and intrapersonal ambiguity about preferences, identities, experience, and meaning. The worlds that confront decision makers appear to be systematically less orderly, more ambiguous, and more symbolic than the worlds that are portrayed in most of the theories considered up to now.

5.1 Order and Ambiguity in Decision Making

The ideas discussed in the earlier chapters see decision making processes as orderly exercises of human coherence. Those chapters differ in how they imagine that order to be created and maintained, but not in a conception of decision making as discerning, exploiting, and affecting a coherent world. The present chapter considers a set of ideas that locate decision making in a confusing world, ideas in which the standard emphasis on coherence is questioned.

5.1.1 Conceptions of Order

Classic conceptions of order in decision making involve three closely related ideas. The first is *reality*, the idea that there exists an objective world that can be perceived, and that only one such world exists. An object either exists or does not. An event either has happened or has not. Actions that are taken and outcomes that follow can be related to each other in a unified, consistent way. History is real.

The second idea is *causality*, the idea that reality and history are structured by chains of causes and effects. Within such a conception, choices affect consequences, and decisions are means to desired ends. Causal relevance links solutions to problems. Learning stems from comprehensible experience and causal inferences about that experience. Conflict is joined and resolved by making a causal connection between negotiation, bargaining, or exchange and their consequences.

The third idea is *intentionality*, the idea that decisions are instruments of purpose and self. Rational choice, learning, rule following, bargaining, and exchange all serve preferences and identities. Preferences and identities are imposed on actions through the evaluation of anticipated consequences (as in rational choice), through the evaluation of experience (as in learning), or through the matching of identities to situations (as in rule following). History is interpreted in terms of prior intentions and identities, each stemming from a conception of self.

Variations on those three ideas permeate thinking about decision making. They permeate this book. Conceptions of rational, consequential action depend on commitments to reality, causality, and intentionality as central organizing ideas. Conceptions of appropriateness and rule following depend on the notion that there is an orderly link between history and the evolution of rules. Students of decision making harbor an affection for order in general, and a particular affection for order based on those three ideas.

5.1.2 Confusions and Complexities

Such conceptions of order seem, however, to underestimate the confusion and complexity surrounding actual decision making. The observations are familiar. Many things are happening at once; practices, forms, and technologies are changing and poorly understood; preferences, identities, rules, and perceptions are indeterminate and changing; problems, solutions, opportunities, ideas, situations, people, and outcomes are mixed together in ways that make their interpretation uncertain and their connections unclear; decisions at one time and place appear to have only a loose tie to decisions at others; solutions seem to have only modest connection to problems; policies are not implemented; decision makers seem to wander in and out of decision arenas and seem to say one thing while doing another.

Decision histories are often difficult to describe. When (and even whether) a decision was made, who made it, with what intentions, and with what consequences are all often obscure. Many decisions are made by default, and decision processes often exercise problems without solving them. Decisions are made outside of an explicit decision process, and decision processes often fail to make decisions. The attention of participants is difficult to predict simply from the properties of the choice being considered. Participants fight for the right to participate, then don't exercise it. Decision makers ignore information they have, ask for more, then ignore the new information. Organizations buffer the process of decision making from the processes of implementation. Participants argue acrimoniously over policy, but once policy is implemented the same participants seem indifferent to its implementation.

On the basis of such observations, organizational decision processes have been described as funny soccer games: "Consider a round, sloped, multi-goal field on which individuals play soccer. Many different people (but not everyone) can join the game (or leave it) at different times. Some people can throw balls into the game or remove them. While they are in the game, individuals try to kick whatever ball comes near them in the direction of goals they like and away from goals they wish to avoid."[1]

5.1.3 Ambiguity

These confusions and complexities have led to an interest in "ambiguity." Ambiguity refers to a lack of clarity or consistency in reality, causality, or intentionality. Ambiguous situations are situations that cannot be coded precisely into mutually exhaustive and exclusive categories. Ambiguous purposes are intentions that cannot be specified clearly. Ambiguous identities are identities whose rules or occasions for application are imprecise or contradictory. Ambiguous outcomes are outcomes whose characters or implications are fuzzy. Ambiguous histories are histories that do not provide unique, comprehensible interpretations.

AMBIGUITY AND UNCERTAINTY

Ambiguity is related to, but distinguishable from, uncertainty. In most theories of decision making, *uncertainty* refers to imprecision in estimates of future consequences conditional on present actions. Such theories assume (1) that it is possible to specify all the mutually exhaustive and exclusive states of the world that might exist; (2) that although it is not possible to specify precisely which state exists, some state does, in fact, exist; and (3) that the uncertainty about which state exists will be reduced by the unfolding of information over time. The idea is that there is a real world that is imperfectly understood. It can, in principle, be understood—at least up to some irreducible noise. Uncertainty is a limitation on understanding and intelligence. It is reduced through the realizations of history, search, and negotiation.

When a situation is described as *ambiguous,* on the other hand, what is meant is that a decision maker is less confident that any one thing is true, or that the world can be partitioned into mutually exhaustive and exclusive states, or that information will resolve the lack of clarity. Ambiguity refers to features of decision making in which alternative states are hazily defined or in which they have multiple meanings, simultaneously opposing interpretations. Students of ambiguity argue that information may not resolve misunderstandings of the world; that the "real" world may itself be a product of social construction, thus not so much discovered as invented; that interpretations of experience and desires may be fundamentally ambivalent rather than simply uncertain; and that ambiguity may be used to augment understanding through imagination.

AMBIGUITY AND DECISION MAKING

Ambiguities of experience and desire are challenges to standard notions of decision making order. From a calculus that sees alternative states of the world as mutually exclusive and exhaustive and causality as orderly, we are led to a calculus that allows the simultaneous existence of opposites and causal inconsistencies. From a conception of wants as consistent and clear, we are led to a conception of wants as contradictory and fuzzy.

Worlds in which interpretation and desires are contradictory and causality is unfathomable can be disturbing. They are represented in fairy tales by the forest (dark, forbidding, and dangerous) and in stories of adventure by the sea (dark, powerful, and uncontrollable). Ambiguous worlds are disturbing, but they are also magical. Beauty and ugliness are compounded; reality and fantasy are intertwined; history is created; intelligence is expanded.

In this chapter the story of decision making moves away from concepts tied tightly to ideas of reality, causality, and intentionality in order to explore decision arenas within which meaning is obscure. We leave a decision world with coherent intentions, expectations, identities, and rules. Decisions are seen as vehicles for constructing meaningful interpretations of fundamentally confusing worlds, not as outcomes produced by a comprehensible environment. Decision processes sometimes become means for evading or alleviating ambiguity, sometimes means for embracing and enhancing it.

As in the previous chapters, the discussion here is limited to a sampler of possible ideas. It considers research on organizations that has emphasized loose coupling rather than tight coupling within decision processes, the orchestration of decisions through temporal orders rather than causal orders, and the role of decisions and decision making in the development of meaning and interpretations. The ideas reflect two quite different perspectives on decision order. One emphasizes the ways in which conceptions of disorder in decision making are a product of inadequacies in theories about the world. These ideas assert that an order exists, but it is an order different from the order anticipated by conventional theories of decision making. The second perspective emphasizes the reality of chaos and embraces its meaningfulness.

5.2 Ambiguous Bases of Decision Making

Rational action stems from two guesses about the world. One is a guess about the uncertain future consequences of possible current action. The other is a guess about the uncertain future preferences by which the outcomes of current action will be evaluated in the future. Rule following stems from two other guesses about the world: One is a guess about how to classify the current situation. The other is a guess about what identity is relevant in such a situation and what it requires. In each case, one guess is about a reality external to the self and one is a guess about the self.

Those guesses are sometimes given other names. They are called things like estimations, specifications, or determinations. Such terms are quite reasonable and will sometimes be used here, but they have a deceptive aura of concreteness and precision. Even the more elegant procedures for estimating future consequences, defining current situations, specifying objectives, or determining identities are filled with assumptions and approximations that make them better described as "guesses" than as "best estimates."

5.2.1 Ambiguities of External Reality

Rational action presumes beliefs about the world summarized in such statements as: "If I make this choice, then the following consequences are likely to follow." Such conditional statements are interpretations of the causal order of the world. Rule following also uses interpretations of the causal order of the real world to encode the meaning of experience into enduring rules. History teaches by developing theories of experience. Sometimes the understandings of reality are self-evident, but often they are not.

INTERPRETING REALITY

History and science are formal attempts to provide causal stories about ambiguous events: "How did democracy develop?" "Why are some people rich and other people poor?" "How was the universe formed?" "Why did Xerox fail to develop the personal computer?" On a less formal basis, this process of sense making and storytelling is an essential part of individual and organizational life. It is so common that its familiarity obscures some of the ambiguities associated with comprehending our world. Decision makers routinely make inferences about their worlds and their histories. What are the inferences they make, and how do they make them? Decision makers come to have strong beliefs about their inferences, accepting them as verified by their experience. How is it possible that they might make inferences incorrectly, yet believe in them firmly? Decision makers often believe things that outside observers consider to be contradictory. How do they develop and believe simultaneously opposing interpretations?

In an old fairy tale about beliefs, a sly tailor persuades an emperor (and most of his subjects) that a naked monarch is actually wearing a robe made from a fabric so exquisite (and expensive) that only people of great virtue and sophistication can see it. The story invites discussion of some subtle questions about social beliefs and their connection to reality: If the emperor's clothes did not exist, is it possible that a belief in them might be sustained? Is it possible that such a belief might be desirable? Is it possible to sustain meaningful simultaneous beliefs both in the existence of the clothes and in the true reality of the emperor's nakedness?

The story about the emperor's new clothes is actually less complicated than real life, because the storyteller tells the reader that the fabric is really a fraud perpetrated by the tailor. Thus, the story emphasizes the ways in which social processes of sharing belief can lead to ridiculous beliefs. In ordinary experience, the problems are greater. Instead of knowing the truth and inquiring whether social beliefs are consistent with it, individuals observe social beliefs and ask whether they might be false, despite being widely believed.

Since the processes by which false beliefs are formed, transmitted, and reinforced are indistinguishable from the processes by which true beliefs are, individuals cannot infer much about the validity of beliefs from their universality. As a result, when they confront widely held (or reported) beliefs, for example about the efficacy of medical treatment, the value of education, or the distinctiveness of good wines, they cannot be sure that the beliefs reflect the truth. Indeed, they know that many of the beliefs that historically have been held to be incontrovertible are now believed to be false.

A thoughtful (and somewhat pedantic) reader of fairy tales might well ask: Are there psychological and sociological processes by which an unwarranted belief in the existence of the emperor's clothes can be sustained? If the emperor's clothes did not exist, might intelligent people come to believe in their existence? If variation in the quality of wines is not reliably detected by most human taste buds, might intelligent people come to believe in good wines? Are there features of human inference which, in combination with plausible features of historical processes, are likely to lead human beings to misinterpret their experience and their perceptions? Are there systematic consequences of such potential misinterpretations?

As has been seen earlier in the discussions of human inference, the answer to each of those questions is an unconditional "yes." Ambiguous histories are experienced in a personal and social context that largely accepts the ideas of reality, causality, and intentionality. As a result, human interpretations of history consistently exaggerate the coherence and necessity of realized history, the role of human intention and action in history, and the comprehensibility of historical forces. Historical accounts define historical events and establish causal and personal accountability for the events they define. They fit the world into an interpretive frame that is comfortable and familiar.

Human decision makers exhibit regularities in their interpretations of history. In particular, studies of interpretations indicate three distinct biases:

1. *Belief conservation.* Decision makers conserve belief. That is, they tend to interpret new experiences and information in ways that make them consistent with prior beliefs. Since experience tends to be ambiguous and beliefs tend to be strong, this effect is substantial.

2. *Event certainty.* Decision makers overestimate the probability of events they have actually experienced and underestimate the probability of events that might have occurred but did not. Thus, they tend to learn too much from the precise event that happened and learn too little from the many things that almost happened. They construct theories of history that make observed historical outcomes necessary, certain, and obvious, rather than a draw from a large pool of possible outcomes.

3. *Anthropocentric focus.* Decision makers construct anthropocentric theories of history. That is, they attribute events to the actions and wills of human beings. They attribute history to factors of intention and competence, rather than chance or happenstance. If something happens, they imagine that it happened because someone wanted it to happen or someone made a mistake.

Those three features of interpretation are accentuated by the fact that most decision makers rise to positions of authority by virtue of past successes. Success tends to confirm beliefs and make them less vulnerable to contradictory evidence. Success tends to make it easier to see history as lawful and determinate rather than chancelike. And success tends to reinforce the notion that history is due to human agency. Thus, top-level decision makers are particularly likely to exhibit these interpretive biases.

INCONSISTENT INTERPRETATIONS

A more subtle feature of historical interpretation is the development of simultaneous, inconsistent interpretations. If everything must be interpreted but the evidential basis for interpretation is modest, human actors and institutions will develop repertoires of different interpretations. These interpretations may be quite inconsistent with each other, yet they are sustained through experience with the requirements of ordinary interpretive life. In many ways, human stories about the world can be characterized as strong beliefs in contradictory things. The story that is currently told is told fervently, but it conceals another, quite different story that is also believed.

In organizations, the repertoires of interpretation are often organized around conflicts among subcultures. Subcultures sustain their differences by sustaining conflicting interpretations of the world. The dynamics of their competition with each other encourage them to elaborate distinct beliefs, each subculture developing in contradiction to the others. As a result, decision making organizations are characterized by simultaneous subcultural or subunit commitments to quite different interpretations.

The phenomenon is not limited to differentiation within an organization. One study of administrative reorganization in the United States national government showed, for example, that individuals made two very standard interpretations of administrative change. One pictured change as a rational solution to administrative problems. The other pictured change as a result of self-interested political maneuver *(realpolitik)*. At some points in some arenas, one interpretation was dominant. At other points in other arenas, the other was. However, the two interpretations did not divide participants into two distinct groups. Rather, both interpretations were known to and accepted by many people. Individuals seemed to switch easily from one interpretation to the other.

The switch from one interpretation to another is partly a function of situation. Children present an interpretation of the world to their parents that is different from the interpretation they present to peers. Students readily shift interpretations to reflect the expectations of instructors. Consultants interpret things differently as they move from one world to another. The shifts may be consciously manipulative, but they often are not. Students are often unconscious of the inconsistencies shown in their collection of examination papers if considered as a whole.

THE CONSTRUCTION OF CONTRADICTORY BELIEFS

Contradictory beliefs are a standard feature of life. As individuals develop beliefs in the efficacy of action, they simultaneously lay a basis for a belief in its futility. The description and justification of the former belief contains much of the content of the latter belief. It does not require an enormous wrench of interpretation to transform a wise adviser into a fool, because the basis for the latter interpretation is already present in the former.

This feature of interpretation underlies the emphasis on the simultaneity of opposites in much of literature. Love and hate are not so much opposites as they are a closely linked pair of interpretations. Such ambiguity in the interpretation of human experience compromises any conception of order that presumes the mutual exclusion of opposites. Conceptions of sin and virtue, good and bad, truth and falsity, reality and fantasy are developed jointly rather than separately.

The elaboration of contradictory beliefs can be illustrated by considering the construction of beliefs about leaders. Carlyle said that leaders determined the course of history,[2] and hundreds of books have echoed him. Tolstoy said that leaders had nothing to do with the course of history[3] and hundreds of books have echoed him. As innumerable observers have noted, leaders are more inclined to believe Carlyle in good times and Tolstoy in bad times. They tend to take credit for their successes and attribute their failures to bad luck. Their critics, on the other hand, are inclined to reverse the attributions. It is obvious that the argument between Carlyle and Tolstoy cannot be settled by recourse to the data of history. Each side can cite "evidence" that can be interpreted to justify its beliefs.

Stories told of leaders, like stories of other things, are constructed in a language that encourages simultaneous contradictory beliefs. Consider, for example, the ways in which individual decision makers are characterized. Descriptions of decision makers and their decisions are typically organized around a series of behavioral dimensions. Characteristically, however, those descriptions are couched less in terms of observable behavior than in terms of evaluative labels attached to the behavior. Moreover, each observable behavior has both a positive and a negative label:

Dimension 1   bold *(foolish)*   careful *(timid)*
Dimension 2   independent *(arrogant)* consultative *(indecisive)*
Dimension 3   fresh *(naïve)*   sophisticated *(cynical)*
Dimension 4   honest *(rude)*   sympathetic *(soft)*

Each kind of behavior has simultaneous opposite labels or evaluations. As a result, interpretations can be changed almost instantly. When a decision or a decision maker is successful, one set of labels is likely to be highlighted. When a decision or a decision maker is unsuccessful, another set of labels is highlighted. Boldness becomes foolishness. Honesty becomes rudeness. These radically different labels develop together, each contributing to its contrast and to sustaining contradictory beliefs.

TAUTOLOGY AND BELIEF

Decision makers, like other humans, tend to develop general-purpose weak theories (e.g. "human beings are inherently good") to account for history. The theories are general-purpose in the sense that they can be applied to many situations. They are weak in the sense that they are not easily susceptible to disconfirmation. Indeed, many of the theories used in discussions of decision making are essentially tautologies. They are true by virtue of a circular definition of their key term or terms.

Tautologies abound in ordinary discourse, including the ordinary discourse of social science:

The power story. Powerful people get what they want. How is power measured? By measuring the extent to which people get what they want.

The personality story. People do things because of their basic personalities. How is personality defined? By observing what people do.

The utility story. People choose things because of the value they associate with the outcomes. How are the things people value determined? By observing what they choose.

The culture story. People behave in ways that are consistent with their cultural traditions. How is the culture to which a person belongs determined? By observing what cultural rules he or she follows.

Such theories provide glib *post hoc* explanations for anything that might happen. They provide a story line that allows a certain amount of elaboration. The traditional objection to them is that they do not provide much power for predicting what will happen. Precisely because they can explain anything, they can predict nothing.

Such objections may perhaps miss the obvious point that most story lines are more frequently used to interpret past outcomes than they are to predict future ones. Decision makers, as well as others, devote more time and energy to explaining things, talking about them, and exhibiting intelligence in comprehending them than they do in predicting the future. Tautological beliefs and story lines are valuable frames for conversation. They provide a rhetoric of confidence and irrefutability that fits the identity of a decision maker. Decision makers are supposed to act with confidence in their own understanding of a situation. These tautologies allow them to do so. The costs of predictive ambiguity are relatively minor.

5.2.2 Ambiguities of the Self

In theories of decision making based on a logic of consequence, possible choices are compared in terms of their consequences. The self of a decision maker is found in a set of preferences. In theories of decision making based on a logic of appropriateness, possible actions are compared in terms of their appropriateness. The self is found in a set of identities. Students of ambiguity emphasize the ambiguities of preferences and identities as a critical difficulty in understanding action based on them. Neither preferences nor identities can easily be characterized as either clear or coherent.

AMBIGUITIES OF PREFERENCES

In standard formal theories of consequence-based choice, preferences are not observed. They are inferred from choices and have no independent standing outside of choices. The fundamental premise is that a well-behaved utility function can be discovered in a set of choices. To make the estimation and other technical problems tolerable, formal theories of choice generally assume that preferences have three very restrictive properties:

1. Preferences are assumed to be *consistent*. Preference inconsistency is imaginable only insofar as it does not affect choice (i.e., only insofar as it is made irrelevant by the specification of tradeoffs).
2. Preferences are assumed to be *stable*. Current action is normally assumed to be taken in terms of current preferences. The implicit assumption is that preferences will be unchanged when the future outcomes of current actions are realized.
3. Preferences are assumed to be *exogenous* to the process of choice. Preferences, by whatever process they may be created, are not themselves affected by the choices they control.

The assumptions are useful technically, but each of them seems inconsistent with observations of decision making by individuals and organizations. Preferences are inconsistent. Preferences change over time in such a way that predicting future preferences is often difficult. And while decisions are based on preferences, preferences also often evolve in the process of making choices. To cite only one example, in many practical situations, it is possible to infer the monetary value implicitly placed on life by a decision maker. In order for such inferences to be useful within a standard choice theory framework, the inferred monetary value of a life should be the same for different decisions by the same decision maker or decision making body. In practice, the inferred value of life usually varies by several orders of magnitude depending on the particular choice involved.

Partly because it has not proved particularly easy to infer preferences from choices in complex decision situations, partly because "revealed preference" theories of choice and many consequence-based theories of decision making start from different bases, many students of choice are unwilling to treat preferences as inferred. The language of students of behavior has a rich vocabulary for describing observable preferences (goals, wants, needs, utilities, tastes), and explicit preferences play an important role in an array of theories. These theories treat preferences as intra- or interpersonally observable, that is, they assume that individual decision makers can articulate their own preferences in ways that are to some extent independent of concrete actions and are comprehensible to others.

It is hard, of course, to interpret self-reports of preferences. Since "good intentions" are often valued, individuals will tend to report (even to themselves) preferences that are socially valued, even when they (or others) find little evidence of action consistent with the stated preferences. Because of this, hypocrisy can be seen as an interesting phenomenon for study rather than simply as a measurement or a moral problem. Even without hypocrisy, self-reports of preferences are themselves quite likely to be inferences drawn from self-observation. If those inferences are made by imposing a general cultural presumption of consistency between action and preferences, individual decision makers will, in effect, be estimating their own values from their behavior, and hence will find themselves in approximately the same difficult position in which revealed-preference choice theorists find themselves.

In practice, decision makers often seem to take an active role in constructing and shaping their preferences. They make decisions by considering their effects on future preferences. They are repelled by their own desires and attracted by desires they do not have. They avoid sweets because they "don't want to develop a taste" for them. They endure opera and ballet (or football and beer) in hopes that they will become the kind of person who likes them. They say they like "good" wine but leave "good" undefined. They treat their preferences strategically in an infinite game with themselves as they try to control their less attractive desires. Their deepest feelings tend to be paired in contradictory ways. They experience love and hate, or acceptance and rejection, not so much as opposites as components of each other.

AMBIGUITIES OF IDENTITIES

Identities are similarly ambiguous. An assertion that situations evoke identities and that actors follow rules associated with their identities glosses over some significant lack of clarity. As was observed in Chapter 2, individuals have multiple identities, and determining which identity should be evoked in a particular situation, or what to do when several are evoked, is often difficult.

The ambiguities of identity, however, are not limited to conflict among them. Identities are defined in terms of expectations that are likely to be imprecise, inconsistent, unstable, and endogenous. What it means to be an engineer, an accountant, or an executive is continually being comprehended, even as it is changing. How does a mother know what it means to act as a mother? Partly, she learns how to be a proper mother by observing other mothers. Partly, she interprets her own instinctive behavior. Partly, she is instructed by others in the society. Partly, she engages in discussions with herself and with others as she tries to fulfill the role.

Similarly, decision makers learn to be proper decision makers by observing others, by interpreting their own behavior, by instruction, and by discourse. There is consistency enough so that the identity of "decision maker" is meaningful, so that asking someone in an organization to play a decision making role is a meaningful request. As different people fulfill the decision maker identity, they do many of the same things. But exactly what is to be done, or how it is to be done in a specific situation, is often ambiguous.

An identity is like a folk tale. If a storyteller is asked to tell a particular story and responds by telling a different one, the audience can tell that it is not the right story. Still, each storyteller tells the same story in a different way, emphasizing some things, adding details, omitting others. And each storyteller shapes the story to be appropriate for an audience. A folk tale is different when told in different voices, or to different audiences, though it is at the same time recognizable as the same story. For example, the ethnic and scatological content of folk tales seems to be added and subtracted routinely to accommodate audience sensibilities, but a sense of story integrity remains. Gradually over time, a story changes. Each change is small and local, but the cumulative drift can lead to a transformation large enough that only scholars can recognize a story's history in a current tale.

Identities evolve in a similar way. Individuals and societies struggle to discover, interpret, and create the meaning of identities. Consider, for example, the efforts of Western societies to understand and shape gender identities over the past forty years. Those efforts have been political, ideological, and personal. They have included public debate and political pressure to change ways of acting and thinking. They have involved uncounted articles and books detailing what it means to be a woman or a man in modern society. Those works have proposed, proclaimed, celebrated, and bemoaned changes in gender identities. They have become the bases of uncounted conversations and encounters molding individual and social understanding. The efforts have involved millions of individuals trying to make sense of how to act in day-by-day concrete situations.

As a result of all of those efforts, gender identities have changed. Society and individuals think of women and men in ways different from only a few decades ago. And those differences make an appreciable difference to the lives of men and women. Being a woman or being a man means something in these societies. They are not empty terms. At the same time, neither are they terms with precise, consistent meaning. They are ambiguous. They include contradictions, confusions, and obfuscations. The ambiguities are often sources of frustration, sorrow, and amusement. As men and women try to figure out what gender identities mean and how they relate to other identities—parent, friend, executive, soldier, nurse, engineer—they develop and interpret the idea of gender as identity. That identity is a set of social and personal expectations that accumulate meaning through social experience but are always somewhat fuzzy.

The gender identity example is familiar to individuals living in contemporary society, but it is simply one of many identities that are continually being developed through social interaction and experience. Though they provide rules of behavior, and though individuals can be seen reliably as pursuing one identity or another and criticized meaningfully for failing to follow the rules properly, each identity is filled with ambiguity about its meaning. Each involves constant interpretation and reinterpretation.

5.2.3 *Ambiguity and Theories of Decision Making*

Neither rational theories of choice nor rule-following theories of identity fulfillment deal particularly well with ambiguity. The contradictions, inconsistencies, and fuzziness of reality, preferences, and identities are largely ignored. The problems of ambiguous realities are either denied or treated as special cases of uncertainty. And while the problems associated with ambiguous preferences and identities, as well as their significance, are well known, they have not as yet led to substantial modifications either to rational perspectives on choice or to theories of rule following. Although it is hard to keep the structure of either theory intact in the context of preferences and identities that are imprecise, inconsistent, changing, and endogenous, it has been even harder to find acceptable replacements that preserve the other assumptions.

5.3 Loose Coupling in Organizations

Organizations have many features that move them toward coordinated action, particularly hierarchical control structures and standard operating procedures. Nevertheless, they do not reliably display consistent decision coherence. Rather than have decision processes that proceed from consistent intentions, identities, and expectations to coordinated decisions and actions, organizations exhibit numerous symptoms of incoherence. Decisions seem unconnected to actions, yesterday's actions unconnected to today's actions, justifications unconnected to decisions. Beliefs are often unconnected to choices, solutions unconnected to problems, and processes unconnected to outcomes. Organizations frequently have ambiguous preferences and identities, ambiguous experiences and history, ambiguous technologies, and fluid participation in decision making. They are loosely coupled.

Observations of the loose coupling in organizational decision making have led some people to argue that there is very little order to it, that it is best described as chaos. The attribution of disorder to experience, however, results from trying to make sense of observations within standard theories. Perhaps the problem of understanding decision making lies in the fact that the ways in which organizations bring order to disorder is different from that anticipated by conventional theories. Perhaps there is order, but it is not conventional order. The remainder of the present chapter examines some suggestions for discerning order in an apparently disorderly world of loose coupling.

5.3.1 Decentralization and Delegation

Organizations face confusing, inconsistent environments. Loose coupling through decentralization and delegation are designed to solve the motivational and informational problems of coping with those environments. Since knowledge of local conditions and specialized competencies are both essential and more readily found in decentralized units, control over the details of policy implementation and adaptation of general policies to local conditions are delegated to local units. From the standpoint of general management, the strategy is usually seen as one of gaining the informational and motivational advantages of using people with local involvement and knowledge, at the cost of accentuating problems of central coordination and control.

The great triumphs of organizational design—departmentalization, decentralization, and hierarchy—are, however, partly devices for concealing, tolerating, and stimulating useful incoherence. As was observed earlier, the problems of decentralization are not simply informational and motivational. They are also problems of managing a coalition of conflicting demands. The demands on one part of the organization are inconsistent with the demands on another part. Sustaining the coalition involves organizing to obscure inconsistencies in preferences and identities and to take advantage of variations in attention.

By loosening the links among subunits, decentralization buffers inconsistencies in the organization and protects those inconsistencies from centralized monitors of coherence. By delegating responsibility for attending to demands, it makes it possible for different subunits to attend to different demands. If attention from coalition members is sporadic (as it almost certainly must be), an organization can maintain the support of a fairly heterogeneous constituency by limiting its responsiveness to those parts of the coalition that are locally and currently active.

The cost of such a strategy is inconsistency among the various actions of the organization over time and from one subunit to another. The process yields a set of actions that cannot easily be rationalized as stemming from a coherent set of autonomous organizational objectives. Moreover, decentralization and delegation generate a long-run dynamic of differentiation that accentuates organizational-level loose coupling. Subunits develop their own objectives, information sets, clients, and identities. They create subcultures of belief that are different from those found in other subunits. They maintain their distinctiveness by contrasting their careers, stories, and practices with those found in other parts of the organization.

Those centrifugal forces on organization are well known both to the research literature on organizations and to practical managers. They are usually seen as pathologies, however, or at least as unfortunate costs. Such a portrayal of decentralized inconsistency as pathological stems from a particular conception of organizational order. It is a conception that emphasizes internal coordination in the name of a clear, shared objective, rather than flexible adaptation to an environment of conflicting demands.

An alternative view sees the problems of local adaptation as responding to demands and developing preferences and identities as well as responding to local information. From that perspective, effective organizations involve decentralized elaboration and adaptation of goals as well as decentralized implementation of policies and adaptation of tactics. It is a view that is likely to interpret the loosely coupled inconsistencies produced by decentralization and delegation as essential to organizational health, rather than as a sign of organizational sickness.

5.3.2 Decisions and Implementations

Conventional theories of decision making assume that ambiguity in decisions normally stems from some kind of inadequacy in decision making. Applying such a judgment to ambiguity in organizational decision making ignores much of what is known about the making of decisions. Decisions are the result of negotiation among members of a coalition. Participants may share some objectives, but characteristically their coalition is a negotiated coalition of convenience as much as it is one of principle. The clarity of a negotiated decision is more a consequence of negotiation than a technical matter of competence.

One standard procedure for securing support is to make the meaning of a proposed decision ambiguous. Typically, a close decision requires different supporters to be individually optimistic about the way the decision or its implementation will serve their interests or confirm their identities. Such optimism is facilitated by enthusiasm and unrealistic expectations, which in turn are facilitated by ambiguity. Disagreements are resolved by vague language and vague expectations. As a result, an extended decision process is more likely to add to ambiguity than to reduce it.

Although ambiguities of meaning and expectations can increase support for a decision, they often lead to unpredictabilities in implementation. As was noted in Chapter 4, decisions and actions are often loosely coupled because they involve different coalitions of actors. Coalitions, particularly coalitions built on the basis of mutual indifference (logrolls) are likely to be unstable over time and place. When decisions are implemented, many members of the original coalition are likely to be busy elsewhere or uninterested in the implementation of the decision. Other members of the coalition, as well as observers, are likely to fantasize a meaning of the original agreement that is inattentive to its deliberate ambiguity. Ambiguities of intentions and expectations combine with turnover in attention and coalition membership to force a renegotiation of support within a new set of actors.

This loose coupling of decision and implementation is accentuated by the extent to which both decisions and actions involve symbolic commitments. Those who participate in decision making not only pursue personal and group advantage but also personal and group affirmation. Studies of decision making suggest that the act of supporting a policy with appropriate symbolic meaning can be more important to decision makers than its adoption, and its adoption can be more important than its implementation. Decision makers interested in building viable coalitions are likely to seek and find allies who will be vigorous in supporting symbolic decisions and lax in implementing them.

Loose coupling between decisions and their implementations is neither a new phenomenon nor newly discovered. It has been observed in all kinds of institutions for many years. As a result, it is reasonable to expect decision making institutions to have adapted to the realities of ambiguity in policy formation and decision making. As those responsible for implementation experience ambiguity in decisions, they come to treat decisions as palettes for new administrative imagination. They develop techniques for elaborating decisions and for developing new coalitions in support of the elaborations. Similarly, decision makers learn from their experience with imaginative implementation. The skill of implementors in continuing the policy debate and coalition formation into the implementation phase encourages the use of ambiguity in formulating decisions and provides a handy scapegoat for failures. The mutual learning of decision makers and decision implementors is likely to lead to a tendency toward ambiguous decisions and imaginative interpretations of them.

5.3.3 Talk and Action

Organizational decision making is a combination of talk and action.* Both are important, but talk and action are often loosely coupled. Indeed, they are often mutually exclusive rather than mutually supportive. Some things are more readily discussed than decided. Anyone who has participated in late-evening college discussions of religion, philosophy, politics, or personal relationships is aware of the phenomenon at the individual level. The discussions rarely yield conclusions and are seen more commonly as a combination of social bonding and educational development than as an opportunity to resolve issues. Participants exercise personal intelligence, expose personal sentiments, learn arguments, and confirm a common commitment to fundamental values.

Decision processes in organizations have many similar properties. They provide arenas for displaying attitudes and coaching beliefs—the fabric of understandings that tie a community together. Discussions of decisions allow individuals to define, communicate, and enforce virtuous sentiments. They clarify the principles by which individuals wish to be guided. Since those uses of decision processes in constructing meaning will be considered somewhat more fully in section 5.5, only one aspect will be noted here: This talk of decision making is not always closely connected to the action of decisions.

The making of concrete decisions in an organization is an exercise of practical, contextual judgment. It applies conflicting principles of ambiguous relevance to specific situations that confound beliefs. Organizations decide to make some investments rather than others, hire some employees rather than others, set some prices rather than others, settle some disputes and continue others. In principle, these specific decisions in specific situations are derived from some more general decisions about more general situations, sometimes called policies or guidelines. The derivations, however, are typically not straightforward. Policies are more likely to establish contradictory ten-

---

*The tension between talk and action is a favorite topic of Nils Brunsson, and these paragraphs have profited from his comments (perhaps poorly).

sions than to resolve them. Policy decisions to treat employees decently seem to conflict with policy decisions to reduce payrolls. Policy decisions to abandon nuclear power seem to conflict with policy decisions to expand energy availability. Policy decisions to sustain full employment seem to conflict with policy decisions to limit inflation.

Talk and action are loosely coupled, because talk tends to deal with principles one at a time and action tends to deal with many principles simultaneously but only in a specific limited situation. Talk achieves clarity by ignoring the complications of specific contexts. It reminds decision participants of their beliefs. Action achieves clarity by ignoring its implications for contradictory beliefs. It sustains the beliefs but bends them to meet the exigencies of action. As a result, some things that are easily said are not easily done. Other things can be easily done but not easily said.

5.4 Garbage Can Decision Processes

In an environment characterized by complex interactions among actors, solutions, problems, and choice opportunities, the simplest source of order is that of time. Activities can be ordered in time and connected by their temporal relations. Temporal sorting is commonplace in human affairs. Events that occur at the same time are associated with each other. Events that are distant in time are treated as distant in connection. Among the many categories available for sorting people, things, activities, or outcomes, temporal categories are conspicuous by their ubiquity. In important ways, decision processes build on these temporal categories, combining people, problems, and solutions in terms of their simultaneity. Those elements of temporal sorting are exemplified in garbage can decision processes.

5.4.1 Temporal Sorting Perspectives

Any decision process involves a collection of individuals and groups who are simultaneously involved in other things. What happens depends not only on what the activities are but also on how they fit together. The apparent loose coupling that is observed results from a shifting intermeshing of the lives of an array of actors. Any particular decision is a combination of different moments of different lives. Understanding decisions in one arena, therefore, requires an understanding of how participation in those decisions fits into the lives of participants. Each life is itself embedded in a complex mixture of other activities, concerns, and identities that makes a particular decision incomprehensible without attention to the full context. It is a daunting task.

A more limited version of the same fundamental idea focuses on the allocation of attention. The idea is simple. Individuals attend to some things, and thus do not attend to others. The attention devoted to a particular decision by a particular potential participant depends on alternative claims on attention. Since those alternative claims are not homogeneous across participants, and since they change over time, the attention received by any particular decision can be both unstable and remarkably independent of the properties of the decision. The same decision will attract much attention or little, depending on the other things that possible participants might be doing. As the distribution of attention changes, so also does the decision. The apparently erratic character of decision making is made somewhat more explicable by placing it in this context of multiple changing claims on attention and an order imposed on that context by time.

Researchers have identified the effects of temporal sorting in numerous settings, including military engagements, personnel and location decisions in universities, accident prevention efforts in business, the setting of agendas in legislative decision making, and publications decisions in the textbook industry. All of these situations are described as "organized anarchies." There are unclear preferences, and success is often ambiguous. The technology contains no clear rules for producing success. And participation in decisions is fluid; there is turnover of decision makers in decision arenas.

5.4.2 The Garbage Can Model

The general ideas of temporal sorting have been used to deal with flows of solutions and problems, as well as with participants in what has come to be called a garbage can decision process. In a garbage can process, it is assumed that there are exogenous, time-dependent arrivals of choice opportunities, problems, solutions, and decision makers. Problems and solutions are attached to choices, and thus to each other, not because of any means–ends linkage but because of their temporal proximity. At the limit, for example, almost any solution can be associated with almost any problem—provided they are evoked at the same time.

GENERAL PROPERTIES OF GARBAGE CAN PROCESSES

The "garbage cans" in the garbage can model are such choice opportunities as contract meetings, budget committees, and compensation decisions. Choice opportunities collect decision makers, problems, and solutions. Problems are concerns of the people with access to the decision. Problems are signaled by failures or impending failures. They may involve such things as logistics, resource allocation, or scheduling. They may involve issues of lifestyle, fairness, or correctness. They may involve conflicts among participants or between them and outsiders. Problems can be characterized by their arrival times, the amount of energy required to solve them, and their access to choice opportunities (for example, certain choice opportunities may not allow the discussion of certain problems—there are socially enforced rules of relevance). Solutions are answers to problems that may or may not have been recognized. They can be characterized by their arrival times and their access to choice opportunities, as well as by the resources they provide to decision makers who are trying to make choices.

Within this process, decision makers are involved in one choice opportunity at any one time, but they move from one choice opportunity to another. Decision makers are characterized by their arrival times (when they first enter the system), by their access to choice opportunities (decision structure), and by their energy (ability to solve problems). Their participation in a particular decision arena depends on features of the alternative choice opportunities, in particular on the apparent nearness of a choice to decision. A decision maker moves from a choice opportunity that is far from decision toward one that is closer to decision. Such a movement, of course, pushes the decision maker's new choice opportunity even closer to decision (because of the additional energy provided to its resolution) and slows the rate of decision resolution in the former choice opportunity.

Problems, solutions, decision makers, and choice opportunities are linked initially by virtue of the times of their arrivals on the scene and the possibilities available at those times. The linkages change over time as problems, solutions, and decision makers move from one choice opportunity to another, and as choices are made. Thus, the results produced by the system depend on the timing of the various flows and on the structural constraints of the organization.

SIMULATION OF GARBAGE CAN PROCESSES

The garbage can model can be specified more precisely and exercised in a computer simulation. In one illustrative set of simulations,[1] it is assumed that a choice is made whenever the decision makers present at a choice opportunity (aided by whatever solutions are available) have enough "energy" to overcome the problems that are present.

Within the simulations, most choices are made. In that sense at least, the system "works." Choices are made in three different ways:

1. *Oversight.* Sometimes a choice opportunity arrives and no problems attach themselves to the choice. All the problems in the system are attached to other choices. In this situation, a choice is made with a minimum of time and energy. It resolves no problems.
2. *Problem resolution.* Sometimes there are problems associated with a choice opportunity, and the decision makers attached to the choice bring enough energy to meet the demands of those problems. The choice is made and the problems are resolved.
3. *Flight.* Sometimes a number of problems are associated with a choice opportunity for some time. Since they collectively exceed the energy of the decision makers attached

to the choice, the choice is not made. When another choice opportunity becomes available, the problems leave the initial choice to attach themselves on another (e.g. people take their salary grievances to another forum). After the problems are gone, the original choice is made. It resolves no problems.

In these simulations of a garbage can decision process, most choices are made by flight or oversight. Resolution of problems is not typical except when the system load is very light (the energy level of decision makers is high relative to the energy requirements of the problems needing to be solved) or when there are severe restrictions on the movements of problems, solutions, and decision makers. As decision makers abandon one choice in search of one nearer to decision, problems also move in the same search. As a result, decision makers, problems, and solutions tend to track each other through the system. After problems leave one choice to attach themselves to another, the original choice is made. But it resolves no problems.

In some access structures, it is possible to identify which problems and choices are more "important." An important *problem* is one that has access to many choices. In simulations of the garbage can model within such a structure, important problems are more likely to be solved than unimportant problems. More important problems (which have access to many choice opportunities) are able to find arenas in which there are decision makers with enough energy to resolve them. The system thus tends to produce a queue of problems in terms of their importance, to the disadvantage of late-arriving, relatively unimportant problems. An important *choice* is one that is accessible to only a few problems and a few decision makers. In the simulation of the model, important choices are less likely to resolve problems than unimportant choices. And although most choices are made, failures to make choices are concentrated in the most important and least important choices, the former because they allow too few decision makers, the latter because they attract too many problems.

There are three general measures that can be used to assess the performance of a garbage can decision process:

1. Problem *activity* is the amount of time that problems spend attached to choice situations without solution. This might provide a rough measure of the potential for conflict in an organization, as choices are bogged down by an unsolvable set of problems.
2. Problem *latency* is the amount of time problems spend activated but not linked to choices. This might provide a rough measure of the responsiveness of the system, the extent to which participants might complain that the organization ignores their problems.
3. *Decision time* is the amount of time that choices remain unmade. This might provide a rough measure of the apparent efficiency of the system in meeting its explicit decision requirements—allocating resources, making budgets, hiring personnel, etc.

Presumably a good organizational structure would allow problems to appear and be solved and decisions to be made quickly, reducing problem activity, problem latency, and decision time as choices are made and problems move quickly to resolution. In a garbage can process, it is hard to improve on all three measures simultaneously. As problems become more difficult relative to the competencies of decision makers and the solutions available, the system faces increasing problems. Decisions become more difficult. The overall likelihood of solving any given problem drops, it takes longer to make choices, and decision makers spend more time moving from one choice opportunity to another.

Segmenting the access structure of problems to choices reduces the number of unresolved problems in the organization, but at the cost of increasing problem latency and the time devoted to reaching decisions. Segmenting the access of decision makers to choices tends to reduce problem latency but at the cost of increasing problem activity and decision time. That is, segmentation reduces the tendency of decision makers and problems to interfere with each other, but it also reduces the capability of decision makers to share variations in load.

Finally, and perhaps most importantly, the garbage can model is frequently sharply interactive. Although some broad phenomena, such as those described above, seem to be regular and fairly general, some seem to depend on particular arrival times or combinations. For example, although a highly segmented access of problems to choices generally produces long decision times, when such a structure is combined with an unsegmented access of decision makers to choices, decisions are made quickly.

RESTRICTIONS ON GARBAGE CAN PROCESSES

Much of the discussion of garbage can processes found in the literature on decision making emphasizes situations in which the access of problems, solutions, and decision makers to choice opportunities are unrestricted. Any problem, solution, or decision maker is able to intrude on any choice opportunity. These situations produce some of the more dramatic consequences of temporal sorting and are approximated in some real-world situations. There are probably many more situations, however, in which garbage can processes exist but are constrained by social norms, organizational structures, and networks of connections that restrict the process in important ways.

There are shared beliefs and social norms that regulate the linkages formed and the choices made. The soccer field metaphor (see subsection 5.1.2) can be extended by noting that the field is located on a slope, so some outcomes are more likely than others—though predicting precisely which outcome will occur is not easy. In the real world, that slope is reflected in cultural expectations, in rules of conventional practice, and in the host of other taken-for-granted things that shape decision behavior.

Organizational structures restrain the abilities of problems, solutions, and decision makers to interact with choices. Although most of the attention to garbage can processes in the literature emphasizes situations in which the access of problems, solutions, and decision makers to choice opportunities is unrestricted, the model treats several more restricted cases easily. For example, consider the access of decision makers to choice opportunities. In an unsegmented structure, any decision maker can have access to any choice opportunity. In a specialized structure, only certain decision makers have access to any particular choice (e.g. certain forms may require the signatures of certain employees). In a hierarchical structure, important decision makers have access to many choices, and less important decision makers have access to fewer choices.

The same kinds of access structures can be specified for solutions and problems. For example, solutions or problems can be restricted by a segmented structure, where certain solutions or problems have access to only certain choice opportunities (e.g. technological changes can be proposed only at engineering meetings), or they can be restricted by a hierarchical structure, where minor solutions (e.g. those proposed by outsiders) can attach themselves only to unimportant choice opportunities. There are other restrictions on the decision process, particularly deadlines. There are constraints on the arrival times of problems, solutions, choice opportunities, and decision makers.

Each of these restrictions introduces some kind of limit to the pure garbage can process. The outcomes of a garbage can decision process are produced by the interaction of these restrictions with the time-dependent flows of problems, solutions, and decision makers. The restrictions are cautions against assuming that the distinction between garbage can processes and other processes depends on the free flow of problems, solutions, and decision makers. The critical element of a garbage can process is that there are elements of temporal sorting. Linkages are formed, in part, because of simultaneity.

5.4.3 Instrumental Action in Garbage Can Worlds

The contradiction between the logical order anticipated by conventional thinking about decision making and the "disorder" produced by temporal sorting invites an engineering response. How should a decision maker behave in a garbage can world? Decision makers seem to fall into one of three prototypical response types:

1. *Reformers* try to eliminate garbage can elements from the decision process. They see garbage can processes as inherently

inimical to proper decision making and as avoidable. They seek to eliminate temporal sorting of problems, solutions, and decision makers, to impose a coherence based on principles of reality, causality, and intentionality. They advocate more systematic attempts to define objectives, establish knowledge about the world, coordinate among different aspects of a decision, and exercise control in the name of some central vision.

2. *Pragmatists* try to use garbage can processes for their own ends. They see garbage can processes as unavoidable but susceptible to exploitation. They seek to take advantage of the fact that attention is scarce in order to arrange the arrival of solutions, problems, and choice opportunities to serve their own interests. They persist, knowing that the mix of participants in a particular situation changes. They overload the system to protect their interests. They provide garbage cans to attract other decision makers and problems away from choices of interest to them.

3. *Enthusiasts* try to discover a new vision of decision making in garbage can processes. They see those processes as having elements of beauty and instrumentality. They seek to discover the intelligence in temporal sorting as a way of organizing attention, to see the flows of problems and solutions as a form of market, to find elegance in the ambiguity of preferences and identities and in the unfolding nature of the linkages between problems and solutions. They ascribe advantages to flexible implementation, uncoordinated actions, and cognitive confusion.

It is not really necessary to choose among those alternatives. Each has a certain charm. Each has some blind spots. The blind spots of reformers stem from their confidence in a vision of consistent action and their optimism about the possibilities of reform. The blind spots of pragmatists stem from their tendency to assume that everyone else in the world is naïve (less intelligent than they are) and their enthusiasm for a self-indulgent view of human morality. The blind spots of enthusiasts stem from their tendency to see every feature of observed organizational behavior as having hidden virtue and their overestimation of human tolerances for confusion.

5.5 Decision Making and the Construction of Meaning

This book is built around two alternative visions of decision making: The first is a vision of rationality in which actions stem from expectations of their consequences and preferences for those consequences. The second is a a vision of rule following in which actions stem from a matching of the demands of identities with a definition of the situation. Each vision assumes that decision makers interpret their situations and their experiences, that they make sense of them in order to make decisions. Rational actors—whether acting alone or in negotiation with other rational actors—interpret their situations and experiences to predict future consequences of current actions and their future feelings about such consequences. Rule-following actors—whether acting alone or in concert with other rule-following actors—interpret their situations and experiences to identify appropriate identities and rules. They interpret history to develop the rules they follow.

Such interpretations are not always easy. Experience, expectations, preferences, and identities are all likely to be ambiguous. As a result, students of decision making devote much of their energies to discerning the ways in which decision makers resolve or ignore the ambiguities they face in making decisions. Uncertainties are reduced through the accumulation and retrieval of information. Information systems are designed, and information is used to facilitate judgments about consequences or appropriateness. Meaning is established in order to make decisions.

From such a perspective, decisions are important because they allocate resources and produce measurable consequences for the decision maker. Information is meaningful if it resolves uncertainties about preferences, consequences, situations, and identities. What are the implications for profits, costs, and sales in a business firm? What are the implications for victory in a military organization? In those terms, meaning serves action and action serves the purposes of preferences and identities.

This section considers a different conception of the construction of meaning in decision making processes. Interpretation is treated as central, sense making as a basic need. Humans spend much of their time gathering information, spinning explanations, and gossiping about the motives and the behavior of others. In this view, meaning is not established to make decisions; decisions are made to establish meaning.

5.5.1 The Elaboration of Meaning

Ambiguities of experience and interpretation make the construction of meaning critical to life. The events of experience do not automatically have clear meaning. Increasing the participation of younger faculty members in the governance of a university department can be viewed either as an extension of democracy or as the drafting of involuntary cheap labor. Computer-based word processing can be described as augmenting the status and skills of secretaries or as deskilling their jobs. When a business firm abandons a product line, the meaning of that action is unclear until it is interpreted. When an organization changes from one accounting firm to another, the action requires interpretation to achieve meaning. People develop meaning in the ordinary activities of life. They gossip and engage in idle talk. They rely on professional gossipmongers—journalists and historians. They construct myths, exercise symbols, develop rituals, and tell stories.

THE INSTRUMENTS OF MEANING

The instruments of meaning are myths, symbols, rituals, and stories. They are the ligaments of social life, establishing links among individuals and groups, across generations and geographic distances. They give a context for understanding history and for locating oneself in it. Not only do they reflect social structure and process, they create them.

Myths. A myth is "any real or fictional story, recurring theme, or character type that appeals to the consciousness of a people by embodying its cultural ideals or by giving expression to deep, commonly felt emotions."[5] Myths are constructed to provide broad explanations of life and models for behavior. Myths explain the roles of gods (CEOs, boards of directors) and nature (the competition, customers, the market). They explain how much predictability is to be expected in the world and how to placate the powers that control individual destiny (through prayer, humility, or deregulation). They celebrate, or denigrate, human intention and human agency. For example, one of the more common myths in organizations is a creation myth, a stylized story of the founding of the organization, with its mythic heroes, events, and explanations.

Symbols. Symbols are objects, practices, or signs that evoke something else by association, similarity, or convention. Symbols link organizational experience to deep feelings or to abstract definitions of human dilemmas. Clothes and language symbolize power and status. Exclusion from decision making symbolizes loss of personhood. Meetings symbolize thought. Slogans and hugs symbolize solidarity. As these symbols are elaborated and interpreted within a decision context, a particular decision takes on meanings that tie it to a more extensive, and often less predictable, corpus of understanding and feeling. Choices of technologies or resource allocation become not only concrete decisions but also symbols of whether truth will win over ignorance, and whether justice will prevail. The introduction of the personal computer was portrayed by some of those who developed it not as a technological innovation, but as a force for individual freedom in a world of oppression.

Rituals. Rituals are sets of ceremonial forms by which traditions are preserved and meanings sustained. Decision making is a highly ritualized activity. The signature ritual that pervades decision making is an example. By endorsing a message, a decision, or a birthday card with a signature, an individual certifies personal responsibility and authority for the act. The development of a "business plan" is another common ritual of modern business life. It certifies the legitimacy of decisions linked to it, much in the way the words of a marriage ceremony certify the legitimacy of a marital decision by a couple. Rituals signal the transition from one state of organizational existence to another (promotion, retirement) or from one set of loyalties to another (transfers, reassignments). Rituals of consultation, analysis, discussion, and choice surround the process of decision making.

Stories. Stories are tales of what is happening, what has happened, or what might happen. They are elaborations of explanations of why things happen. They are the fuel of decision making and of social life more generally. Most of what individuals know about the world comes in the form of stories told to them by others. Some of those stories are created by professional storytellers: journalists, writers, teachers. Others are a part of daily discourse. Public relations departments try to tell stories that cast a good light on events. Others develop a clientele for stories that define events in terms of vile motives, conspiracy, and corruption. As storytellers compete for attention and approval, stories about decisions are molded to match the intellectual and emotional needs of the listeners. Winners encourage stories that describe events in terms of virtue rewarded. Losers encourage stories of villainy and perverse gods.

THE SOCIAL BASIS OF MEANING

Meaning comes from social interaction and takes both its coherence and its contradictions from its social basis. Interpretations are shared through communication, and their character is transformed through the social process by which they are shared. Social exchange leads a community, group, or organization toward internally shared understandings of experience. Stories, paradigms, and frames come to be widely believed and thereafter are generally sustained by social interpretation of historical events. Idiosyncratic individual interpretations are typically changed by exposure to the interpretations of more conventional others. As a result, there is a tendency for social groups to move toward reliable, but not necessarily valid, interpretations of history. Inferences from the experiences of history are stored in collective memory, in routines and rules, beliefs and stories. The learning is conserved by socialization of new members and maintenance of social control.

This picture of stability and conservation of belief is substantially correct, but reliability is not assured. Some inferences from history are not recorded. Routines, rules, beliefs, and stories are sometimes ambiguous, requiring interpretation that leads to inconsistencies and gradual transformation of meaning. Different individuals have different experiences and different theories for interpreting those experiences. The differences are often organized into active subcultures. As those subcultures act internally to sustain their own internal integrity, they are likely to support differentiation in interpretation within the larger society. In particular, conflicts of interest or world view stabilize conflicting interpretations in subgroups. Conflict over meaning is as socially based as is agreement.

To say that meaning is socially constructed is not to say that it can be arbitrarily transformed. On the one hand, meaning is contested. One vision competes with another. At the same time, the contest occurs within a historical path of beliefs and interpretations. The contemporary meaning of Catholicism in Guatemala reflects not only the outcomes of competition between Mayan rulers and Spanish conquistadors but also the way the historical foundations of thinking by missionaries from Rome (via Spain) encounter meanings encapsulated in Mayan traditions.

THE ROLE OF LANGUAGE

Among the various mechanisms by which meaning is made social, none is more important than language. It is not just that language is the vessel by which meaning is transported. Natural languages are also instruments for creating meaning. Natural language is used to clarify distinctions, to discriminate, and to reduce uncertainty. Language is also used to create new meanings out of old, to make metaphorical leaps, to discover what a person might come to understand. Ambiguity and equivocality are essential to the process, as are irony, paradox, playfulness, and metaphor. Meaning evolves within them through an interplay of precision and evocativeness.

As a result, understanding decision making involves understanding the ways in which language carries, elaborates, and creates meaning. Consider, for example, the process of judicial interpretation—the ways in which judges apply general principles to specific situations. There is ample evidence for the proposition that judges exploit the openness of language to develop interpretations that are convenient to their own class, ethnic group, gender, or nation. But there is also ample evidence that the language of law is neither a completely empty vessel into which any interpretation can be forced, nor simply a passive barrier to change. It is an invitation to extract what is buried in the deep recesses of linguistic experience.

Decision making, like legal interpretation, extracts meaning from language. As decision makers look for meaning in words, they draw on the subtleties of linguistic undertones, finding new interpretations that are immanent in words rather than imposed on them. It is a process that is demeaned by its frequent corruption in the service of bias, but it echoes the process by which readers find meaning in poetry. Meaning not fully comprehended by the poet is implicit in poetic genius. Like judges, readers of poetry or interpreters of decisions may exploit ambiguity in the service of interests or ideology, but the best of them, like the best of judges, use language to evoke deeper meanings.

5.5.2 The Symbolic Importance of Decision Making

The meanings elaborated in decision making have importance beyond the mundane realities of rendering decisions. Decision making and the activities surrounding it have considerable symbolic importance. In the course of making decisions, decision makers develop and communicate meaning not only about decisions but also more generally about truth, about what it is happening in the world and why it is happening. They define what is morally important and what is proper behavior. They elaborate a language of understanding and describe how actions are properly explained and justified. They allocate and define individual worth—who is powerful, who is smart, who is virtuous. Thus, the process affects individual and organizational self-esteem and standing. It helps to mold and sustain a social order of friendships and antagonisms, trust and distrust.

Dale Carnegie saw selling (and more generally influencing decisions) as involving a fundamental trade: In return for buying a product, a buyer is offered self-esteem.[6] "If you will buy my pots and pans, I will give you respect and love." The heart of the Carnegie theory lies in two assumptions about self-esteem: The first is the *meaning* assumption: Decisions have symbolic significance for self-esteem. The second is the *scarcity* assumption: For most people, self-esteem is a scarcer (thus more desired) good than are specific product properties. The implication is that one who wants to influence a decision is well-advised to spend less time extolling properties of the preferred decision and more time articulating its symbolic meaning for the self-esteem of the person being influenced.

The symbolic elaboration of decision making is not a blemish on an otherwise neutral instrument. It is one of the more important aspects of decision processes. Some treatments of symbols, myths, and rituals in decision making portray them as perversions of the decision process. They are presented as ways in which the gullible are misled into acquiescence, as the basis for manipulation of the unwary by the clever. Such pictures are incomplete. Although there is no question that symbols, myths, and rituals are often used strategically, it is hard to imagine a world of decision making that would be free of symbolic meaning. It is hard to imagine sustaining human motivation and attention to decision making without linking it symbolically to deeply felt sentiments. And it is hard to imagine a society with modern ideology that would not exhibit a well-elaborated and reinforced myth of choice, both to sustain social orderliness and meaning and to facilitate change.

Consider, for example, acquisition decisions of a business firm, tactical decisions of a military organization, research design decisions in a research organization, personnel decisions in a school system, or diagnostic decisions in a medical organization or an automobile repair shop These occasions are not just occasions for deciding what to do. They are also occasions for talking about what goals the organization should pursue, what makes an argument legitimate, who is a smart analyst, who is tough, who is not, who is sensitive and who is not, who supports whom, how a decision maker talks, thinks, and acts. Understanding a decision and a decision process involves seeing how these symbolic meanings pervade decision making.

THE MEANINGS OF DECISION OUTCOMES

Decisions gain symbolic meaning from their outcomes and from their processes. The meanings of decision outcomes are most commonly associated with the standings of people, groups, and causes. Every contested choice divides participants into winners and losers. In this sense, at least, decision processes are basically forms of trial by combat—tests of strength and standing for the various participants. The phenomenon is illustrated by contemporary journalistic accounts of political or business decision making in the United States. Such reports are overwhelmingly oriented to describing winners and losers in a presumed struggle for primacy: "The President has suffered a defeat." "The merger is a victory for the CEO."

The trial-by-combat symbolism of decision making holds particularly true for cultures (such as traditional male culture) in which the world is ordered by domination/subordination relations and pecking orders of strength or power. Where pecking order is important, occasions for decision making will be created in order to provide opportunities for establishing personal standing, and participants in a particular decision situation will recall who won more easily than they will recall what the substantive outcome was. Potential losers will be inclined to withdraw from the contest rather than risk exposure of their weaknesses, thereby making agreement appear to be more general than it is.

Domination/subordination visions of social relations are, of course, not the only possible visions. Rather than see decision outcomes as reflecting victories in a test of strength, it is possible to see them as exhibiting affiliation, cooperation, and accommodation. Then outcomes are interpreted in terms of the extent to which they reflect the affiliative character of the group.

THE MEANINGS OF DECISION PROCESSES

Like decision outcomes, decision processes exhibit and communicate meanings. They are occasions for the presentation of self and for validation of the social order. Decision processes are opportunities for individuals to exhibit personal attributes of organizational or cultural importance. They show their intelligence, their cleverness, their coolness. They demonstrate their interpersonal attractiveness. They proclaim their values—at least those of their values that are highly cherished socially. Where such things are important, occasions for decision making will be created to provide opportunities for exhibiting and enjoying proper behavior. Potential outcasts will be inclined to withdraw from the process rather than risk exposure of their lack of social graces, thereby reducing the risks of unpleasantness. Participants are likely not to recall substantive outcomes but to remember the process associated with it.

An individual's participation in decision making intertwines these personal messages with substantive policy positions. The former should not be viewed as inimical to the latter, but an individual's decision making performance is often dictated more by presentation-of-self requirements than by a substantive concern about decision content. As a result, personal styles tend to be more stable than personal positions on issues. Personal styles also tend to vary more as a function of the audience than as a function of the topic under discussion.

Because decision arenas are sites for presentation of the self, they naturally also become sites for educating and socializing the young. People come to build an image of themselves through participation in decision processes, through observing and mimicking the behavior of valued others. A future manager learns how to behave as a manager. A young faculty member learns how to talk like a faculty member. Decision making is a public opportunity to exhibit proper attitudes and to give approbation to them.

Since decisions are educational forums, many problems take on importance because they are discussible rather than because they are necessarily solvable. This is a generally recognized feature of college bull sessions on ethics, equity, and intimate relationships. It is also a common strategy in universities in training research workers and social analysts. It gives understanding to discussions among business managers about the market, the firm, politics, and the future.

DECISIONS AND SOCIAL REASSURANCE

In a society based on faith and revelation, the church is a sacred institution. It symbolizes the glorification of the gods and the subordination of human will to divine guidance. In a society based on reason, rationality, and a conception of intentional human control over destiny, decision making is a sacred activity. The world is imagined to be produced by deliberate human action and responsive to human intention. Intention is imagined to be transformed into action through choice and power. And choice is imagined to be guided by reason.

These traditions of rationalism and anthropocentrism find mythic and ritual manifestation in the idea of decision making. As a result, the process of making a choice in a modern setting is surrounded with as much symbolic and ritual paraphernalia as the divining of God's will in the Middle Ages. The rituals of choice tie routine events to beliefs about the nature of things. They give meaning. They emphasize the centrality of human agency—humans are responsible for choices and thus for the course of history. They validate that the world is organized by choice.

The social interaction that is a part of a decision process is also important in providing more specific social reassurance to decision makers, reassurance that they have done proper and just things. Social beliefs are validated by argument, confirmation, and information gathering. Decision makers ask for more information than they could conceivably use. Though they subsequently ignore the content, the act of gathering information provides reassurance that they have acted properly. Collective decision making meetings allow participants to rehearse arguments and to develop justifications. Groups often engage in considerable discussion even after a decision has been made or could be made. This "irrelevant" discussion provides an opportunity for joint development of rationalizations, but it also provides an opportunity for individuals to reduce their own internal uncertainty about difficult decisions.

Reassurance is particularly important when there is ambiguity. The point is illustrated by a study of a Danish elementary school. The school was created by a group of parents with a strong ideology emphasizing the creation of a socialist society, direct democracy, and nonintellective skills. The ideology was important to the parents. It connected their children and themselves to a vision of a way of life, to their self-perceptions as deviant members of an oppressive society, and to their commitments to education and to their children. When a particular curriculum decision in the school was made, most people (parents, faculty, students) connected to the school were involved heavily in the discussions and debate. The arguments were highly elaborated, deeply felt, and passionately expressed. After extended and forceful debate, a decision was taken. The striking thing about the decision, however, was that it was never implemented. People who participated passionately in the discussion and who insisted on the decision were essentially indifferent to its implementation. In this case, at least, the decision process was much more connected to the generation of reassurance than to the generation of a substantive action.

It is a story that fits—perhaps in somewhat less pure form—throughout decision making. The processes of choice reassure those involved that the choice has been made intelligently; that it reflects planning, thinking, analysis, and the systematic use of information; that people have acted appropriately as decision makers; that the choice is sensitive to the concerns of relevant people; and that the right people are involved. At the same time, the processes of choice reassure those involved of their own significance. In particular, the processes are used to reinforce the idea that decision makers and their decisions affect the course of history, and do so properly.

5.5.3 Life as Interpretation

Theories of choice usually assume that a decision process is to be understood in terms of its outcome, that decision makers enter the process in order to affect outcomes, and that the point of life is choice. The emphasis is instrumental; the central conceit is the notion of decision significance. As the construction of meaning in decision making has been explored in this chapter, the argument has been developed that a choice process does many things beyond providing a basis for action. It provides an occasion for defining virtue and truth, for discovering or interpreting what is happening, what decision makers have been doing, and what justifies their actions. It is an occasion for distributing glory and blame for what has happened; and thus an occasion for exercising, challenging, or reaffirming friendships, antagonisms, power or status. It is an occasion for socialization, for educating the young and the ignorant.

These observations prompt a view that moves meaning to the center of the analysis, rather than one that sees meaning as instrumental to action. It is possible to argue that life is not primarily choice; it is interpretation. Outcomes are generally less significant—both behaviorally and ethically—than process. It is the process that gives meaning to life, and meaning is the core of life. The reason people involved in decision making devote so much time to symbols, myths, and rituals is that they care more about them.

The argument is therefore twofold. On the one hand, it is an argument that any attempt to "improve" decision making must see decisions as instruments of meaning. On the other hand, it is an argument that understanding and explaining decision behavior requires recognition of the centrality of interpretation. Decision making involves symbols, myths, rituals, and stories in the development of meaning. Coming to appreciate the symbolic drama of decision making as fundamental to decision making, rather than an epiphenomenon, leads students of decision making not only to value the elegance, dignity, charm, and beauty of decision rituals as aesthetic qualities but also to understand decision making better.

5.6 Ambiguity and Understanding

Ambiguity is a central feature of decision making life, and theories of decision making almost always underestimate its importance in organizations. Both the world and the self are ambiguous; the link between actions and decisions or thoughts is less direct than is assumed in conventional theories; garbage can decision processes and other forms of temporal sorting confound the ties between problems and solutions.

Attention to ambiguity has forced students of decision making to a more careful look at the way in which meaning is constructed in organizations, for most theories of decision making assume some basis in interpretation. At the outset, this was largely a consideration of the ways in which organizational and behavioral factors affected expectations, preferences, interpretations of history, and identities—the factors underlying logics of consequence and appropriateness. The focus was on ways in which judgments were shaped by the social and experiential construction of meaning.

Some students of decision making go farther, however. They are convinced that decision processes are better seen as parts of a world directed less to action than to interpretation. From this perspective, decisions are instruments for the development of meaning, and the development of meaning is the central organizing activity in decision making. The symbolic interpretations of decision outcomes and processes are critical to their dynamics.

It is a tempting manifesto. But even granting that substantive outcomes can be appreciated only through an interpretive and symbolic filter, there may be some point to maintaining a distinction between the manifest substantive consequences of decisions and consequences that might be called "symbolic." Ignoring the substantive consequences of decisions and contests over them seems as blind as ignoring the symbolic interpretations of those decisions or the processes by which they are generated.

CHAPTER SIX

Decision Engineering

Previous chapters have subordinated questions about the quality of decisions or their improvement to understanding decisions and decision processes as individual and social phenomena. This chapter considers some aspects of the former questions. It examines a few basic complications that arise as decision makers try to achieve intelligence.

Claims of intelligence have been used to justify various decision procedures, including both anticipatory rationality and history-based rule following. Advocates of rational action emphasize the intelligence provided by explicit calculation of future consequences. They decry the blind conservatism of rule following. Advocates of rule following, on the other hand, embrace the intelligence captured by accumulated experience represented in rules. They criticize the excessive informational and cognitive requirements of rationality.

The argument between the two sides echoes an old debate in social philosophy between those who see wisdom in willful, calculated action and those who see wisdom in the lessons of history as coded in traditions. The argument is not settled in this chapter. On the contrary, the discussion here suggests that many forms of decision making, including both rationality and rule following, are useful procedures for decision making, but no form guarantees intelligence.

That conclusion is embedded in a simple introduction to decision engineering. Section 6.1 considers the problems of defining decision intelligence in terms of the outcomes decisions produce and the complications of making the tradeoffs required when outcomes are realized across time and space and in the form of both symbolic and substantive returns. Sections 6.2, 6.3, and 6.4 examine some of the possibilities for enhancing decision intelligence, considering some aspects of how decision engineering can improve adaptiveness, the use of knowledge, and the creation of meaning.

6.1 Defining Decision Intelligence

Decision engineering is dedicated to producing decisions that are intelligent, but the definition of intelligence is often left unclear. Students of decision making oscillate between process and outcome definitions of intelligence and have never been able to resolve satisfactorily some difficult issues associated with key tradeoffs underlying the definition of good outcomes. The problems are deep enough and have been known long enough to suggest that hopes for their early resolution are probably misguided.

6.1.1 Outcomes and Processes

Discussions of decision making and decision engineering are plagued by confusions over the multiple meanings of "intelligent," "rational," "learning," and various similar terms. In this book, and particularly in this chapter, distinctions are made among these terms. The distinctions—though not necessarily any particular nomenclature—are essential to discussions of decision engineering.

Words like "rational" and "learning" are used in two quite distinct ways. Past actions are sometimes described as "rational" or "substantively rational" if they resulted in outcomes that were deemed good. Alternatively, actions are sometimes described as "rational" or "procedurally rational" if they were made by a procedure that assesses expected consequences and chooses actions that are expected, on average, to lead to desired outcomes. Similarly, an organization is sometimes described as "learning" or "substantively learning" if its performance improved (regardless of the process by which that improvement was realized) and is sometimes described as "learning" or "procedurally learning" if it used inferences drawn from previous outcomes to adjust behavior (regardless of whether those inferences led to adjustments that improved outcomes).

The confusions between process and outcome definitions of rationality, learning, and other forms of decision making are understandable. It seems natural to believe that decision makers will generally do well if they choose actions that are expected to lead to desired consequences. Similarly, it seems natural to believe that outcomes will improve if a decision maker adjusts behavior by avoiding actions that in the past have been associated with bad things and reinforcing actions associated with good things.

Convictions that good outcomes will be achieved if decision makers follow a particular preferred process underlie much of the normative literature on decision making. In standard treatises extolling the beauties of analytical decision making, the preferred procedure is rational calculation. In standard treatises extolling the beauties of learning, the preferred procedure is experimentation and incremental change. In standard treatises extolling the beauties of fundamentalist ethics, the preferred procedure is literal consultation of sacred texts. The possibility that following the rules of decision theory, learning, or fundamentalist ethics may sometimes lead to poor outcomes is obscured by a definitional sleight-of-hand that equates outcome intelligence with process reliability.

Observations of decision making, as well as more precise specifications of the models, suggest that these presumptions are not, in general, warranted. The links between processes and outcomes cannot be assumed. They must be demonstrated.

This chapter examines questions of whether and when decision processes are likely to lead to good outcomes and the possibilities for improving those processes. The intelligence of an action is defined in terms of its *outcomes*. An action is defined as intelligent if, after all the results are in (including possible changes in preferences and identities), it has satisfied the wishes of relevant parties. In this view, intelligence is an *ex post* concept. Intelligence cannot be determined until the results are known. An outcome-based definition of intelligence excludes statements of the form: "She acted intelligently but the outcomes were poor."

An outcome-based definition of intelligence not only makes intelligence an *ex post* assessment but also makes intelligence subjective. Since the intelligence of an action is determined by the value of its outcomes, it depends on the preferences and identities of the relevant actor or actors. Normally, of course, an action is associated with a specific decision maker or set of decision makers, and its outcome is assessed in terms of the values of those decision makers (or those for whom they acted as agents). In assessing multiple actor actions, however, it may be difficult to specify the relevant decision makers, and the relevant values may be obscure. Outcome intelligence, as a result, may be indeterminate.

Rationality, learning-based rule following, coalition formation, imitation, and temporal sorting decision making are all treated here as *processes*. For example, a decision is described as "rational" if it is made by a process that follows standard procedures for choosing among alternatives in terms of expectations about future consequences. Decisions by a financial organization are rational, in these terms, if the organization makes a systematic analysis of the probable future consequences of possible alternatives and selects that alternative that maximizes expected value (regardless of whether the decisions lead to good outcomes).

Similarly, a decision process is described as being a form of "learning" if it involves changing behavior incrementally in response to feedback about performance. Thus, a manufacturing organization is described as learning if the organization responds to negative feedback on its performance by increasing the chance of changing its standard rules and responds to positive feedback by decreasing the chance of changing its standard rules (regardless of whether the learning led to improvement in performance).

Those definitions make rationality and learning *ex ante* concepts, properties of procedures and not defined by their outcomes. Rational procedures may lead to good outcomes or to poor outcomes. The remainder of this chapter examines the opportunities and limitations of various possible procedures for making decisions in organizations, including rationality, learning, multiple actor conflict, and ambiguity.

6.1.2 The Tradeoffs of Intelligence

If intelligent decision making means decision making leading to outcomes that contribute to a decision maker's well-being or to the well-being of a group, organization, or society, three difficult questions need to be addressed: (1) To what extent should a decision process and a decision be judged by their contributions to action and the consequences of action as opposed to their contributions to the development of meaning and an interpretation of life? (2) How should outcomes that are distant in time be weighted in the overall evaluation relative to outcomes that are near? (3) How should the wants, values, and needs of different individuals and groups be weighted? None of the questions has an obvious answer.

SYMBOLS AND SUBSTANCE

Decision making allocates scarce resources and achieves some of its importance in that way. At the same time, however, decision making also displays values and interprets life. Decision making is a central part of modern Western ideology. It is linked to key concepts of the Age of Reason, such as intentional human control over destiny and human will. Decision processes are imbued with symbolic content. They exhibit and reassert social beliefs, dramatize commitments to a faith of deliberate and effective human action, and provide opportunities for making individual statements that fit an individual into that faith. Decision making is organized to share stories, explanations, and symbolic meaning as well as to take action.

For example, decision makers often seem to treat the gathering and use of information as part of the pursuit of symbolic meaning rather than as part of the resolution of decision uncertainties. Gathering information and making decisions are signals and symbols of competence. The possession and exhibition of information symbolizes (and demonstrates) the ability and legitimacy of decision makers. A good decision maker is one who makes decisions in a proper way, who exhibits expertise and uses generally accepted information. Competition for reputations among decision makers stimulates production and conspicuous displays of information well beyond what is used to resolve substantive uncertainties. Decision makers gather information and do not use it; ask for more and ignore it; make decisions first and look for relevant information afterward; gather and process a great deal of information that has little or no direct relevance to decisions.

The symbolic significance of decision making can be seen as a corruption. There is little doubt that the symbolism of decisions results in misallocation of decision energy, in manipulation of the innocent by the sophisticated, and in "armaments races" as purveyors of technological and organizational gadgets induce competition in their own versions of conspicuous information consumption. From this standpoint, decision engineers may want to resist the introduction of symbolic elements into decision processes or buffer the making of decisions from their effects. The former is difficult to accomplish on a unilateral basis, but the latter offers some hope. It is sometimes possible to segregate the symbolic and substantive aspects of decision making. For example, information gathering and analysis, with its heavy symbolic significance, is sometimes buffered from the making of choices. Choices are frequently negotiated outside the context of explicit decision processes, where the rituals are more heavily symbolic. Observations of garbage can decision processes indicate that decision processes exercise problems more often than they solve them, and that the substantive choices made are frequently made outside formal decision processes.

Alternatively, decision engineers can see the development of adequate rituals and symbolism as a primary responsibility. The symbolic aspects of decision making can be embraced and elaborated as reflecting a fundamental aspect of decision intelligence. Decision making can be seen as developing myths and interpretations of life and as modifying the diffuse beliefs and cultural understandings that make events comprehensible. With that in mind, decision engineering may want to be concerned with improving the effectiveness with which decision symbols develop and maintain social beliefs about choice, reason, power, conflict, and intelligence. The object is to improve human commitment to rationality and identity, to build bases for community and diversity. Decision rituals can be constructed and performed to accomplish such ends. The main impediment is an inability of decision makers to think about meaning as fundamental, thus an inability to focus on the design of rituals and the organization of symbols.

COMPARISONS ACROSS (NESTED) TIME

Decision outcomes unfold over time. The short run is nested in the long run. Many actions that contribute to short-run well-being are deleterious in the long run, and vice versa. Moreover, preferences and identities change over time, partly as a result of taking actions. Are outcomes to be evaluated in terms of preferences and identities that existed at the time of the decision or in terms of those that exist at the time at which the effects of the decision are realized?

The complications of weighting consequences that are distributed across time constitute a prime topic in both the psychology and the economics of choice. Psychologists of individual development have long noted the difficulties involved in delayed gratification, in forgoing current pleasures in order to lay the basis for future pleasures. Individual eaters implicitly compare the immediate delights of eating chocolate cake with the more uncertain future costs of weight and health problems. Subsequently, they make the same comparison from the vantage point of time. The problem is defined as one of learning to give more weight to anticipations of delayed pain and pleasure and to give less weight to immediate pleasures and pains.

The same problem is discussed in the literature of economics, particularly in consideration of the choice between current consumption and savings (future consumption). As numerous critics of delayed gratification have observed, there is no necessary reason for giving more or less weight to expectations of future pleasures and pains then to current ones. There are pathologies of saving as well as pathologies of consumption. In standard economic treatments, the choice between savings and consumption depends on some discounting factors that are partly based on individual values (weights) and partly based on the fact that savings accumulate earnings.

Economic discussions emphasize comparing present and future costs and benefits in terms of their "present values." The idea of present value calculations is to make present and future expectations monetarily equivalent by estimating the amount of current money, properly invested, that would grow (or decline) to the level of the future expectation by the time the future has arrived. Since present value calculations are normally made in terms of money, rather than the value to the decision maker of the goods money buys, they avoid the more difficult complications involved in evaluating the future subjective value of future realizations.

Comparisons across time are particularly difficult because preferences and identities are not stable. They are changing, and changing in part as a result of decision making. It is frequently argued that the intelligence of an action should be an *ex ante* concept, that is, that a decision should make sense from the standpoint of the preferences, identities, and time values of the decision maker at the time of the decision. Such a position, however, has the disadvantage of ignoring the obvious fact that many decisions that are judged "intelligent" *ex ante* will subsequently be assessed as "unintelligent" when all of their outcomes and effects on values are finally realized.

Alternatively, it is possible to argue that the intelligence of an action is ultimately an *ex post* concept, to be assessed in terms of future values and experiences. In that case, decision intelligence cannot, in general, be determined at the time decisions are made. It can be approximated, however, particularly if decision makers attend not only to the unfolding consequences of their actions but also to the unfolding effects of their actions on their preferences and identities.

COMPARISONS ACROSS (NESTED) DECISION MAKERS

Students of decision making intelligence have ordinarily been uncomfortable with the idea of intelligence when applied to decisions involving multiple inconsistent actors. Intelligence has generally been treated as requiring consistent preferences or identities. The well-being of a decision maker may be inconsistent with that of others, as well as with the well-being of an organization or a larger community of which the decision maker is a part.

A limited form of intelligence has been found in the Pareto-preferred criterion. Where an action will not hurt anyone (in his or her own terms) and will help at least one person (in his or her own terms), taking the action seems unquestionably more intelligent than not taking it. The classic Pareto procedure is a form of unanimity in which all persons vote "yes," "no," or "don't care," and action is taken only if there are no "no" votes and at least one "yes" vote. Bilateral voluntary exchange is one such procedure.

Given the severe restrictions imposed on choice by Pareto decision rules, some social welfare theorists have sought to define procedures for weighting the preferences and identities of various people. For most decision theorists, however, interpersonal comparisons of value seem to have create unresolvable problems. How is it possible to decide whether gains to one person, measured in terms of that person's values, are greater or less than losses to another person, measured in terms of that person's values? Modern students of choice are agreed that ordinary individuals and societies do, in fact, routinely make such comparisons, but there is no agreement on a justification or procedure for doing so.

The ways in which the organization of attention provides an implicit solution to these problems was discussed earlier in the context of inconsistency in multiple actor decision making. Multiperson decision making procedures such as exchange, bargaining, coalitions, and power achieve some of their success by being embedded in a system of limited attention. If everyone could attend to everything, and did so, the possibilities for irreconcilable conflict, that is, for the failure of decision procedures to achieve acceptable choices, would be greater than they are.

Incomplete attention to inconsistencies in preferences and identities is aided by mechanisms that conceal the contradictions. Organizations are divided into departments, and labor is divided among specialists, thereby reducing the likelihood that inconsistencies cutting across divisional or specialty lines will impinge on decision making. Inconsistencies are ignored through ignorance. In this way, limited attention sacrifices global consistency for local consistency. Since not all inconsistencies are evoked, loosely coupled decision making systems operate successfully in the face of potential conflict when those that seek integration fail. The old folk wisdom is: Good fences make good neighbors.

The assessment of intelligence across individuals and groups is further complicated by their nested character. Decision making individuals are parts of decision making groups. Decision making groups are parts of decision making organizations. Decision making organizations are parts of decision making societies. Outcomes that are favorable to individuals may not be favorable to the groups, organizations, or societies of which they are parts; and vice versa.

For example, consider the problem of deciding on socialization and turnover rates in an organization. An organization socializes its members, instructing them in the organizational code. Convergence of individual beliefs and an organizational code is generally useful both for individuals and for an organization. Individuals profit from learning the rules of the organization quickly. The organizational code profits from individual experiments with new beliefs that turn out to be useful. However, a serious threat to the effectiveness of the system is the possibility that individuals will adjust to an organizational code before the code can learn from them. A combination of relatively slow socialization of new organizational members and moderate turn-over sustain needed variability in individual rules. Thus, the socialization and turnover rates that are desirable from the standpoint of the development of the organizational code are not necessarily desirable from the standpoint of every individual in it.

6.1.3 Decision Making Myopia

The dispersion of consequences over time and space is a funda-mental complication in defining decision intelligence. Actions taken here and now have consequences here and now, but they also have consequences somewhere else and some time later. Since the distant consequences, in particular, are not easily pre-dicted, tradeoffs across time and space invite some biases and prejudices.

OUT OF SIGHT, OUT OF MIND

Although moralists and decision theorists are sometimes con-cerned with the dangers of sacrificing immediate and close in-terests to those more distant, deploring excessive savings or misguided parochialism, they generally see larger perversities in biases favoring realizations that are close in time and space. The immediacy and clarity of the present and the nearby tend systematically to disadvantage the spatially and temporally dis-tant. The symbolic and substantive pleasures of the process of decision making and its immediate, nearby consequences come to dominate.

The bias toward effects that are clear and close undoubtedly introduces a tendency for decision making procedures to be in-appropriately inattentive to important concerns that are fuzzy and distant. Correcting the bias is, however, complicated by the fact that favoring the clear and the close is sometimes necessary to survive. In that sense, at least, concerns about long-term and global intelligence must always be subordinated to valid con-cerns about short-term and local intelligence.

In any event, the story of bias against the distant is told about both individuals and social systems. Individuals seem often to sacrifice their long-run interests for short-run pleasures. Brief gastronomic, alcoholic, pharmacological, symbolic, and sexual pleasures seem irresistible at the moment despite their conspicuous longer-run costs. Individuals indulge in practices when young that have adverse consequences when they are old. When consequences are dispersed among individuals, the actions that produce pleasures for some often cause pain to others. Decision makers seem to find it systematically easier to empathize with the feelings of close relatives, colleagues, compatriots, and currently visible strangers than with the feelings of more distant people. In short, there is a tendency to respond to present, local concerns and to leave the resulting long-run and more distant problems for subsequent or more distant decision makers. For example, the budget director who presided over the largest expansion of the national deficit in United States history has been quoted as saying that the job of every subsequent administration "is to distribute and administer pain." [1]

APOSTLES OF RECKONING, APOSTLES OF PROGRESS

Making an assessment of decision intelligence involves a judgment with respect to distant consequences of actions taken here and now. In this regard, the deepest division among students of decision making intelligence is the division between those who see decision making as affecting the distribution of symbols and resources over time and space but not their total amount and those who see decision making as affecting both the distribution and the total amount of symbols and resources available.

The former group might be called the apostles of *reckoning.* Their beliefs are typified by a principle: The world's resources are fixed. Whatever gains are made at one time and in one place must be paid for at another time or in another place. Ultimately, there is conservation of symbolic and substantive assets. The latter group might be called the apostles of *progress.* Their beliefs are typified by an alternative principle: The world's resources are expandable. By suitable inventions and exchanges everyone can be made better off. Symbolic and substantive assets can be augmented.

Three important modern variations on the theme of reckoning are found in theories of divine judgment, economic exploitation, and environmental tampering. The basic idea of divine judgment is that any temporal, earthly rewards and penalties for actions taken here and now have compensatory rewards and penalties in a heavenly eternity. The basic idea of economic exploitation is that spiritual or physical wealth in one place is made possible only through compensating poverty elsewhere, that richness for individuals and for states results from redistributing limited resources. The basic idea of environmental tampering is that human interventions into the ecology of the earth in order to better the lives of contemporary humans in some parts of the world inexorably reduce the quality of life for later and more distant humans. The common thread of all three theories is the idea that every gain is a loss somewhere else.

The theme of progress is basically a theme of expanding resources (or increasing efficiency in exploiting them). It finds modern representations in theories of religious conversion, theories of economic growth, and theories of scientific and technological development. The basic idea of religious conversion (or education) is that virtue can be expanded indefinitely. Each additional person who is led to Truth increases the aggregate amount of virtue in the world. The basic idea of economic growth is that allocations of disproportionate wealth to some persons at one time increase the pool of resources over time and thus ultimately the wealth of others. It is possible for everyone to be made better off and for gains now to translate into the possibility of even greater gains in the future. The basic idea of scientific and technological development is that knowledge and its practical applications increase over time, and those increases lead to increases in aggregate available symbolic and substantive resources. The common thread of all three theories is the idea that resources are expandable, that gains for one person can lead to gains for all others.

The prophets of progress are clearly less depressing than the prophets of reckoning. They offer hope that the whole universe indefinitely, rather than just a part of it briefly, can be made better. Although beliefs in the axioms of progress can be found in many places and times, they seem to be disproportionately expressed through the voices of the young, the West, and the rich. The discouragements of age, life away from the mainstream of organizational and technological elaboration, and persistent poverty all make progress seem more fantastical than believable.

Understanding the bases for divisions between the apostles of reckoning and the apostles of progress is useful for monitoring contemporary debates over religion, economic systems, science and technology, and the environment, but a resolution of the debate still leaves the criteria for intelligence ill defined. For whether one accepts a vision of reckoning or a vision of progress, one is still left with problems of intertemporal and interpersonal comparisons. One is still left with problems of the unstable and endogenous nature of preferences and identities. And one is still left with the necessity of deciding whether decision making is to be seen as an arena for developing interpretations of life or an arena for directing life.

Faced with the intractability of these problems in defining intelligence, decision engineering for the most part ignores them. It asks how decision making intelligence can be improved even in the face of uncertainty about exactly where intelligence lies. The implicit presumption is that some techniques of improvement are robust vis-à-vis alternative conceptions of intelligence. The implausibility of the presumption is counterbalanced by its necessity. In such a spirit, the remainder of the chapter examines three sets of problems involved in decision engineering. The first is the problem of improving adaptiveness, of making a more consistent match between decision makers and their environments. The second is the problem of using knowledge, of bringing what is known and knowable to bear on decisions. The third is the problem of creating meaning, of using decision making as an occasion for expanding perceptions, constituting selves, and eliciting human commitment.

6.2 Improving Adaptativeness

Decision processes strengthen their claim to intelligence when they improve the match between decisions and the demands of the decision environment. As a result, decision engineering is tied closely to an understanding of fundamental issues in theories of adaptation.

6.2.1 *Adaptive Inefficiencies*

Traditionally, the search for adaptive decision intelligence has involved trying to discover decision procedures that lead to unique and stable decisions that are (by some plausible criterion) best in a particular environment. If such procedures can be specified, they may be appropriately described as "intelligent" or "efficient." Such claims are often made for rational decision procedures and for history-dependent rule following, for example.

Assumptions of efficiency are, however, suspect. Decision processes may sometimes lead to decisions uniquely required by a decision situation, but they often will not. In fact, modern understandings of adaptive processes identify several ways in which decision processes result in outcomes that are not implicit in environments or are not unique. Those inefficiencies in matching the environment stem from some very general features of adaptation that are shared by many decision processes :

1. *Lags in matching.* Adaptation takes time. Although it is possible to imagine that decision processes improve the match between decisions and the environment, there is no guarantee that complete convergence will be achieved by any particular time. If the environment is changing, there is not even any assurance that adaptation will be fast enough to improve the match.
2. *Multiple equilibria.* Most theories of decision making are theories of local adaptation. They assume a process in which considerations close in time and close in cognitive or social distance dominate those that are more distant. Such decision making is essentially "hill-climbing," responding to local feedback, and is subject to becoming stranded at local (rather than global) maxima.
3. *Path dependency.* Decisions and outcomes in a particular environment depend not only on that environment but

also on previous environments and the ways in which they have been experienced. The historical path makes some outcomes unrealizable in the future, including some previously realized. Relatively unlikely events, if they occur, change the structure in permanent ways.

4. *Networks of diffusion.* Outcomes depend on the ways in which information spreads. Information structures isolate some decision makers and produce outcomes attributable to elements of isolation and integration. This makes the outcomes of a decision making process sensitive to patterns of connection in information networks, to changes in information technology, and to the ease with which information is incorporated by decision makers.

5. *Mutual adaptation.* Decision makers adapt to their environments at the same time as their environments are adapting to them. They discover what parts of the environment are exploitable, but the exploitability of the environment changes as a result of their having discovered it. They receive social approval or disapproval as a function of making particular decisions, but the level of approval or disapproval shifts as the number of other decision makers making similar decisions changes. These forms of mutual adaptation are likely to lead to stable outcomes that are predicted neither by the initial environment nor by a recent one.

6. *Ecologies of adaptation.* Decision makers are tied into communities of other decision makers and their decisions. Their histories are intertwined by competition, cooperation, and other forms of interaction. History cannot be seen as simply a product of one decision maker and his or her own exogenous environment. Decision makers and their environments coevolve.

The idea that history is a locally adaptive, branching process with multiple equilibria is a central feature of modern theories of change. There are irreversible branches, hence path-dependence and decisive minor moments. The branch-points often seem almost chancelike in their resolution, yet decisive in their effects on subsequent history. Though the course of development is explicable in terms of a comprehensible process, its realized course is difficult to predict.

6.2.2 *Exploration and Exploitation*

A central concern of adaptive intelligence within a path-dependent, meandering history is the relation between the exploration of new possibilities and the exploitation of old certainties. Exploration includes things captured by such terms as search, variation, risk taking, experimentation, play, flexibility, discovery, and innovation. Exploitation includes such things as refinement, choice, production, efficiency, selection, implementation, and execution. Explicit choices between exploration and exploitation are found in calculated decisions about alternative investments and strategies. Implicit choices are buried in many features of decision making rules and customs, for example, in procedures for accumulating and reducing slack, in search rules and practices, in the ways in which targets are set and changed, and in incentive systems.

In rational models of choice, the relation between exploitation and exploration is basic to theories of rational search. Choices must be made between gaining new information about alternatives and thus improving future returns (which suggests allocating part of the investment to searching among uncertain alternatives), and using the information currently available to improve present returns (which suggests concentrating the investment on the apparently best alternative). The problem is complicated by the possibilities that new investment alternatives may appear, that probability distributions may not be stable, or that they may depend on the choices made by others.

In theories of limited rationality, discussions of exploration and exploitation emphasize the role of targets in regulating risk taking and allocations to search. The usual assumption is that risk taking and search are inhibited if the most preferred alternative is above (but in the neighborhood of) the target. On the other hand, risk taking and search are stimulated if the most preferred known alternative is below the target. Because of the role of targets, discussions of risk taking and search in the limited rationality tradition emphasize the significance of the adaptive character of aspirations themselves.

In learning and selection models of rules, discussions of exploration and exploitation are framed in terms of the twin processes of variation and selection. Elimination of inferior forms, routines, or practices is essential to survival, but so also is the generation of new alternative practices, particularly in a changing environment. Because of the links among environmental turbulence, decision diversity, and competitive advantage, the efficiency of any decision process is sensitive to the relation between the rate of exploratory variation reflected by the practice and the rate of change in the environment. For example, it has been argued that the persistence of garbage can decision processes in organizations is related to the diversity advantage they provide in a world of relatively unstable environments, when paired with the selective efficiency of conventional rationality.

6.2.3 Finding a Balance

Ordinary experience teaches that social institutions often suffer from a failure to exploit what is known. Enthusiasms for creativity, new ideas, and change lead decision makers to be lax in assuring that the plumbing works, that telephones are answered, that the logistics are well managed. Glorification of exploration obscures the fact that most new ideas are bad ones, most changes are detrimental, and most original inventions are not worth the effort devoted to producing them. Decision systems that engage in exploration to the exclusion of exploitation are likely to find that they suffer the costs of experimentation without gaining many of its benefits. They exhibit too many undeveloped new ideas and too little distinctive competence. Conversely, systems that engage in exploitation to the exclusion of exploration are likely to find themselves failing to discover and develop new capabilities and new opportunities. In a changing world, they are likely to become obsolescent.

Understanding the choices and improving the balance between exploration and exploitation are complicated by the fact that returns from the two options vary not only with respect to their present expected values but also with respect to their variability, their timing, and their distribution within and beyond the organization. Processes for allocating resources between them therefore embody intertemporal, interinstitutional, and interpersonal comparisons, as well as risk preferences.

The difficulties involved in making such comparisons lead to complications in specifying appropriate tradeoffs, and in achieving them. Defining an appropriate balance is made particularly difficult by the fact that the same issues occur at several levels of a nested system—at the individual level, the organizational level, and the social system level. Achieving an appropriate level is made particularly difficult by dynamics that tend to trap decision makers in cycles of accelerating exploration or exploitation.

On the one hand, exploration can become a trap. If failure usually leads to exploration and exploration usually leads to failure, a decision maker can be trapped in a cycle of exploration, trying one new thing after another without spending long enough exploiting any innovation to secure the gains from experience that are necessary to make it fruitful. When decision processes lead to a string of inadequately exploited experiments, they are likely to be improved by interventions that inhibit exploration.

On the other hand, exploitation can also become a trap. The essence of exploitation is the refinement and extension of existing competencies, technologies, and paradigms. Its returns are positive, proximate in both time and space, and predictable. The essence of exploration is experimentation with new alternatives. Its returns are uncertain, distant in both time and space, and often negative. Strategies of exploitation that lead to locally positive outcomes are likely to come to dominate over exploratory strategies that are globally better but locally inferior. That is not an accident; it is a consequence of the temporal and spatial proximity of their effects, as well as their precision.

Those traps to exploitation stem not from stupidity but from learning. Refinements and improvements in competence associated with improving standard paradigms, conventional knowledge, and established methods provide local gains that are compelling. As they develop greater and greater competence in using existing technologies, knowledge, routines, forms, or strategies, however, decision makers become less and less willing or able to change to newer ones that offer longer-run superiority. They become better and better at an inferior practice. In this sense, at least, adaptation is self-destructive. When adaptive processes lead to greater and greater competence at existing procedures, they are likely to be improved by interventions that protect or stimulate exploration.

6.3 Using Knowledge

Decision processes presume the exploitation of knowledge. For example, rationality involves anticipating the future consequences of present actions, as well as future preferences for those consequences when they occur. The ability to use knowledge to anticipate consequences and establish preferences for them is essential. In a similar way, rule-based action demands coherent adaptation to the past. The adaptation of rules and procedures to experience involves forming inferences about the world from the events of history. The ability to use knowledge in making those inferences validly is essential.

Knowledge is a social construction. It is developed and certified within social institutions. Those institutions help to make knowledge both valid and reliable, valid in the sense that it portrays reality correctly and reliable in the sense that it is shared and reproduced among knowledgeable people. There are rules for certifying knowledge, and those rules are maintained in social institutions of research and education. The rules and their integration into institutions make knowledge inaccessible to unilateral manipulation. It is not easy for individuals or small groups to dictate what is believed. On the other hand, knowledge changes. Often knowledge at one time becomes ignorance and prejudice at another, as anyone who has read fifty-year-old textbooks in any field can testify. Those changes result from tensions between old knowledge and new challenges to it and are orchestrated in such a way that knowledge rarely wanders very far from broad socially acceptable understandings.

Decision makers try to involve themselves in the social process of forming and transmitting knowledge in order to translate that knowledge into effective action. From time to time they make mistakes or are misled. They leave some things unknown or incorrectly known. Knowledge is often elusive, and using it is often difficult, but ordinarily the benefits from knowledge make its pursuit worthwhile. Difficulties in gaining and using knowledge are mitigated by improving techniques for extracting knowledge from experience and from others.

6.3.1 Extracting Knowledge from Experience

It is well known that individuals are not particularly good interpreters of evidence, and their limitations undermine the intelligence of decision making. They make a variety of mistakes and simplifications. They learn lessons inadequately, recall memories incompletely or incorrectly, estimate futures inaccurately. They learn superstitiously, assigning causal significance to actions that are correlated with effects but not affected by them. They remember history in ways heavily dependent on their current beliefs. They confound their wishes and hopes with their expectations. They ignore useful information out of concern that it may reflect deliberate falsification.

Some features of the processes of human inference have been reviewed in earlier chapters. The limitations on inference, however, are not simply human frailties. They are also due to structural features of the environments in which decisions are made. Decision makers face four principal structural problems in understanding either the future or the past: the paucity, redundancy, ambiguity, and strategic nature of information. Mistakes of inference in the face of those problems do not simply produce random error. They also produce systematic biases.

PAUCITY OF INFORMATION

Predicting the future or learning from the past requires information adequate to assess the causal structure of the environment. Decision makers try to understand their environments on the basis of inadequate information. History is not generous with observations. Sample sizes are small. Furthermore, different samples drawn from historical experience are not easily comparable. Pooling across events involves pooling relatively dissimilar things.

For example, consider the case, discussed in Chapter 1, of situations involving very low-probability events of very high consequence. Examples might include important innovative discoveries or large-scale nuclear disasters. Most decision makers will never experience the occurrence of any particular very low-probability event. Experience is likely to lead them to believe that the chance of that event is even smaller than it is. As a result, ordinary experience is likely to lead a decision maker to be perversely pessimistic in the case of low-probability positive events (e.g. breakthrough innovative discoveries) and perversely optimistic in the case of low-probability negative events (e.g. nuclear accidents).

Systematic sampling bias is also introduced by promoting successful decision makers to positions of power and influence. Successful decision makers are inclined to attribute their own past successes to their own past actions and thereby tend to exaggerate their own capabilities for avoiding risk and producing successful outcomes in the future. By retaining and promoting successful individuals and removing or ignoring individuals who have failed, decision making systems generate strong pressures toward interpretations of the past that reinforce confidence in being able to overcome obstacles and to avoid pitfalls. Such optimism can sometimes lead to self-confident behavior that is self-confirming. But it can also lead to foolish adventures.

Overcoming the paucity of information involves both trying to increase sample sizes, which is not always easy but is usually viewed as uncontroversial, and trying to extract more information from unique cases, which is often seen as more controversial. Three suggestions have been made for improving the information content of history as it is found within the small samples of natural experience:

1. *Rich histories.* Decision makers can try to experience history more richly. Any particular historical event is a collec-

tion of smaller events, each of which can be experienced. The process of elaboration is a matter not so much of making good statistical estimates of a few variables as it is of accumulating and integrating detail.

2. *Multiple observers and multiple interpretations.* Decision makers can try to interpret experience in more ways. Given the cost of increasing sample size, increasing the number of interpretations of observations will often result in greater net return than will increasing the number of observations. Improvement comes from reducing measurement error rather than sampling error.

3. *Hypothetical histories.* Decision makers can try to experience more of the events that did not happen. Using rich descriptions of actual histories and near-histories to develop models of the processes of history, they can simulate alternative histories and estimate the likelihood not only of the realized history but also of other histories that might have happened.

Each method attempts to deal with what appears to be a small sample problem by squeezing more information out of a single case. In effect, they are criticisms of standard (large-sample) methods, which tend to extract only a single bit or two of information from a complicated event.

REDUNDANCY OF INFORMATION

Information about the world is produced by past actions in it. Past actions tend to be repeated, leading to observations that are concentrated in the same or similar situations. As has been detailed in the earlier discussion of exploration and exploitation and of risk taking, decision makers generally repeat successes. When decision makers repeat successes, their experiences become increasingly redundant. They gain little experience doing other things. Decision reliability limits evidence to phenomena in the neighborhood of current practice.

Overcoming the redundancy of information involves increasing the willingness to experiment. One way of increasing experimentation is by adding noise to measures of performance. Performance feedback that is noisy leads to arbitrary failures, thus to experimentation. The same kind of result may be achieved by sustaining other elements of confusion into the system—breakdowns of socialization, memory, and social control. When new technologies or new organizational forms make retrieval easier or harder, they disturb the balance between remembering history and forgetting it and change the rate of experimentation.

A second way to increase experimentation among successful decision makers is to increase the rate at which aspirations adjust to success. The same performance will be interpreted as either success or failure depending on a decision maker's aspiration level. Raising aspirations increases the failure rate and thus the experimentation rate. Investigations of the effects of adaptive aspirations indicate that very rapid or very slow adaptation of aspirations to past experience is usually less desirable than an intermediate rate of adaptation and that the rate of aspiration adjustment has long-run implications not only for an individual decision maker but also for populations of them.

As was observed in the discussion of risk taking in Chapter 1, however, the relation between success (or failure) and experimentation is more complicated than the simple "failure produces experimentation" hypothesis. For example, persistent failure may have deadening effects rather than stimulating ones; interpretations of outcomes may persistently exaggerate performance, thus reduce the failure rate; and experimentation may be stimulated not only by failure but also by the personal security and illusions of invulnerability produced by persistent success. As a result, managing exploration by controlling patterns of success and failure is more complicated than it might appear at first blush.

AMBIGUITY OF INFORMATION

Natural experience is difficult to interpret. As history unfolds, the drawing of inferences is seriously compromised by the difficulty of isolating causal effects from random or extraneous forces. The experimental designs of history leave many relevant variables uncontrolled. The outcomes of history occur within an endogenously changing environment that complicates the making of valid inferences about it. Measurement procedures are poorly specified and are subject to substantial subjectivity.

Overcoming the ambiguity of information involves trying to improve the experimental design of experience. When decision makers change things, they often make several small changes at the same time. Such incrementalism has much to recommend it, but it is not a very good strategy for gaining knowledge in a noisy world. Incremental decision makers find it difficult to disentangle the effects of multiple small changes in a complex environment. The effects of one change confound the effects of other changes, and the smallness of each change means any effects it may have produced tend to be lost in the confusions of history. Such problems suggest a strategy of decreasing the number and increasing the scale of changes that are made.

They also suggest a strategy of slowing the rate of adaptation to experience. In a world where there is both considerable noise in observations and simultaneous adaptation by others, fast learners tend to track noisy signals too closely and to confuse themselves by making changes before the effects of previous actions are clear. Those disadvantages of fast adjustments are often overlooked in the face of enthusiasms for fast learning as a tool of intelligence. The translation of premature inferences into action is likely not only to lead to decision mistakes but also to confuse subsequent inferences. Patience, in combination with decisiveness, is likely to yield greater gains than an alternative strategy that combines quick learning with incrementalism.

6.3.2 Extracting Knowledge from Others

Many of the capabilities of individuals are connected to their abilities to profit from the experiences, knowledge, and practices of others. Many of the capabilities of organizations are connected to their abilities to store knowledge in rules that are widely accessible. As a result, improving decision processes involves understanding how individuals and organizations appropriate the knowledge of others and what the traps and limits of appropriation may be.

Imitation leads to shared practices and beliefs, but the intelligence of the process depends not only on the speed and comprehensiveness of diffusion but also on the "quality" of the information or practice being diffused. If bad ideas spread easily, knowledge will be shared, but the sharing will not lead to intelligence. If imitation devalues the ideas or practices being diffused, the sharing of knowledge will lead to decreases in legitimacy rather than increases.

A basic advantage of knowledge is that bad ideas spread more rapidly among the ignorant than among the informed, and good ideas spread more rapidly among the informed than the ignorant. In particular, good ideas spread slowly if the knowledge necessary to their comprehension or utilization is not widely shared. This creates complications for decision makers seeking to use good new ideas generated elsewhere and for societies seeking to ensure the development, storage, and retrieval of knowledge about possible technological and policy alternatives in the absence of a current demand for them.

Individuals, business firms, schools, and public bureaucracies are able to make effective use of new ideas that are consistent with their existing competencies and technologies. If decision makers have not invested in knowledge inventories, they are not able to evaluate, adopt, and adapt new ideas. Lacking necessary knowledge, they may adopt the form but not the substance of new concepts (most recently things like "quality circles," "just-in-time" inventory and delivery systems, and "total quality management"). To facilitate the spread of ideas and their timely availability, individuals and organizations develop stockpiles of knowledge. Organizations, for example, invest in knowledge acquisition through policy analysis, libraries, experts, expert systems, and file cabinets of contingent action plans.

Determining an optimal level of investment in knowledge inventories is not easy. How can it be determined, for example, whether a decision maker is "overinvesting" in knowledge? Libraries have many books that are infrequently used; research laboratories generate knowledge that has no impact; and management information systems carry files that are rarely tapped. Does society "overinvest" in library books? In research? In information? Optimizing on investments in knowledge is particularly troublesome because the costs and benefits of knowledge are distributed quite differently over both time and space. Having knowledge when it is needed often requires an investment in knowledge that is not known to be needed at the time it is acquired. The returns from knowledge may occur in a part of the system quite different from the part where the costs are paid.

Knowledge-based abilities to imitate provide both a negative incentive for exploration (because of the difficulty of capturing the gains from one's own discoveries), and a simultaneous positive incentive (because of the resulting ease of capturing the gain's from the discoveries of others).² When the positive effects of spillover exceed the negative, decision makers should invest in the development of irrelevant fundamental knowledge. In this case, the investment in fundamental knowledge is not directed primarily toward making discoveries or inventing new policies but to developing the knowledge base required for profiting from policies and discoveries made by others.

There are two relatively stable equilibria in this story of knowledge inventories and absorptive capacity. In one equilibrium, everyone devotes substantial resources to exploring for new ideas. Most of the returns of exploration for each individual, however, do not come from that individual's discoveries—which are unlikely to be significant enough to warrant the investment. The returns come from building capacity to absorb the occasional significant discovery by others. Those returns from knowledge and absorptive capacity sustain the exploration that occasionally produces the discoveries required. In this situation no individual decision maker has an incentive to decrease exploration, nor can a new entrant gain by forgoing exploration. That is true even though the direct returns of one's own exploration are less than the costs. The equilibrium is sustained by the advantages of imitation and the inability to separate the processes that build knowledge and absorptive capacity from the processes that underlie discovery.

In the second stable equilibrium no one invests in exploration. Since the returns of exploration are primarily returns from absorbing ideas generated elsewhere, those returns are insignificant if no one else is engaging in exploration. As long as no one else is engaging in exploration, there is inadequate incentive for any individual participant—or potential new entrant—to do so.

The knowledge inventory and absorptive capacity story suggests that the problems of intelligent imitation are not only individual problems but also system problems. Any system of decision makers is at a serious disadvantage if it is trapped at an equilibrium with low investment in accumulating knowledge. The advantage of the high-investment equilibrium comes in the first instance from the increased ease of appropriating and using good new ideas effectively and, as a byproduct, the generation of occasional good ideas. If the high-investment alternative is the better one, it cannot easily be achieved through autonomous action of intelligent individual actors starting from a low-investment equilibrium.

PROFITING FROM THE RULES OF OTHERS

Students of decision making have studied the spread of practices, forms, and norms through populations of decision makers. They emphasize the importance to any given decision maker of acting in a way that is appropriate. The argument is that decision makers who follow appropriate rules gain legitimacy as decision makers, and that legitimacy facilitates survival.

The spread of rules, forms, and practices is sometimes imposed by edict of governmental agencies, customers, or professional or trade associations. It sometimes results from contacts among decision makers. This copying is facilitated by involvement in a network and influenced by position in that network. That is, decision makers who are embedded in networks of other decision makers use those networks not only to improve information flows and channels of influence, but also to learn how to behave in a way that makes them legitimate decision makers. Occupying similar positions in a network makes imitation more likely, and imitation across status differences is more likely to occur from high status to low status than in the other direction.

The spreading of rules follows a natural dynamic. In the most common situation, increases in the number of adopters of a rule increases the likelihood of adoption by any particular decision maker who is not currently using the rule. The more universal the rule, the greater the value in using it. In such a situation, each current user of a rule gains legitimacy from each other user. This gain provides a strong incentive to encourage imitation, and users seek to convert nonusers. In some situations, however, the relation between legitimacy and the spread of rules is more complicated. Secrets, for example, have the property that they lose value as they gain converts. Fads have the property that, up to a point, an increase in users increases the legitimacy of each, but beyond that point additional users decrease the appeal.

MATCHING SITUATIONS TO REPERTOIRE INVENTORIES

When decision making is organized by a logic of consequence, problems and alternatives are ordinarily taken as given, and the information problem is primarily a matter of establishing the likelihood of various possible consequences conditional on choice of one of the alternatives. That is the conception underlying the design of many decision support systems. It emphasizes information about the future in order to allow choice in the present.

Such uses of information are certainly common, but they are probably less characteristic of decision makers than a somewhat different mode. Rather than look for information about consequences to resolve a choice among alternatives, decision makers scan their environments for surprises and solutions. They often do not recognize a "problem" until they have a solution. They operate in a recognition/appropriateness mode. They look for a match between a situation and practices, preferences, and identities they have in their repertoire library.

In such a mode, identities and response repertoires are ordinarily taken as given, and the information problem is primarily one of recognizing a situation. A rule-following decision maker is more interested in timely information about the state of the world as it unfolds than in probability estimates of a possible future. The presumption is that appropriate action will be known immediately, once the situation is revealed. As a result, monitoring support systems emphasize early warnings of clear opportunities and dangers over estimates of distant possibilities.

A monitoring system scans the environment for current events that require a change in performance routines. It thrives on networks of informers, gossip, disorderly information, and quick, clear signals of surprises. A consequence assessment information system tries to organize systematic information relevant to understanding possible futures. It thrives on analysis, orderly information, and deliberation. Both types of information systems are useful to decision intelligence, but a system designed to do the first will not do a very good job on the second, and vice versa. Since information-monitoring systems tend to receive less attention than information-analysis systems in theories of decision, the panoply of formal information retrieval and communication, as well as the technology of information, tends to be oriented to the latter.

An information strategy of monitoring for surprises implies that the response repertoires of a decision maker are adequate to deal with whatever situations may be discerned. This, in turn, implies a second aspect to decision information. Since rule-following decision makers want to respond quickly to new situations, they must continually update their capabilities for response, gathering information and training in competencies that may be needed in the future. Those inventories of programs imply a view of information that is more like that of a good library than that of a system pointed to a small set of specific decisions.

As a result, ideas about the engineering of decision making should include "early warning" systems and systems to facilitate timely response and effective imitation. They probably need to be oriented less to anticipating uncertain future consequences than to scanning and interpreting ambiguous environments; tied less to evaluating a specified set of alternatives than to a wide spectrum of knowledge relevant to actions impossible to anticipate precisely; less likely to illuminate the consequences of known alternatives for known goals than to recognize situations and pair them with established routines.

6.3.3 Complications of Knowledge

Intelligence is inconceivable without knowledge, but knowledge also poses problems for decision intelligence. In particular, it is worth noting that substitutes for knowledge can interfere with improving knowledge, that knowledge does not always yield advantage in a competition for primacy, and that the political nature of knowledge gives advantages to some decision makers at the expense of others.

KNOWLEDGE SUBSTITUTES

As was noted in the discussion of competency traps, competence at one technology or procedure can substitute for, and therefore inoculate against gaining competence at and using, another, possibly superior, one. In the same way, when other available capabilities can substitute for knowledge, knowledge is less likely to be pursued. Knowledge substitutes make knowledge less valuable, at least in the short run. People who can see are, by virtue of that competence, less likely to learn sign language. Two conspicuous forms of knowledge inoculation are found in technique and power.

Substituting Technique for Creativity. Much of knowledge is arranged hierarchically, proceeding from basic principles or paradigms through intermediate propositions to immediate observables. As decision makers seek to increase knowledge, they deal simultaneously with several levels of their knowing. For example, students learn how to function within a given paradigm and simultaneously to learn what paradigm to use. The latter learning is sometimes called higher-order learning, double-loop learning, insight, creativity, or consciousness raising. The former might be called gaining competence or technique.

New higher-order knowledge is particularly valuable but is also a particularly difficult kind of knowledge to gain from either education or personal experience. Normal processes of education tend to strengthen awareness of socially accepted basic principles and paradigms and to protect against alternative frames. A well-educated physicist or geographer is one who knows well what is accepted as knowledge within those fields. Similarly, experience ordinarily protects higher-order beliefs. As experience is accumulated, improvements in technique *within* a schema confuse comparisons *among* schemata. In the course of augmenting knowledge about how to function within a set of principles or frames, decision makers compromise their willingness and ability to consider alternative paradigms.

In this way, the process of becoming more competent is self-destructive. Michael Polanyi, commenting on one of his contributions to physics, observed: "I would never have conceived my theory, let alone have made a great effort to verify it, if I had been more familiar with major developments in physics that were taking place. Moreover, my initial ignorance of the powerful, false objections that were raised against my ideas protected those ideas from being nipped in the bud."[3]

For most decision makers, therefore, the problem of multi-level knowing is a problem of exploring alternative frames in the face of the well-established and well-recognized technique they have at using an existing one. In practice, because technique is an inoculation against a paradigm shift, rather little higher-order learning is secured from experience or from orderly searches for knowledge. Fundamental assumptions come from paradigm peddlers and paradigm politics, social processes of persuasion and reinterpretation that are part of the trade of teachers, preachers, gurus, writers, and consultants. The process, as has often been observed, involves fitful transitions from one stable set of beliefs to another.

Substituting Power for Learning. Adaptive decision making is predicated upon skill at understanding the environment and responding to it. Many adaptive strategies involve monitoring the environment, understanding its causal structure, storing inferences drawn from that understanding, and retrieving the implications of those inferences at appropriate times and places. Decision makers who engage in such activities have abilities that are augmented by their experience in dealing with an uncertain but possibly comprehensible environment. The skills are learnable and vital to intelligent action.

Not all decision makers develop talents in such activities, however. Some decision makers are buffered from attention to the environment by a combination of pig-headedness and luck. They believe they know what is right and pursue their course without attention to signals from the environment. In rare cases, they turn out to be right and conquer the world. In even rarer cases, their luck continues into their next revelation.

Other decision makers are protected from the environment by their power: Domineering parents with children; domineering bosses with subordinates; domineering paradigms with scientists; domineering firms with other firms in their industries; domineering countries in the world order. The powerful do not attend to the environment, because their power makes them immune to its threats. They become the environment, forcing others to adapt to them. They develop skills at unilateral leadership, at command. It is a familiar story in interpersonal life, in science, in markets, and in world politics.

A conspicuous problem with such power, however, is that it is poor preparation for loss of dominance. Children grow up; subordinates revolt; new paradigms arise; new firms challenge market position; national preeminence declines. Decision makers who have little experience with observing, understanding, and reacting to changes in the environment lose the capability to do so. Their power to impose a world undermines knowing how to cope with a world that cannot be unilaterally controlled. As their skills at imposing environments grow, their skills at adapting to an environment atrophy. Subsequent losses of power tumble decision makers into worlds requiring skills that they lack.

There is no magic solution to the inoculations against knowledge provided by technique and power. Efforts to strengthen performance through improving technique or power interfere with efforts to redefine broad principles. It is a variation on one of the most familiar features of the exploration/exploitation dilemma—the competency trap. It is quite possible for technique or power within an established system of knowledge to become great enough to preempt higher-order knowledge or capabilities.

DILEMMAS OF COMPETITIVE DISADVANTAGE

Societies, institutions, and individuals compete with one another, using their knowledge in pursuit of competitive advantage. The consequences of changes in knowledge on the part of one competitor depend on changes in the knowledge held by others in ways that may not be immediately obvious. In particular, as was observed in Chapter 1, knowledge has a mixed effect on competitive advantage. Knowledge makes action reliable and thereby reduces variability, and reductions in variability can be costly in a competition for primacy.

Suppose realized performance on a particular occasion is a draw from a probability distribution of performance. We can characterize this distribution by some measure of average performance, which might be called "ability," and some measure of variability, which might be called "unreliability." Gains in knowledge are typically associated with improving average performance and reliability, thus with increasing the mean and decreasing the variance of the performance distribution. The increase in reliability restricts the competitive advantage to be gained from knowledge, particularly when the number of competitors is large. More precisely, if increased reliability has the effect of reducing the right-hand tail of the distribution, increased knowledge may easily decrease the chance of being best among several competitors, even though it increases average performance. Some highly variable competitor is almost certain to be best.

The question is whether one can do exceptionally well, as opposed to better than average, without leaving the confines of conventional action and socially certified knowledge. The answer is complicated, for it depends on a more careful specification of the kind of knowledge involved and its precise effects on the right-hand tail of the performance distribution. But knowledge that simultaneously increases average performance and its reliability is not a guarantee of competitive advantage. As a result, the role of the pursuit of knowledge in achieving and sustaining competitive primacy is mixed.

THE POLITICS OF KNOWLEDGE

Intelligent decision making requires coping with the political uses and consequences of knowledge. On the one hand, the use of knowledge makes decision makers dependent on knowledge providers, therefore vulnerable to manipulation. On the other hand, knowledge itself is not neutral politically. Knowledge frames approaches to problems and shapes decision possibilities in ways that favor some alternatives and interests and disadvantage others.

Strategic Nature of Knowledge. Decision-related knowledge is rarely innocent. It is tainted by the way it is generated and by the context in which it is presented. Most knowledge is subject to strategic misrepresentation. As a result, systems of information and knowledge are instruments of power that favor those who can control them at the expense of those who cannot.

Those problems become particularly severe in modern contexts where specialization in knowledge and short lead times on decisions cause decision makers to make spot contracts for the provision of decision-relevant knowledge. As organizations move toward knowledge and competence inventories that are represented by markets in contract services, rather than a collection of in-house skills, the politics of knowledge acquisition and utilization becomes particularly germane to intelligent decision engineering.

Procedures for overcoming the strategic nature of knowledge are key elements of classical political theory treatments of the role of experts and of modern economic theories of information. The latter have been considered briefly in section 3.3.3.

Decision makers are sensitive to their vulnerability to the lack of innocence in knowledge and wary of relying on strategically manipulable evidence. Everyone knows that a sales representative has incentives for exaggerating a product's good qualities. Everyone knows that a manager or worker has incentives for underestimating how long a job will take or how much it will cost when seeking to have a job approved, and for overestimating how long it will take or how much it will cost when negotiating a budget for a job once approved.

Because everyone knows such things, everyone makes adjustments in evaluating the evidence. But because everyone also knows that everyone knows such things, sales representatives, managers, and workers are involved in a potentially explosive escalation of biases and counter-biases. Consider, for example, the language of praise in the film industry, where the meaning of unstinting enthusiasm is ambiguous, and anything less than "magnificent" or "genius" is treated (correctly) as an insult.

The pathologies are familiar to anyone who has considered the uses of information and knowledge where preferences or identities are inconsistent. Faced with the possibility of strategically manipulated information, decision makers try to ensure that the preferences and identities of knowledge providers are consistent with their own. They seek to assure either the loyalty of knowledge providers or their neutrality. The neutrality of knowledge providers is a goal of many conceptions of professionalism in which the mark of a professional is seen as the capability to render advice uncontaminated by concern about its decision consequences. Desires to assure the loyalty of information providers make decision makers likely to consult friends or relatives, rather than comparably trained others, and to seek to make those who provide knowledge dependent on them for resources. Loyalty, of course, has the potentially dysfunctional complication that it may shield decision makers from adverse information that might help them to recognize mistakes.

Alternatively, decision makers try to decouple themselves from dependence on knowledge providers. In the course of decoupling themselves from specific knowledge providers, however, they tend to decouple their decisions from knowledge. One response is to use "intuition" or "prior estimates" to make decisions, thus avoiding the updating of basic beliefs with contemporary information. Because the information used in decision making is strategic, it is treated as unreliable and less important for decision making. Decoupling strategies are often characteristic of socially peripheral individuals or groups. They feel sufficiently estranged from prime sources of information that they reject all external claims to knowledge.

The Nonneutrality of Knowledge. Political problems with knowledge extend beyond the conscious manipulation of knowledge by knowledge providers. Knowledge itself plays political favorites. That is well known with respect to technological and scientific knowledge. The computer/information revolution, for example, has considerably disadvantaged public policies of individual privacy. The development of nuclear weapons of mass destruction changed the political position not only of nations but also of groups within nations. The nonneutrality of knowledge is also well known with respect to political and social knowledge. Research on individual voting behavior has transformed not only political campaigning but also the whole structure of democratic responsiveness, to the detriment of citizens who favor a Burkean perspective on representation.

The political biases of knowledge can be illustrated by looking at American economics and sociology. The biases of interest here do not stem from the fact that American economists, as a group, and American sociologists, as a group, exhibit quite different political party preferences. The biases come from the nature of economic and sociological domains of knowledge, the way they are organized, the factors they consider, the visions of humankind they assume, the questions they formulate, and the way they frame answers to them.

Economics imagines the world as a system of voluntary exchange among actors who are endowed with wants and resources and who seek to satisfy their own wants by trading their own resources for the resources of others. It is a conception that favors decisions oriented to improving the conditions of exchange, assuring that no mutually satisfactory trades are overlooked. It tends to treat the initial conditions of exchange (wants and resources) as given. As a body of knowledge, economics is an ally of decision makers who prefer to take individual wants, identities, and resources as inviolate. Decision makers who are concerned about the initial distribution of wants and resources in a system of exchange will find economics as a body of knowledge less helpful.

Sociology, on the other hand, imagines the world as a system of norms, belongings, and identities that sustain themselves through socialization and maintain a social order. It is a conception that favors decisions oriented to modifying the norms, belongings, and identities. It tends to treat wants and resources as subject to social control. As a body of knowledge, sociology is an ally of decision makers who prefer to change individual wants, identities, and resources. Decision makers who are concerned with the problems of arranging efficient exchanges among individuals in a society will find sociology as a body of knowledge less helpful.

The differences are not the standard ones of specialization. It is not so much that economics and sociology look at different things as that they look at the same things differently. The different ways they have of looking at the world translate into decision advantages and disadvantages for others. In a similar way, any body of knowledge fits the needs of some interests and does not fit others. Medical knowledge organized around treating sick people is different in its decision implications from medical knowledge organized around keeping healthy people from becoming sick. Historical knowledge organized around the nation state leads to different decision implications from historical knowledge organized around international networks. Legal knowledge organized around conceptions of "law" has different decision implications from legal knowledge organized around conceptions of "justice." The former privileges legislators, rulers, and judges; the latter privileges vigilantes, zealots, and juries.

6.4 Creating Meaning

Decision making presupposes meaning, an understanding of the way things are and might be, a basis for engaging others in discourse about what is possible and what has happened. Those meanings are often interpretations of fate and nature, but they are human constructions, and decision processes are one of the sites within which the constructions take place.

6.4.1 Expanding Awareness

Decision processes use language and symbols to create and communicate meaning. They are threatened by two dangers in the use of language. The first is that *explicit* meaning will be lost, that what one person intends to say will not be understood by another, that specific knowledge will be degraded and manifest feelings obscured. Concerns over this danger dominate those theories of communication in decision making that draw their inspiration from the transmission of electrical signals. In metaphors taken from such theories, optimal communication is portrayed as the precise reproduction by a receiver of a sequence of overt meanings coded and transmitted by the sender.

The second danger is that *implicit* meaning will be lost, that what one person says without being entirely conscious of saying it will not be heard, that specific knowledge will not be enlarged and interpreted, and that feelings will not be elaborated. The quest for order excludes the ambiguous features of life and those human reactions to them that are at the heart of imagination and artistic comprehension. Sometimes expanding understanding involves taking things that seem clear and making them ambiguous.

Concerns over this second danger dominate those theories of communication in decision making that draw their inspiration from poetry and the arts. The emphasis is on creating and interpreting evocative ambiguity. Evocative ambiguity uses language (or other media) to stimulate meaning. Rich meanings are drawn from the resonances and deep structure of language, meanings that are not transparent to the writer or speaker but are generated from the particular language chosen. Communication, in these terms, is the art of crafting such evocativeness. In this spirit, T. S. Eliot once commented on a critic's discussion of his poem "The Love Song of J. Alfred Prufrock" by writing that the analysis made by the critic "was an attempt to find out what the poem meant—whether that was what I had meant it to mean or not. And for that I was grateful."[4]

Propounding a theory of artistic imagination may be a bit beyond the present book, but it should be noted that artistic meaning draws on a spirit different from that of information theory. It uses evocative ambiguity to expand awareness. Evocative ambiguity is far from noise or arbitrary symbols. The poet creates meaning without fully comprehending the meaning that has been created, but the words are chosen carefully to elicit the imagination of language. Poetry and art encourage the simultaneous adoption of a vision and the recognition of its unreality. They affirm life in the face of absurdity. They are comfortable with multiple, contradictory meanings and with the simultaneous truth and falsity of beliefs. In a similar way, decision makers create ambiguity not to confuse but to stimulate, not to obscure meaning but to discover it. Communications are constructed to gain access to the imagination and to knowledge carried in words and visual stimuli. In the world of evocative decision making, memoranda become forms of poetry; plans become forms of sculpture; meetings become forms of theater.

In order to promote evocative ambiguity to an appropriate place in its repertoire, decision engineering probably should ground part of its character in theories of history, jurisprudence, language, culture, art, and criticism. Historical interpretation involves the exploration of possible histories and understanding the efficiencies and inefficiencies of the accumulation of history in tradition and belief. Theories of legal interpretation consider the ways in which the meanings of laws and legal concepts evolve through an interplay of self-interested pressures and contemplative elaboration of meaning. Theories of language examine the ways in which communication exploits the structure of language to capture and impart meaning that is fully comprehended neither by the writer nor by the reader. Theories of culture explore the ways cultural development reflects adaptation to, and enactment of, a changing symbolic environment. Theories of art and criticism treat good information engineering not as a passive or manipulative activity in a decision scheme or a program of learning, but as an instrument of appreciative interpretation.

The aspirations are, of course, too grand for the instruments at hand, and it would be foolish to imagine that the design and use of decision making processes can result in solutions to such ancient problems. It may be helpful, however, to judge decision making in terms of its evocativeness, its power to provide not just confirmation of familiar orders but also intimations of alternative orders, not just communication of what is known but a transformation of what is knowable.

6.4.2 *Constituting the Self*

Among the many aspects of meaning that are shaped within decision making processes, few are more important than the understandings individuals have of their preferences and their identities. Values, goals, wants, and other conceptions of the self emerge from the process of making decisions. Facilitating intelligent transformations of preferences and identities is a prime task of decision engineering.

Theories of limited rationality and rule following tend to take preferences and identities as given. Decision makers are assumed to be endowed with wants and conceptions of selves and to act upon them, but the sources of those endowments are left unclear. If the origins of preferences and identities are considered at all, they are generally treated as buried in some inexplicable cultural and social process of socialization and development that occurs primarily in childhood.

This sometimes leads to a curious difference in the ways theories of decision making treat adults and children. Adults are assumed to have well-defined preferences and identities. Their decisions are predicated on those givens but do not affect them. Children, on the other hand, are seen as developing preferences and identities. Their decisions are seen as ways in which they develop (or engineer) themselves, moving from a condition in which preferences and identities are ambiguous and inconsistent to a condition in which they are clear and consistent.

The distinction made between adults and children is too sharp. The preferences and identities of adults, like those of children, can be molded within decision making processes. Decision makers can discover values, aspirations, and self-conceptions in the process of making decisions and experiencing their consequences. The aspirations that allow decision makers to distinguish successes from failures can themselves be transformed in the process of decision making. By observing their own actions, decision makers can learn what they want and who they are. When decision makers feel responsible for their actions or feel in a positive mood, they are particularly inclined to see an outcome as successful and to define their preferences and identities in a way that is consistent with it.

Suppose decision making is treated as a way of creating preferences and identities at the same time as preferences and identities are treated as a basis for decisions and their justification. In order to use decision making as a conscious basis for constructing the self, decision makers have to combine logics of consequence and appropriateness with a technology of foolishness. They need to think about action now as being taken in terms of a set of unknown future preferences or identities. They need ways to do things for which they currently have no good reason. In that sense, at least, they need sometimes to act before they think.

The engineering problem is to find ways of helping decision makers experiment with doing things for which they have no good reason, to construct their conceptions of themselves. Five things have been suggested as possible:

1. *Treat the self as a hypothesis.* Conventional thinking about decision making allows doubts about everything except the one thing about which there is often the greatest doubt—the self. Suppose decision making is defined as a time for testing alternative preferences and identities. Decision makers can treat decision making less as a process of deduction or negotiation and more as a process of gently upsetting preconceptions of what is desirable or appropriate.

2. *Treat intuition as real.* It is not clear what intuition is. Perhaps it is simply an excuse for doing what decision makers want to do when they cannot explain why they want to do it. Perhaps it is some inexplicable way of consulting memories or ideas that are inaccessible to standard theories of thought. Whatever it is,

a belief in intuition strengthens the case for actions that are otherwise indefensible.

3. *Treat hypocrisy as a transition.* Hypocrisy is an inconsistency between behavior and asserted preferences or identities. It incurs opprobrium both because it reflects inconsistency and because it appears to combine the pleasures of vice with the rewards of virtue. The onus on hypocrisy, however, inhibits foolishness. A decision maker with good-sounding talk may be a person experimenting with being good in other ways. It may be more sensible to encourage the experimentation than to condemn it.

4. *Treat memory as an enemy.* Rules of consistency and coherent selves require memory. For most purposes good memories make good choices. Memories accumulate experience and permit learning. But the ability to forget, or overlook, may also be useful. A decision maker who cannot recall what was done yesterday or does not know what others are doing today may act within a system of consistent rationality or rule-following and nevertheless act foolishly.

5. *Treat experience as a theory.* Learning is based on a series of conclusions about history that people have invented to understand experience. Interpretations of history, and thus experience, can be changed retrospectively. By changing the interpretation of history now, decision makers can revise what they learned earlier and reconstruct self-conceptions.

Each of these suggestions represents a way to suspend temporarily the operation of a system of reasoned consistency. They are also potentially dangerous. They make the greatest sense in situations, which occur in much decision making, where there has been an overlearning of the virtues of logics of consequence and appropriateness.

A second requirement for a technology of foolishness is some strategy for suspending imperatives toward consistency. Knowing which of several foolish things might be done is not enough. There is still the problem of actually doing it. The most natural answer is that decision makers escape consistency through playfulness. Play allows action that is "unintelligent," "irrational," "out of character," or "foolish." Such action explores alternative ideas of possible purposes and alternative visions of identities while retaining a basic commitment to the necessity of order and seriousness. In order for individual decision makers to function effectively, organizations and societies need to maintain both playfulness and consistency as aspects of intelligence. Organizations can be playful even when the participants in them are not. Organizational play is encouraged by temporary relief from control, coordination, and communication.

6.4.3 Eliciting Commitment

Decision making normally presumes commitment, the willingness of decision makers both to devote time and energy to deciding and to accept responsibility for the uncertain consequences of their actions. Designing effective decision processes involves creating a motivational basis for such a commitment that is consistent with the human spirit and does not create more problems than it solves.

KNOWLEDGE AND ACTION

The usual modern motivational basis for great action lies in hopes for great consequences, but those hopes are persistently undermined by the many ways in which history frustrates them. The more one knows about the world, the less inclined one is to embrace a vision of deliberate human control over history, and the less one is willing to make the commitment demanded from decision makers. It is a commonplace observation about aging and experience that they undermine confidence in the efficacy of decision making, that only the youthful, the inexperienced, and the very successful retain a belief that they can affect destiny by their own actions. Experience and knowledge convert the ambitious into cynics and encourage either passivity or the crass pursuit of immediate personal pleasure.

Saying when, where, how, or why a decision occurs typically becomes more difficult as one understands decisions better. Showing whether a particular decision fits into a particular identity, or determining the consequences of a decision and attributing consequences to actions, is a complicated problem in historical analysis. As a result, the commitment necessary to make and implement decisions is undermined. Not only is it hard to make intelligent decisions, it is hard to say that thinking about the making of decisions is a sensible way of thinking about life. The ideology of choice conflicts with the realities of knowledge.

It is not necessary to embrace the more extreme forms of this view to recognize that knowledge can be inimical to making decisions. Knowledge seems to increase questions at a faster rate than it increases answers. It provides too many qualifications, recognizes too much complexity. One American President said that he wished he could find a one-handed adviser. Most of his advisers would tell him one thing and then say "but on the other hand" and add several contradictory observations. The more knowledge they had, the more complicated the world seemed to them. They saw the difficulties, the interconnectedness of things, the second- and third-order effects of simple actions.

Decision making seems to invite a different kind of style from that of knowledge. Decisions require clarity, closure, and confidence. As a result, decisive action comes more easily from the ignorant than from the wise, more easily from the short-sighted than from those who anticipate the long run. Hamlet bemoaned the way the "native hue of resolution is sicklied o'er with the pale cast of thought"[5]—the contradiction between thoughtfulness and action. This cliché of literature—that the pursuit of knowledge is inconsistent with making decisions—has some basis. Knowledge creates both arrogance and doubts. Arrogance supports action, but doubts undermine it.

The contrast between the timorousness of knowledge and the assertiveness of decision can be seen in decision making meetings. Meetings often begin by consulting knowledge, by making sure that experts are heard and considerations are aired. But before long, meetings become instruments of confidence building. Participants reassure each other that the decision is right, that it is supported by logic and by evidence. Without such reassurance and the collective curtain it draws on individual knowledge, informed decision making is hard, for knowledge accentuates uncertainty about the efficacy of action.

Despite the encroachments of knowledge, one thing that seems obvious about the human estate is the persistence of human ambitions for significance. Myths of importance, the idea of vision and its implementation, the idea of meaningful action, and the idea of human will are not only ancient traditions but also conspicuous parts of contemporary human faith. Support for decisiveness in decisions in actions normally comes from one of three different sources: hopes for consequence, pursuit of identity, or arbitrary willfulness. Each contributes to maintaining commitment, and each has its difficulties.

Hopes for Consequence. Some people come to believe that there is, in fact, a role for decisive human action in determining the course of history. Some find hope in a general sense that human destiny is within human control. Others find hope in the way in which path-dependent, branching histories are sensitive to small interventions at particular points. Those beliefs may be illusions, as many students of history would say they are; but they are beliefs that are conspicuous and are supported by many other students of history.

A few of the individual and social mechanisms by which decision makers develop confidence in their own capabilities for affecting action have already been described. When great commitment demands great expectations but history cannot provide them with clarity, myths of heroes are invented. Stories are told in which the flow of history is attributed to the intentions, strategies, and virtues of individual decision makers. The routines of decision making are orchestrated to confirm those visions of significance. Information is gathered and reported to symbolize the importance of decision makers. Meetings are held to symbolize that decision makers are in control. Memoranda, procedures, and rhetorics of action symbolize the importance of decision making.

Those rituals and ceremonies of decision making are reinforced by interpretations of the career experiences of decision
makers. People who are successful normally discover ample
grounds in their experience to sustain a belief in their significance. The stories they tell develop a story line that promotes
such a belief among readers and listeners. Hierarchical promotion systems in which individuals compete for decision making
authority on the basis of past performances make it likely that
individuals with decision making authority will be relatively un-
encumbered by doubts about their capabilities for making a difference. People who are promoted in a hierarchy are generally
more resistant to false beliefs in impotence than to false beliefs
in control. Similarly, an educational system organized by promotion on the basis of success predisposes those who are promoted to believe in possibilities for human control.

The usefulness of mythic stories of decision maker significance does not depend entirely on their truth. Any rush to sophisticated doubt about the possibilities for significant action
should not ignore the extent to which a belief in heroic consequences can sustain commitment to meet unreasonable demands on decision makers. "Take away an ordinary person's illusions," says Dr. Relling, "and you take away happiness at the
same time."

The issues extend beyond individual dreams of happiness,
however. There are potential social costs in a loss of confidence
in human significance by decision makers. Consider two general
types of errors a decision maker might make in assessing the
importance of intentional actions in controlling history. A decision maker might make a "false positive" error of coming to believe in considerable personal control over outcomes when, in
fact, that control does not exist. Such a belief would lead to (fu-
tile) attempts to control events, but it would not otherwise affect results. Alternatively, a decision maker might make the
"false negative" error of coming to believe personal control is
not possible when, in fact, it is. Such a belief would lead to self-
confirming withdrawal from efforts to make a difference. The
social costs of the first type of error seem small relative to the
second. Given a choice, most people would probably prefer a

society that errs on the side of making false positive errors in assessing human significance rather than false negative errors.

Heroic myths constructed on ambiguous histories present one important difficulty, however—the vulnerability of decision making to intelligent doubt about the myth. Decision makers of judgment and intelligence find it hard to believe unconditionally in their own significance. Great expectations become questionable, and enduring the frustrations of decision making seems to require either blindness to the ambiguities of history or an irrational acceptance of costs without likely benefits. Hence the standard dilemma of intelligent decision makers: They must choose between maintaining a belief in a myth of history that they see as dubious and abandoning their commitment to the significance of their roles.

Pursuit of Identity. The dilemma posed by belief in decision efficacy is real, but it depends on the assumption that great action requires great expectations. There is another grand human tradition for justifying great action, one that uncouples heroic commitment from hopes for consequence and connects it to a conception of self. The vision is one of obligations rather than expectations, of a logic of appropriateness rather than of consequence, and of a sanity of identity rather than rationality. Enthusiasm and commitment stem from a willingness to embrace the claims of identity, from a desire to achieve consistency with an internal sense of self.

Decision maker identities are learned in the same way other social identities are learned, though instruction, imitation, and elaboration of what it means to be an acceptable decision maker. Those identities are grounded in cultural commitments to individuation through the making of choices and the acceptance of responsibility for them. Personhood is associated with making decisions: choosing an education, an occupation, a marriage, a family, a place to live, and a time to die. When this commitment to life as the making of choices permeates identities, the denial of decision making is tantamount to the denial of self. To question the existence of decision options or to exhibit passivity in the face of them is to reject one's identity as a human being. Action is sustained by socialization into a sense of its necessity.

Obligations form the basis of commitment within old traditions of honor, duty, self-respect, and self-actualization. Those traditions also have problems. They have often been used to justify stupidity, obstructionism, and tyranny. But they offer a counterbalance to exclusive reliance on a logic of consequence. Decision making can be seen as driven less by personal incentives or heroic expectations than by obligation to a sense of self.

Arbitrary Willfulness. In some traditions of human action, commitments to seek a better world do not depend on clear visions of preferences or identities, and willingness to try does not depend on confidence in success or in obligations to self. These bases are, from this point of view, inimical to commitment, because human commitment should be an arbitrary expression of will. It is precisely because decisions are without consequence and are irrelevant to identity that they have significance. By acting decisively in decision making without any legitimate reason, the decision maker creates meaning in an arbitrary expression of aesthetics or faith.

This vision of arbitrary action is reflected in the Kierkegaardian observation that any religion that can be justified is hardly a religion. The conventional word is "faith," an irrational, selfless commitment that achieves its status precisely by its inconsistency with reason or with self. The medical/legal word is "insanity." The decision making structures that have traditionally sustained faith and insanity are the structures of family, ethnicity, religion, and nation.

From this perspective, the irrelevance of decisions and the inconsequential role of human intention in human destiny are not justifications for inaction but a basis for rejoicing in action. If decision making were to make sense because of its consequences, then it would be nothing more than economics. If decision making were to make sense because of its consistency with an identity, then it would be nothing more than sociology. But if decision making makes sense neither as a pursuit of objectives nor as the fulfillment of an identity, then it represents the ultimate declaration of individuality, the right to freedom from concern about consequences and identity, the proclamation of an aesthetic of human life. Don Quixote said: "For a knight-errant to make himself crazy for a reason warrants neither credit nor thanks; the point is to be foolish without justification." [7]

THE PURSUIT OF INTELLIGENCE

The indeterminacies of decision intelligence and the complications in achieving it make the pursuit of decision intelligence frustrating. Although individuals and societies have long struggled with issues of balancing the short run and the long run, coping with the shifting nature of preferences and identities, balancing benefits to some with costs to others, and weaving the symbolic and substantive elements of decisions together, modern theories of collective decision making over time are conspicuous for their failure to resolve such problems in the definition of decision intelligence. The problems of endogenously changing preferences and identities are beyond the reach of any current formulations. And the symbolic content of decision making is alternately treated as corrupt, paramount, or irrelevant.

Efforts to improve the practical procedures of intelligent decision making without worrying about a precise definition of intelligence seem similarly frustrating. A fruitful balance between exploration and exploitation is persistently upset by dynamics of adaptation that lead decision makers to excess of one or the other. Gaining knowledge from experience or from others is persistently confounded by limitations in individual and organizational capabilities. And efforts to develop useful technologies of foolishness and poetic ambiguity to complement technologies of reason and information clarity seem to run into substantial ideological resistance.

Any reasonable contemplation of that record of failure erodes confidence in the idea that decision making and the expectations of meaningful action that it implies are plausible routes to a moral life. It is hard to be confident that any decision process will yield decisions that can be unambiguously described as intelligent. History is cluttered with decisions and decision processes that seemed to offer short-run improvements in some domains but in retrospect created greater problems in the long run or in other domains. And history is filled with evidence of the irrelevance of human actions. In the long run, decision makers are all dead and the species is extinct.

Such a catalog of despair might be seen as an invitation to abandon decision making. Hopes for magic in new technologies or philosophies of decision seem to be as unrequited as they are unquenchable. The issues are ancient. Their resolution is elusive. Knowledge about the difficulties involved in defining and achieving virtue through decision making leads to pessimism about the possibilities for intelligent action. The means by which individuals justify action in the face of such problems might well seem to make the problems more severe. If sustaining action involves colluding in illusions of control, accepting a social ideology of human identity that is disturbingly idiosyncratic to modern Western society, or embracing one or another unreasoning faith, it is easy to conclude that action is not worth sustaining. The alternatives manage to give passivity a good name.

A book on decision making might possibly conclude with such an apostasy, but this one does not. Such an ending would be a mistake for two conspicuous reasons: First, the problems are difficult, but they are not beyond human comprehension and amelioration. It is possible to apply thought to the problems of intelligence, to profit from an understanding of how decisions happen in order to make them happen better. Much of the present book has been devoted to laying a foundation for such improvements. Foundations do not keep the rain out, but they offer some small basis for imagining that a roof is possible.

Second, if human commitment depended on a comprehension of life and on hopes for consequence, commitment would be less beautiful to contemplate than it is. The elegance and beauty of human life is augmented within a vision of decision making, and the human spirit is elevated. The idea of decision making gives meaning to purpose, to self, to the complexities of social life. It ennobles as it frustrates. So it is not despair that is appropriate but a reminder from Sénancour: "Man is perishable. That may be. But let us perish resisting; and if nothingness is what awaits us, let us not act in such a way that it is a just fate."[8]

And if the earthy world of decision making occasionally leads us to the divine world of Ibsen, Cervantes, Kierkegaard, and Sénancour, let us be grateful. But let us not stay in that world too long. It is hard enough to make sense of the simple things without discovering they are really not as simple as they look.

Notes

Chapter 2. Rule Following

1. "Yo sé quien soy." Miguel de Cervantes, *El Ingenioso Hidalgo Don Quixote del la Mancha*, I, 5.

Chapter 3. Multiple Actors: Teams and Partners

1. Omar A. El Sawy and Hisham El Sherif, "Issue-based Decision Support Systems for the Egyptian Cabinet," *MIS Quarterly*, 12 (1988): 551–69.

Chapter 5. Ambiguity and Interpretation

1. James G. March and Pierre Romelaer, "Position and Presence in the Drift of Decisions," pp. 251–76 in James G. March and Johan P. Olsen, *Ambiguity and Choice in Organizations* (Bergen, Norway: Unversitetsforlaget, 1976), p. 276.
2. Thomas Carlyle, *Heroes and Hero-Worship* (1841).
3. Leo Tolstoy, *War and Peace* (1865–69).
4. Michael D. Cohen, James G. March, and Johan P. Olsen, "A

Garbage Can Model of Organizational Choice," *Administrative Science Quarterly*, 17 (1972): 1–25.

5. William Morris, ed., *The American Heritage Dictionary of the English Language* (Boston: Houghton Mifflin, 1981), p. 869.

6. Dale Carnegie, *How to Win Friends and Influence People* (New York: Simon & Schuster, 1936).

7. Kristian Kreiner, "Ideology and Management in a Garbage Can Situation," pp. 156–73 in James G. March and Johan P. Olsen, *Ambiguity and Choice in Organizations* (Bergen, Norway: Unversitetsforlaget, 1976); Soren Christensen, "Decision Making and Socialization," pp. 351–86 in March and Olsen.

Chapter 6. Decision Engineering

1. Sidney Blumenthal, "The Sorcerer's Apprentice," *New Yorker*, July 19, 1993, p. 29.

2. Wesley M. Cohen and Daniel A. Levinthal, "Absorptive Capacity: A New Perspective on Learning and Innovation," *Administrative Science Quarterly*, 35 (1990): 431–57.

3. Michael Polanyi, "The Potential Theory of Adsorption: Authority in Science Has Its Uses and Its Dangers," *Science*, 141 (1963): 1013.

4. T. S. Eliot, *On Poetry and Poets* (New York: Noonday Press, 1961), p. 126.

5. Act 3, Scene 1, Line 56.

6. "Tar De livsløgnen fra et gjennomsnittsmeneske, så tar De lykken fra ham med de samme." Henrik Ibsen, *Vildanden*, V.

7. "Que volverse, loco un caballero andante con causa, ni grado ni gracias; el toque está en desatinar sin ocasión." Miguel de Cervantes, *El Ingenioso Hidalgo Don Quixote del la Mancha*, I, 25.

8. "L'homme est périssable. Il se peut; mais périssons en résistant, et, si le néant nous est reservé, ne faisons pas que ce soit une justice." Sénancour, *Obermann*, xc.

Additional Reading

Preface

For a general introduction to the study of decisions, see:

Allison, G. T. *Essence of Decision: Explaining the Cuban Missile Crisis.* Boston: Little, Brown, 1971.

March, J. G., "Introduction." In *Decisions and Organizations.* Oxford: Blackwell, 1988.

————. "Decisions in organizations and theories of choice." In A. Van de Ven and W. Joyce, eds., *Perspectives on Organizational Design and Performance.* New York: Wiley, 1981, pp. 205–244.

————. "How decisions happen in organizations." *Human/Computer Interaction,* 6 (1991): 95–117.

Witte, E., and H.-J. Zimmermann, eds., *Empirical Research on Organizational Decision Making.* Amsterdam: Elsevier, 1986.

For a general introduction to the study of organizations, see:

Grandori, A. *Perspectives on Organization Theory.* Cambridge, MA: Ballinger, 1987.

Leavitt, H. J., and H. Bahrami. *Managerial Psychology: Managing Behavior in Organizations.* 5th ed. Chicago: University of Chicago Press, 1988.

Perrow, C. *Complex Organizations: A Critical Essay.* 3d ed. Glenview, IL: Scott, Foresman, 1986.
Scott, W. R. *Organizations: Rational, Natural, and Open Systems.* 3d ed. Englewood Cliffs, NJ: Prentice Hall, 1992.

Chapter 1. Limited Rationality

For an introduction to ideas of limited rationality, attention, and search, see:

Cyert, R. M., and J. G. March. *A Behavioral Theory of the Firm.* 2d ed. Oxford: Blackwell, 1992.
March, J. G. *Decisions and Organizations.* Oxford: Blackwell, 1988, Ch. 1–3.
March, J. G., and H. A. Simon. *Organizations.* 2d ed. Oxford: Blackwell, 1993.

For more detail on the psychological study of decision making under uncertainty, see:

Janis, I. L., and L. Mann. *Decision Making: A Psychological Analysis of Conflict, Choice, and Commitment.* New York: Free Press, 1977.
Kahneman, D.; P. Slovic; and A. Tversky, eds. *Judgment under Uncertainty: Heuristics and Biases.* Cambridge, England: Cambridge University Press, 1982.
Nisbett, R., and L. Ross. *Human Inference: Strategies and Shortcomings of Social Judgment.* Englewood Cliffs, NJ: Prentice-Hall, 1980.

For discussions of risk and risk taking from a behavioral perspective, see:

Douglas, M., and A. B. Wildavsky. *Risk and Culture.* Berkeley: University of California Press, 1982.
MacCrimmon, K. R., and D. A. Wehrung. *Taking Risks: The Management of Uncertainty.* New York: Free Press, 1986.
March, J. G. *Decisions and Organizations.* Oxford: Blackwell, 1988, Ch. 4.

For an indication of the ways in which limited rationality is found in economic theories of the organization, see:

Arrow, K. J. *The Limits of Organization.* New York: W. W. Norton, 1974.
Holmstrom, B. R., and J. Tirole. "The theory of the firm." In R. Schmalensee and R. D. Willig, eds., *Handbook of Industrial Organization.* Vol. 1. New York: Elsevier, 1989, pp. 61–133.
Williamson, O. E. "Transaction cost economics." In R. Schmalensee and R. D. Willig, eds., *Handbook of Industrial Organization.* Vol. 1. New York: Elsevier, 1989, pp. 136–82.

Chapter 2. Rule Following

For further elaboration of rule following as a basis of action, see:

Anderson, J. R. *The Architecture of Cognition.* Cambridge, MA: Harvard University Press, 1983

Burns, T. R., and H. Flam. *The Shaping of Social Organization: Social Rule System Theory with Applications.* London: Sage, 1987.

March, J. G., and J. P. Olsen. *Rediscovering Organizations: The Organizational Basis of Politics.* New York: Free Press, 1989, Ch. 2.

For more on identities and their development, see:

Elster, J. *The Multiple Self.* Cambridge, England: Cambridge University Press, 1986.

Hogg, M. A., and D. Abrams. *Social Identifications: A Social Psychology of Intergroup Relations and Group Processes.* London: Routledge, 1988.

Kondo, D. K. *Crafting Selves: Power, Gender, and Discourses of Identity in a Japanese Workplace.* Chicago: University of Chicago Press, 1990.

For examination of various ways in which rules and the population of rules change over time, see:

Axelrod, R. *The Evolution of Cooperation.* New York: Basic Books, 1984.

Hannan, M. T., and J. Freeman. *Organizational Ecology.* Cambridge, MA: Harvard University Press, 1989.

Holland, J. H.; K. J. Holyoak; R. E. Nisbett; and P. R. Thagard. *Induction: Processes of Inference, Learning, and Discovery.* Cambridge, MA: MIT Press, 1986.

March, J. G. *Decisions and Organizations.* Oxford: Blackwell, 1988, Chs. 8–11.

Nelson, R. R., and S. G. Winter. *An Evolutionary Theory of Economic Change.* Cambridge, MA: Harvard University Press, 1982.

Chapter 3. Multiple Actors: Teams and Partners

For elaboration of basic ideas on inconsistency in social systems, see:

Coleman, J. S. *Individual Interests and Collective Action.* Cambridge, England: Cambridge University Press, 1986.

Elster, J. *Interpersonal Comparisons of Well-Being.* Cambridge, England: Cambridge University Press, 1991.

March, J. G. *Decisions and Organizations.* Oxford: Blackwell, 1988, Ch. 5.

————. "Decisions in organizations and theories of choice." In A. Van de Ven and W. Joyce, eds., *Assessing Organizational Design and Performance*. New York: Wiley Interscience, 1981, pp. 205–44.

For an introduction to teams and partnerships, see:

Levinthal, D. A. "A survey of agency models of organization." *Journal of Economic Behavior and Organization*, 9, (1988): 153–85.
Marschak, J., and R. Radner. *Economic Theory of Teams*. New Haven: Yale University Press, 1972.
Milgrom, P., and J. Roberts. *Economics, Organization and Management*. Englewood Cliffs, NJ: Prentice-Hall, 1992.
Rasmussen, E. *Games and Information: An Introduction to Game Theory*. Oxford: Basil Blackwell, 1990.

Chapter 4. Multiple Actors: Conflict and Politics

For more discussions of power and its role in understanding decision making, see:

Bachrach, P., and M. Baratz. *Power and Poverty*. New York: Oxford University Press, 1970.
March, J. G. *Decisions and Organizations*. Oxford: Blackwell, 1988, Ch. 6.
Nagel, J. H. *The Descriptive Analysis of Power*. New Haven, CT: Yale University Press, 1975.
Pfeffer, J. *Managing with Power*. Boston: Harvard Business School Press, 1992.

For a discussion of coalitions, conflict, and problems of implementation, see:

Bardach, E. *The Implementation Game*. Cambridge, MA: MIT Press, 1977.
March, J. G. *Decisions and Organizations*. Oxford: Blackwell, 1988, Ch. 7.
Pfeffer, J., and G. R. Salancik. *The External Control of Organizations*. New York: Harper & Row, 1978.
Riker, W. H. *The Theory of Political Coalitions*. New Haven, CT: Yale University Press, 1962.

Chapter 5. Ambiguity and Interpretation

For further elaboration of the general ideas of ambiguity, contradiction, and interpretation, see:

Brunsson, N. *The Organization of Hypocrisy.* Chichester, England: Wiley, 1989.

Cohen, M. D., and J. G. March. *Leadership and Ambiguity: The American College President,* 2d ed. Boston: Harvard Business School Press, 1986.

March, J. G. *Decisions and Organizations.* Oxford: Blackwell, 1988, Chs. 15–17.

Weick, K. *The Social Psychology of Organizing,* 2d ed. Reading, MA: Addison-Wesley, 1979.

For more discussion of the symbolic aspects of decision making, see:

Arnold, T. *The Symbols of Government.* New Haven: Yale University Press, 1935.

Edelman, M. *The Symbolic Uses of Politics.* Urbana: University of Illinois Press, 1964.

March, J. G. *Decisions and Organizations.* Oxford: Blackwell, 1988, Chs. 18–19.

For more descriptions and discussions of garbage can decision processes, see:

Kingdon, J. W. *Agendas, Alternatives, and Public Policies.* Boston: Little, Brown, 1984.

March, J. G. *Decisions and Organizations,* Oxford: Blackwell, 1988, Ch. 14.

March, J. G., and J. P. Olsen, eds. *Ambiguity and Choice in Organizations.* Bergen, Norway: Universitetsforlaget, 1976.

————. "Garbage can models of decision making in organizations." In J. G. March and R. Weissinger-Baylon, eds. *Ambiguity and Command.* Cambridge, MA: Ballinger, 1986, pp. 11–36.

For more on the construction of meaning, see:

Agger, B. "Critical theory, poststructuralism, postmodernism: Their sociological relevance." *Annual Review of Sociology,* 17 (1991): 105–31.

Berger, P. L., and T. Luckman. *The Social Construction of Reality: A Treatise in the Sociology of Knowledge.* New York: Doubleday, 1966.

Fiske, S. T., and S. E. Taylor. *Social Cognition.* Reading, MA: Addison-Wesley, 1984.

Krieger, S. *Social Science and the Self: Personal Essays on an Art Form.* New Brunswick, NJ: Rutgers University Press, 1991.

Powell, W. W., and P. DiMaggio, eds. *The New Institutionalism in Organizational Analysis.* Chicago: University of Chicago Press, 1991.

Chapter 6. Decision Engineering

For general discussions of the ambiguities of decision intelligence, see:

Elster J. *Choices over Time*. New York: Russell Sage Foundation, 1992.
———. *Sour Grapes: Studies in the Subversion of Rationality*. Cambridge, England: Cambridge University Press, 1983.
———. *Ulysses and the Sirens: Studies in Rationality and Irrationality*. Cambridge, England: Cambridge University Press, 1979.
Sen, A. K. *On Ethics and Economics*. Oxford: Blackwell, 1988.

For more elaboration of the problems and pitfalls of adaptive intelligence, see:

Hirschman, A. O. *Exit, Voice and Loyalty*. Cambridge, MA: Harvard University Press, 1979.
March, J. G. *Decisions and Organizations*. Oxford: Blackwell, 1988, Ch. 12–13.
March, J. G. "Exploration and exploitation in organizational learning." *Organization Science*, 2 (1991): 71–87.
Schelling, T. C. *Micromotives and Macrobehavior*. New York: Norton, 1978.

For discussions of the intelligence of routines and rules, see:

Stinchcombe, A. L. *Creating Efficient Industrial Administration*. New York: Academic Press, 1974.
———. *Information and Organizations*. Berkeley: University of California Press, 1990.

For some general suggestions on how to improve decision intelligence, see:

Argyris, C., and E. Schön. *Organizational Learning*. Reading, MA: Addison-Wesley, 1978.
George, A. L. *Presidential Decision Making in Foreign Policy: The Effective Use of Information and Advice*. Boulder, CO: Westview Press, 1980.
Hedberg, B. L. T.; P. C. Nystrom; and W. H. Starbuck. "Camping on seesaws: prescriptions for a self-designing organization." *Administrative Science Quarterly*, 21 (1976): 41–65.
March, J. G.; L. S. Sproull; and M. Tamuz. "Learning from samples of one or fewer." *Organization Science*, 2 (1991): 1–13.

For some exploration of poetic, artistic, and jurisprudential approaches to meaning, see:

Eliot, T. S. *On Poetry and Poets.* New York: Noonday Press, 1961.

Levi, E. H. *An Introduction to Legal Reasoning.* Chicago: University of Chicago Press, 1949.

Rosenberg, H. *Art on the Edge: Creators and Situations.* New York: Macmillan, 1975.

Sontag, S. *Illness as Metaphor.* New York: Farrar, Straus, & Giroux, 1978.

Index

283

About the Author

James G. March is the Jack Steele Parker Professor of International Management and a professor of political science and sociology at Stanford University. He is the author and co-author of numerous books and hundreds of journal articles on organizations, decision making, and leadership. He lives in Stanford, California.